Educational Psychology and Child Development

Educational Psychology and Child Development

Edited by

Suchitra Deshprabhu

KANISHKA PUBLISHERS, DISTRIBUTORS
NEW DELHI-110 002

KANISHKA PUBLISHERS, DISTRIBUTORS
4697/5-21A, Ansari Road, Daryaganj
New Delhi -110 002
Phones : 2327 0497, 2328 8285
Fax : 011-2328 8285
E-mail : kanishka_publishing@yahoo.co.in

Educational Psychology and Child Development

First Published-1998
Edition-**2017**

PRINTED IN INDIA

Published by Madan Sachdeva for Kanishka Publishers, Distributors, 4697/5-21A, Ansari Road, Daryaganj, New Delhi-110 002, Typeset by Sunshine Graphics, Delhi, and Printed at Rajdhani Printers, Delhi.

Preface

Education has been described as the process of drawing out the best in a person. The process is a complex one, involving the definitive, cognitive and intuitive aspects of the growth and development of the child and its consciousness. It also brings into focus the overall environment of the child-home and family, school and formal instruction, class-room and peer-groups, community and society, and younger and older persons. A vital part of the entire process is the formalisation of educational psychology, the enabling body of principles and practices that equip teachers, educators and policy-makers with the necessary skills and approaches, insights and attitudes to creatively and constructively handle pupils of all mental and physical dimensions. The crucial inter-relationship between educational psychology and child development can never be underestimated.

In the process of education, the psychological variables that interest teachers the most are those which help, or impede, learning. In particular, they like to know how 'intelligent' a child is. A teacher usually makes a reasonable comparison of one child's ability with that of others and sees him as 'average' or 'below average' or 'above average' for the group. He does this both empirically as well as subjectively; the child learns more quickly or more slowly than the others, or he behaves 'sensibly' or 'foolishly' compared with others. In all educational contexts the question of intelligence is central to the formalisation of educational psychology. Definitions of intelligence are numerous; it is believed that there are atleast six traditional definitions and teachers can have their pick. The acid test occurs when a teacher is required to educate children with learning disorders and difficulties.

The present publication attempts to bring together articles, papers, discussion notes and educational footnotes from a wide range of sources for the benefit of students and teachers of education.

The materials together provide a body of readings that are both interesting and useful and collectively afford the student, the teacher and the policy-maker a holistic view of the entire subject of educational psychology and child development. The topics cover aspects such as: learning patterns in infancy; intelligence development in the pre-adolescent child; growing child and challenge of policy formulation; learning and discrimination; approaches to decision-making curriculum; children and mathematical concepts; learning skills in handicapped; major factors in learning and learning disorder; educational approaches and new technologies; child development perspectives and mass media; and understanding the value of children. These are understood to be subjects of much significance in any planned educational curriculum and the readings in the publication will go a long way in supplementing the current body of important literature in the area.

Editor

Contents

CHAPTER 1

Policy Imperatives for Child Development

I

Introduction: Health, Nutrition and Development

It is widely agreed that inadequate physical growth and poor development of children are prevalent and important problems world-wide. In most countries, the situation is worse for the poor and the deprived than for the more affluent section of the population. For a long time health workers and others have taken action to attempt to influence better growth and to foster optimum child development. Other than the few who argue that "small is healthy," by far the majority wish to find the means to help families help their children grow well physically, socially, and psychologically. This colloquium is designed to examine current strategies, to review successes and failures, and most important, to suggest new directions to achieve the objective of improved growth and development for children at risk.

Currently, many different strategies, many different programmes, many different actions by international agencies, national governments, individual families, and others are taken to promote good growth and development. But there is one strategy, above others, that both in its name and in its stated objectives focuses very specifically on the growth of children. This is growth monitoring, now better termed *Growth Monitoring and Promotion* (Hendrata 1988). This strategy has become controversial (Anon. 1985) with strong proponents and opponents (Gopalan and Chatterjee 1985; Rohde 1984 and others). The many other actions taken to support or promote growth and development, although very widely practised, are not as visibly advocated as strategies for growth promotion. Because of this, growth monitoring as practised is deserving of attention, but this should not be at the expense of limiting consideration of other actions that foster good child growth and development. Recognition also needs to be given to the fact that good growth is often related to other aspects of good child development and that those situations, environments, and actions that promote good child development, also usually help promote optimum physical growth. The two are intertwined. But because physical growth is relatively easy to measure, much more reliance (Stephenson *et al.* 1983) is placed on physical growth than on other aspects of child development, as a gauge of childhood well-being.

Growth Monitoring and Promotion

For several decades the periodic weighing of infants and children to assess their growth has been advocated and used within health systems. Sometimes measurements other than weight, including especially length or height, arm circumference, and skinfold thickness, are also used either to determine development or assess nutritional status (Latham 1979; Jelliffe 1966). These secular determinations, if periodic, are strictly speaking anthropometric growth monitoring. The term monitoring means literally "to keep watch over" or "to check systematically."

However, the term "growth monitoring" now usually refers to the periodic weighing of children and the plotting of each measurement on a "growth chart" or child health card. The information on the card is meant to influence actions by the health worker making the measurements and the mother or guardian who brings the child to be measured (Latham 1991).

The recording of a child's weight on a growth chart in itself serves no useful purpose, unless accompanied by some action (Latham 1984). This has long been recognised, but in many growth monitoring programmes this is about all that is done. Under these circumstances the potential benefits of growth monitoring are not and cannot be achieved. A realisation of this led to the use of the term *Growth Monitoring and Promotion* (Hendrata 1988). This is potentially important because the promotion of good growth clearly should be the main objective of regular weighing.

Wherever a growth monitoring and promotion (GMP) programme at the local or national level concentrates on weighing and charting, but does not use the chart in a coherent positive manner, then it clearly is an exercise in futility. This is assuming that growth monitoring is being used mainly to influence growth of the individual child. Growth monitoring could be used simply to generate data for purposes of nutritional surveillance, or programme evaluation. That is a different matter, and is not the subject of this colloquium.

Growth measurements have been used as a means of judging growth and health of children for many years. In several industrialised countries, well baby clinics included child weighing as a means to judge proper development. Morley *et al.* (1968), on the basis of work in Nigeria, advocated in the 1960s, the use of growth charts in developing countries, and this can be regarded as the birth of the growth monitoring movement. The view was that "maintaining an adequate rate of growth" was replacing "prevention of malnutrition" as the goal towards which child clinics might direct their work (Anon. 1968). Morley stressed the use of the chart to promote growth and not to cure malnutrition; he advocated the mother, rather than the clinic, hold possession of the chart; and he later stressed that the health worker and the mother should be more interested in growth velocity than in the child's position on the chart. The term "road to health chart" became widely accepted (Morley 1973).

Currently, many different weight charts are in use around the world. Debate exists about which kind of growth chart to use. These are usually based on "reference standards," and unless accepted national standards exist, it is recommended by WHO and others that National Centre for Health Statistics standards be used (Stephenson *et al.* 1983).

GMP includes sequential weighing and it is used to help caretakers maintain good growth in the individual child. A useful definition (Hendrata 1988) adopted by the Indian Integrated Child Development Service is:

> Growth monitoring and Promotion can be defined as an operational strategy of enabling mothers to visualise growth or lack of growth and to receive specific, relevant and practical guidance in ways in which she, her family

and community can act assure health and continued regular growth in her child. GMP implies a regular and sequential measurement of growth, recognising it to be the result of overall health, nutrition, environment, psycho-social and development factors in the child.

GMP is based on a strategy aimed at behavioural change and adoption of improved self-help actions within the family and the community in order to promote optimal health. In short, GMP is a communication strategy for making health and nutrition education more individualised, more convincing and more effective.

A current view is that GMP should, where possible, be closely integrated into Primary Health Care (PHC) activities, and it should not usually be a separate programme. It should concentrate on maintaining good growth in infants and children, and not, as is often the case, be used mainly for rehabilitating children whose growth is poor. If this is to be the focus, then it is essential that infants enter the programme soon after birth because, in general, infants 0-5 months of age who are breastfed have satisfactory growth. GMP is then a preventive not a curative strategy; it is designed mainly to promote good growth and health, not to deal with malnutrition and ill health. Workers should be obtaining information on how mothers and families are managing to achieve good growth rather than mainly finding the reasons for growth failure. Praise and reinforcement should be an important feature of the programme. Although the major emphasis is on maintenance of good growth, which can be viewed as a pre-emptive strategy, nevertheless, the programme should include a strategy for dealing with those hopefully few cases where the programme has failed and where children are not doing well and need special attention. This will usually involve some special advice from health workers involving behavioural change aimed to achieve rehabilitation and in some cases will necessitate treatment or referral. Growth monitoring then is viewed as a strategy to empower mothers to maintain good nutritional status in their children and to prevent growth retardation.

In GMP programmes, much of the action should consist of positive reinforcement rather than corrective action. As a diagnostic exercise, it should be as much to find out what mothers are doing right and what is going wrong. It is also used to detect early growth faltering, to find the likely reasons for this, and to suggest to mothers corrective actions that are realistic and that they might try. It is likely to be relatively unsuccessful if used mainly to try to "correct" the growth of older children who are moderately or severely stunted, especially if these children are not wasted. In all cases, meaningful involvement of mothers and families should be the heart of a growth monitoring and promotion programme. It is a participatory exercise; it involves dialogue and discussion, not lecturing and scolding; and mothers should help in decision-making, for example, about the location, the hours, and the organisation of GM sessions. Mothers need also to be consulted about such matters as the need for privacy and confidentiality and whether it is appropriate in their culture to weigh children nude or clothed.

This is a view of the concepts of what good GMP should be, rather than what it usually is in practice in countries in Africa, Asia, and Latin America (Latham 1991). This author continues to see growth monitoring in action that ignores these principles. Too often growth monitoring is used mainly as a weighing exercise and advice is given only to mothers whose children are doing badly. Often, the mothers are scolded publicly and advice is frequently impractical and does not recognise what would be useful to them. Inadequate time is devoted to dialogue, to advice, and to education. In some parts of the world, GMP is regarded by health workers mainly as a tool for diagnosis of malnutrition. In other places, it is used to select children to receive free or subsidised weaning foods. Feeding can be a component of a GMP programme but the full potential benefits will not be realised without the level of communication, dialogue and empowerment of mothers and communities described earlier. At worst, growth monitoring consists of the routine exercise of weighing and weight charting with no advice given and with no use made of the chart. Those conducting the GMP session may not have time to do anything more than weighing and charting; and they may not have the training or knowledge to use other needed interventions properly. Where this is the case, then GMP is a useless exercise, and one that is wasteful of resources including mothers' time. Elsewhere, there may be societies with cultural prejudices against weighing of young children, which may be a reason for not introducing GMP or atleast for sensitive efforts to overcome this difficulty.

The differences between growth monitoring on the one hand and nutritional surveillance on the other, have been pointed out by Rohde ((1984). This view may not be consistent with the current UNICEF approach to nutritional surveillance. Nutritional assessment using growth data for surveillance may, for example, require only small subsamples of the population of the communities involved. In this case, quite a large number of children can be weighed per day because diagnosis and communication is not an important feature. In addition, surveillance may require precise, accurate measurements done by a highly trained worker with the measurements repeated at long intervals. In contrast, GMP programmes hope to enrol all children under a particular age; the groups of children at a weighing session should be relatively small because diagnosis and dialogue are important; the measurements made need not be as precise and can be performed by a person with less education and training (sometimes even by mothers themselves); and children should if possible come for weighing and growth promotion sessions at much shorter intervals. If the main objective of a programme is nutritional surveillance and not growth monitoring, then the programme should be different.

In a properly run GMP programme, most infants should be enrolled as soon after birth as possible. Children seen for the first time in their second or third year of life often will already have evidence of growth failure, and GMP can at this stage do relatively little to improve the situation, especially in stunted older children. Infants under 6 months of age when breast milk is adequate and breastfeeding is the normal feeding practice, usually show good growth. This, therefore, is a period when dialogue is most useful. GMP can provide positive reinforcement, but it can also be a time when dialogue becomes established. This becomes most useful in the months ahead, during the nutritional danger period, which is usually between 6 and 18 months of age. A mother should tell the health worker about what she plans to do, when she intends to introduce other foods, how long she expects to breastfeed, whether she wants to get the infant immunised, and how she will deal with illnesses such as diarrhea and respiratory infections. The worker at the GMP session should now cautiously guide the mother and discuss with her a strategy for maintaining good growth and health in her infant during the danger period, rather than concentrating on the rehabilitation or cure of malnutrition.

If this is to be the heart of the programme then it is important that the health worker has a good understanding of existing child raising practices and the local cultural, social, and dietary environment of the community. Without this, the messages may not be relevant, practical, or feasible for mothers to implement and may not even be credible to them. The health worker must also have a minimum of knowledge about the factors most likely to lead to growth faltering. For example, he or she should understand that after about 6 months of age breastfeeding alone often provides inadequate nutrition and needs to be supplemented; that too much supplementation may reduce suckling and lead to insufficient milk; that certain foods are bulky and have low energy density, but that there are ways to increase energy density; that as breastfeeding becomes less important, frequent feeding with other foods is important while breastfeeding should continue for as long as possible; that infections may themselves lead to growth faltering, but that starvation as a treatment for diarrhea and other infections contribute to this; and that breastmilk and other foods should be provided during most illnesses. To discuss this properly, the health worker needs to have enough time with each mother, adequate training, and understanding of health and nutrition beyond charting. Above all, he or she needs to have the right temperament.

An operational rule then might be that the health worker requires adequate time to talk to each mother (at least 5-15 minutes) and needs to have a certain basic knowledge and reasonable communication skills. It is important that he or she knows how to listen and to elicit information from the mother and how to provide positive feedback and encouragement plus appropriate advice. This takes some skill and some of these skills can be imparted in training. But obviously some individuals are better listeners and communicators than are others.

Another operational rule that follows is that GMP be integrated into Primary Health Care. Many of the messages and advice suggested are an integral part of PHC. Mothers should, in general, not have to attend separate sessions on a different day for treatment of common infections and to have their children immunised, to receive vitamin A or anthelminthics, to get advice about oral rehydration, or to attend for prenatal examination or get family planning advice. In fact, it should be the duty of the GMP staff to ensure that all children attending have been immunised against the six diseases covered in the Expanded Programme of Immunisation, that mothers know how to use oral rehydration therapy, etc. Growth monitoring and promotion can be a part of PHC or, alternatively, it can encompass PHC activities. Hendrata (1988) has stated that "GM and P can help to shift the emphasis from professionals to parents, from clinics to homes, from dependence to empowerment. And in so doing it can help to build a genuine primary health care system." GMP can serve as an activity that at frequent intervals brings the child into contact with the health services.

A good principle is that advice, nutrition, and health education should be rather specific and aimed at the particular circumstances of each mother and child. The dialogue should give the mother the feeling that she herself is developing a realistic achievable strategy to maintain the good growth and health of her child and in this way she will see the benefits of the time that she has invested in the exercise. The content of the messages should be simple, and must take account of the child in a family situation.

Finally, GMP should be conducted as near as possible to people's homes; at a time convenient to parents; in small enough groups to allow adequate individualised dialogue and short waiting periods; and be conducted in a way mainly to suit parents not health workers. For example, in an urban setting where mothers work away from home, the sessions could be on a Sunday and the health workers have Monday off. Unless some means are provided for combining GMP with simple therapy and other preventive services, attendance may be poor. This might include, for example, deworming, administration of vitamin A, provision of ORT packets, availability of anti-malarial drugs, and possibly also simple treatment of common illnesses. In all cases, rural GMP activities based in a small village must be linked with and have back-up from a health centre, dispensary, or clinic. Rohde (1984) and others have stated that food supplements should not be provided at GMP sessions even if the child is faltering, because supplements may have negative consequences for the programme. This view is not shared by all those involved in GMP. In the much heralded Tamil Nadu Integrated Nutrition Project (TINP) funded by the World Bank in India, free food supplements are provided and are targeted to the most needy children, and this targeting is based largely on the weight charts.

Under some circumstances, GMP may be conducted not at a health centre, but by visits to people's homes. This will often be popular with mothers, and it will result in a wider coverage especially of the most neglected families, but will usually be more expensive, because one fieldworker can cover fewer children per day. Although GMP can act as a catalyst in the strengthening of primary health care activities, it is also true that it is much easier to have GMP as part of a well functioning PHC system. Therefore, efforts to strengthen and improve primary health care will also make well run GMP a more feasible possibility.

Although growth monitoring is simple in concept, and is a relatively low cost technology for helping to reduce the extent of malnutrition, it is very seldom done well. It takes good organisation, adequate resources, an appropriate existing infrastructure, and careful training and proper supervision of workers. In some geographic locations, it may involve overcoming cultural barriers.

Growth monitoring (and less frequently, growth monitoring and promotion) is being widely practised, and with the blessing and financial assistance of UNICEF and other agencies, the number of children included in GM programmes has greatly increased in the last 8 years, UNICEF as an advocate claims many successes of growth monitoring in developing countries around the world (Grant 1987).

The success or failure GM depends on how the information and the chart are used. The weighing and the plotting have to result in action if there is to be a benefit. Those taking action in general are likely to be either the mother (or parents or guardian) of the child or the health worker. Growth monitoring is one among several means of attempting to achieve the desired goal of healthy growth. Are there other ways that are easier, cheaper, and more feasible than GM to promote good health and development in poor societies?

Evaluation of Growth Monitoring and Promotion

Many governments, funding agencies, and nutritionists and pediatricians strongly believe that GMP is a very important strategy in the fight against malnutrition. There are also serious critics of growth monitoring who state that its value has not been demonstrated and that it is too costly a project for poor countries, considering the very limited financial resources available for health and nutrition services.

The unfortunate fact is that there have been very few scientific attempts to evaluate growth monitoring and most of these have flaws in their design. There are studies that suggest that illiterate women can be taught to understand growth charts (Pelemeier 1985). In some studies, where growth monitoring appeared to be of value in terms of improved health or nutrition, it was not possible to separate benefits from the growth chart, per se, from benefits resulting from other interventions introduced as part of the growth monitoring programme, activities such as immunisations, oral rehydration therapy, supplementary feeding, treatment of disease, and others (Morley 1973).

A detailed review of GM in India suggests major problems and a few successes, but illustrates that no well-conducted evaluation has been undertaken (Gopalan and Chatterjee 1985). In the case of Indonesia, both the World Bank funded project covering 225,000 people and designed to examine the impact of community-based GM, and the ever-expanding UPGK (Usaha Perbaikan Gizi Keluarga) programme covering a large population using volunteers termed "Kaders," have been described at length (Griffiths 1985). In the former project, it is claimed that based on 600 programme households and 400 comparison households, there was a significant improvement in mothers' nutritional knowledge and practices, and in the nutritional status of the children. Unfortunately, there were many differences between the two groups, and it is not possible to judge how much improvement was due to the major efforts of nutrition communication and behaviour change and what exact role was played by the growth chart as part of GM.

Studies in Jamaica, in Lesotho, and elsewhere also have problems and produced results that are unconvincing. The book length publication "Use of Growth Charts for Promoting Child

Nutrition—A Review of Global Experience" by Gopalan and Chatterjee (1985) concludes that the effectiveness of GM has not been proven, but also suggests that good evaluation studies have not been undertaken. In 1985, Rohde stated that the statistical proof of the efficiency of growth monitoring had still not been demonstrated.

The literature to date does not include very many well-controlled, well-designed studies to evaluate the effectiveness of growth monitoring. There are even fewer reports of research that has attempted to evaluate the benefits of the weighing and charting component of growth monitoring, in comparison with the benefits from the nutrition education and primary health care interventions which should also be a part of GMP programmes. There are not many studies on the relative time and resources devoted to the weighing part and the order GMP activities. In Zaire, Gerein and Ross (1991) evaluated three child health programmes that included growth monitoring. They concluded that the "theoretical gain in health service efficiency by targeting was largely lost" and that the "programme did not exploit the potential of growth monitoring as an educational and motivational tool." They conclude from their study and other recent reports that "the introduction of growth monitoring into future child health programmes appears difficult to justify at present."

In contrast, excerpts from a report for the Tamil Nadu Integrated Nutrition Project (TINP) as reported by Beg (1992), describe the great benefits of targeting supplementary feeding on the basis of weighing as a part of its programme. In the project, selective supplementary food is provided on the basis of poor growth, as judged by serial weight determinations. The report states that "being weighed, selected, fed and graduated appears to have a profound educational impact on the beneficiaries and on staff." The report states that" TINP demonstrated that growth monitoring can be done in large-scale nutrition projects, provided workers perceive it to be the centrepiece of the project" and that "the project must be able to prove to mothers that regular weighing will promote healthy growth" and "by demonstrating the ways in which such problems can be overcome."

A recent study also in Tamil Nadu, but conducted in collaboration with the Christian Medical College and Hospital in Vellore, and not a part of TINP, has attempted to evaluate the benefits of weighing and charting, separate from PHC and other interventions (George *et al.* 1992). The research suggests that a package of interventions including nutrition and health education and PHC improves the knowledge of mothers and the growth of young children with or without the use of weighing and growth charts. So the weight chart, even when well used, showed no additional benefits in growth when compared with not using the growth chart in families where other interventions were provided. This study used home-based, not clinic-based GMP and did not include supplementary feeding.

An editorial in the *Lancet* (1985) suggests, any system "is only as good as the workers who operate it." Unlike oral rehydration, GM is not a curative approach with quick results and unlike immunisation, it is not a magic bullet requiring little behavioural change. Rather, it is intended as a means by which a simple technology can help people help their children and can in theory empower mothers. The unanswered questions remain:

(a) What conditions need to exist for it to be effective? and

(b) Can equally good results be obtained at lower cost using similar interventions without frequent weighing?

Conclusion

A review of published data on GMP suggests that it is very seldom being done well. The principles described here as being essential or important are usually ignored. Most GMP is so focused on weighing and charting and so little on growth promotion, as to raise serious doubts about its use as generally practised. In many instances, the health workers do not appear to have the time to provide the education and other interventions that are essential for the promotion of good growth and development. Often, they lack training, motivation and supervision. In many cases, GMP workers are not provided the resources to allow them to help the mothers and children attending. The primary health care component is frequently weak or almost non-existent. No wonder sceptics doubt whether GMP is a strategy worth supporting.

Added to these problems is the fact that despite much reported evaluation of GM programmes, practically none of these have evaluated the added benefits resulting from the weighing and the growth charts, rather than the benefits which accrue from other interventions. Even in the growth monitoring projects, reported to be most successful, the actual role of the weighing and the growth chart have not been evaluated. Thus, TINP in India used regular weighing as the centrepiece of the project and feeding targeted to unsatisfactory weight gain in children as an important intervention. Reports state that nutritional status improved, that relapses into malnutrition were reduced over time, and that the selection of children on the basis of growth was very important in effective nutrition education (Berg 1992). What we do not know is if the selection of young children for special attention had been based on something other than weighing, it would have resulted in equal "success." What would the results have been if the basis of selection had been the weight for age of the child at say 12 months of age, or a mother's perception at each visit that the child was not doing well, or had reported poor appetite, or that the health worker made a judgment on the basis of the history provided by the mother and the appearance of the child, or if arm circumference rather than weight had been used? We do not have the answer to these questions, either for TINP or elsewhere.

The results from the research by George *et al.* (1992) suggest that in a situation in India where considerable effort is expended to ensure that reasonably good levels of PHC, health and nutrition education, immunisations, deworming, and other interventions are available to rural families, then the addition of weighing provides no further benefits as judged by anthropometry. At the other end of the scale, the Zaire study of Gerein and Ross (1991) and reports from elsewhere would suggest that weighing and charting not accompanied by an adequate level of effective nutrition and health education, or other interventions, is unlikely to produce benefits to child nutrition or health and is not worth doing.

Are there situations between these two extremes where weighing and charting would be very beneficial, because it greatly helped the other interventions, and these other interventions were well implemented? We do not have an answer to this question; certainly not one that would be acceptable to the sceptics. On the other hand, perhaps the advocates of GMP and the critics could agree on a minimum set of circumstances that are deemed essential or near essential for GMP to have any likelihood of success in improving health and nutrition. For example, if the weighing and charting for one mother and child takes less than 10 minutes, perhaps double that time needs to be available for advice, education, and other interventions.

If the health or clinic workers do not have that amount of time, or if the desired interventions are not feasible in a particular setting, then perhaps the weighing and charting is not desirable. Perhaps particular trajectories on the growth cart should be tied to particular counselling, and sets of counselling cards for different situations are important or essential. Perhaps time and resources spent on GMP are not appropriate in communities where levels of immunisation against measles or other preventable diseases are under, say 75%.

Are there ways to identify countries or districts or communities where other ways of screening children for interventions may be easier and more effective than child weighing? Have we adequately (either with or without GM) used the mother's opinion on the health and well-being of her child as a way to select children at risk? Could the child's weight at a particular age, perhaps 6, 9, or 12 months, be the basis for action over the next 12 months, rather than the practice of time consuming weighing at frequent intervals? Could a measure of poverty, or of mother's education or nutritional or health knowledge provide the basis for selection of children for special attention? Could a Paulo Freire approach, where communities themselves play a major role in assessing both their own problems and suggesting appropriate local actions, be preferable and more effective than GMP imposed on them (Freire 1972; Drummond 1975)? Could such an approach combined with mothers weighing their own children as part of growth promotion be an integral part of community development, as suggested by Morley (1992)?

II

A Development Strategy

The growth monitoring and promotion (GMP) programmes were expanded in many countries during the early 70s without having the benefit of a solid body of principles and guidelines for implementation. Policy-makers and programme managers developed their programmes primarily on the basis of their own understanding and vision and learning from each other's experiences.

It is to be expected, therefore, that the understanding of the principles and their functioning varied widely from programme to programme. This paper examines those principles in the light of recent developments in nutrition strategies with a view to finding the linkages between GMP and the broader strategy of growth promotion.

Basic Principles

Among many definitions of GMP the one adopted by the Integrated Child Development Services, India, is perhaps the most comprehensive. It defines GMP as "an operational strategy of enabling mothers to visualise growth or lack of growth and to receive specific, relevant and practical guidance in ways in which she, her family and community can act to ensure health and continued regular growth in her child."

Three basic principles could be derived from the above definition:

* GMP is a preventive and promotive strategy aimed at action before malnutrition occurs.
* GMP is a behaviour change strategy carried out through effective communication to achieve adequate growth through home and community action.
* GMP deals with the total environment of the growing child, encompassing not only food but health, physical environment, psychological development, and intellectual stimulation.

Operational Implications

GMP as a Preventive and Promotive Strategy

Most nutrition programmes have suffered from the same curative bias found in health programmes in general. Both the providers and the community perceive it to be curative. The attitude has too often been to find the malnourished and try to rehabilitate them, basically by giving them food. This approach, clearly, cannot bring satisfactory results over the long term. Malnourished children are identified frequently in their 3rd, 4th, or even 5th year of life and their rehabilitation is difficult, expensive, and partial at best.

One of the key operational implications of the GMP Strategy is the importance to reaching young infants soon after birth, for the following reasons:

* Most children under 6 months will show a rapid growth pattern. This period is, therefore, ideal to give positive reinforcement to mothers and to demonstrate to them the value and feasibility of maintaining good growth in their children.
* Responses of early growth faltering are usually effective, because mothers have more control over the child's environment and more home-based, effective actions are available to overcome growth faltering while the child is still on the breast (*e.g.*, introduction of complementary feeding, increased frequency of feeding).
* Although the *prevalence* of malnutrition is generally highest in older children, above age 2, the *incidence* of growth faltering (the process of *becoming* malnourished) occurs maximally from about 6 months to 2 years. Beyond this age, growth trends are nearer to normal, although attained size may be far below the desired norm. Thus, the promotion of continued good growth and early action in the case of faltering, even before any malnutrition is evident, prevents the development of malnutrition.

GMP as a Behaviour Change Strategy

One fundamental flaw in our communication/education strategy is that it is basically a knowledge dissemination strategy.

It is based on a faulty assumption that dissemination of factual knowledge will in itself bring about changes in practice and behaviour. The best example of this approach in nutrition education is the promotion of the "four food groups" to bring about changes in the diet of the population. The approach has generally failed because no clear behavioural objectives were formulated.

To be effective in its behaviour change impact, a communication exercise should fulfil the following requirements:

* It must be based on sufficient knowledge of the existing behaviour pattern and the reasons behind it.
* The messages must take into account the environment (socio-cultural, economic) in which the changes are to take place. This is to guarantee the credibility and relevance of the message and feasibility of the recommended practice.
* It must be action-oriented, dealing primarily with "what to do" and the reasons behind it. It must be presented in a convincing and persuasive way.
* It must be specific and individualised.
* The proof of benefits must be available within a relatively short period.

The GMP strategy has great potential in translating those principles of communication into practice. *Firstly,* a problem must be identified and recognised. Here is the vital role of *assessment* of *growth,* to measure and actually *see* the problem. Hence, the importance of weight plotted on a card—the *visualisation* of a problem otherwise not seen or even perceived. Here too lies the value of the trend line of growth, rather than the more commonly used nutritional status lines (or colours)—we want to *see* the problem early, before malnutrition is obvious. *Secondly,* we must facilitate the mother (and others concerned) to analyse *why* growth is not occurring as expected and desired. This analysis and understanding must precede any effort at advice or action, in order to ensure the mother accepts the logic or reasoning behind the suggested action.

Advice based on an understanding of the problem behind the growth faltering is by its very nature specific and action-oriented: it deals with that particular child. Every month, communication in GMP should, therefore, start with listening to what mothers have to say about the child's health and nutrition situation in the context of the family situation. It is a dialogue between the mother and the "counsellor" in analysing the possible reasons behind the child's failure to grow. In this process, the mother is empowered to deal more effectively with the problem. Three major groups of issues are relevant to be examined: the household food availability, the child care and feeding practices, and infections.

As part of developing a positive environment to support the individual communication, a demand for "growth" must be created. Basically, this is an effort to market growth intensively as something valuable and desirable for every child. Only if the significance of growth is fully understood and growth is demanded by the community can the individual interaction be more effective. In short, unless the clients *want* our "product," it will never sell. When mothers seek growth, they will anxiously watch the assessment (weighing and plotting to visualise growth) and be open to discuss and take action to achieve the desired goal. Without an understanding of the importance of growth or an appreciation for its overall reflection of child well-being, a mother cannot be expected to mobilise constrained resources of time, money and effort in an attempt to obtain the product we are promoting—regular healthy growth.

GMP: The Total Child Environment

In analysing the possible causes for growth faltering, one must examine the areas of food availability, child care, and health/infection. The underlying causes could be in any of those areas. This will lead to action that will go beyond the traditional prescriptive advice.

It may involve action by the mother but, more often, will require the concurrence of her family decision-makers (husband, mother-in-law, etc.). Invariably, it will call for some type of resource mobilisation, and women seldom control resources. Be it her own time (increased frequency of breast-feeding or other food), family diet (set aside a reasonable portion of food for the child), other family resources (build a latrine, consult a doctor), or even community action (a child care crèche, loan of a garden plot, small credit), action will require collaboration and mutual help.

Hence, the importance of conducting GMP in the community itself where, in small groups, mothers can hear, participate, and understand. Here too is the reason to separate GMP from the widely held expectation of food supplement distribution, an activity that will throttle any chance of meaningful analysis and household or community action. By addressing the total environment of the child the growth of the child becomes the indicator of the well-being of the family (and, quite logically, the sum total of the growth of the youngest children is a sensitive indicator of the well-being of the community). The mother, family, and community are encouraged and empowered to identify the actions within their control that can give a measurable improvement in the quality of life of the most sensitive and vulnerable member of the family. GMP is, in reality, a development strategy.

III

The Nyerere Declaration

The participants at the Colloquium on Growth Promotion for Child Development in Nyeri, Kenya, 12-13 May, 1992 recognised that it is morally unacceptable that malnutrition is a major contributing cause in 10 million out of the 15 million deaths of children in the world each year. The World Summit for Children and the International Convention on the Rights of the Child affirmed as a global ethic that the protection, development, and survival of the child is a human right. Nations should give priority to children in the allocation of resources.

The Colloquium recognised that growth monitoring is being implemented in many countries for millions of children. Too often this monitoring has not promoted growth because the weighing and charting has not been followed by appropriate action.

The Colloquium recommends that:

* Growth promotion for child development should use cyclical problem solving approaches based on assessment, analysis, and action.

* Physical growth is normally a reflection of child development. Cognitive and psycho-social development also need attention. Causal factors of poor growth and development need to be understood for effective action to be taken within local resource constraints.
* All levels of society should support families in their responsibility for promoting child growth and development and should strengthen the capacity and resources of households in providing food security, appropriate care and protection from infection, and other illnesses.
* Communities have responsibility for identifying and analysing the factors causing poor child growth and development, and mobilising resources for sustainable action to provide better.child care, feeding, and health.

  Communities should be empowered to demand support from governmental and non-governmental agencies. International agencies should facilitate this process.
* Supportive services should work with communities to ensure that resources reach the most needy children. This requires mechanisms to identify populations and sub-groups where growth faltering is most prevalent, to define major causes of poor growth and to mobilise resources and actions.
* National responsibility for growth promotion should include macro-analysis of factors contributing to growth faltering, supportive policies, and a framework for planning and action at all levels.
* These objectives will be achieved if appropriate management information systems and applied research are used to build capacity for improved problem-solving and decision-making at all levels.
* Use of information for growth promotion falls into two general categories:

  (a) Growth promotion for individual children involves information from, and assessment by, mothers, community volunteers, and service personnel using:

- * Growth monitoring by weighing and charting to reflect the dynamics of individual growth in the early years of life.
- * Occasional weighing without the use of growth charts.
- * Other methods of assessment including traditional practices and measurements other than weighing.

(b) Community-based nutrition surveillance using periodic assessment of nutritional status, either by anthropometric or other surveys of populations, to focus on children in greatest need.

References

Anon. 1968, The Ilesha Health and Weight Chart, *Nutr Revs*, 26: 267-69.
1985, Growth Monitoring: Intermediate Technology or Expensive Luxury, Editorial, *Lancet,* ii: 1337-38.

Berg, A. 1992, The Borrower's Perspective Supplement to *New and Noteworthy in Nutrition* (No. 16), Report from IBRD, Washington, D.C.

Boulder, Waterview Press, pp. 82-93.

Drummond, T. 1975, Using the Method of Paulo Freire in Nutrition Education: An Experimental Plan for Community Action in Northeast Brazil, Cornell International Nutrition Monograph Series Number 3, Ithaca, New York.

Freire, P. 1972, Pedagogy of the Oppressed, Penguin Books, London.

George, S., Latham, M.C., and Abel, R. 1992, Effectiveness of Growth Monitoring in Indian Villages, The *FASEB Journal,* Abstracts 6(5): 1498.

Gerein, M.N. and Ross, D.A. 1991, Is Growth Monitoring Worthwhile? An Evaluation of its use in Three Child Health Programmes in Zaire *Soc. Sci. Med.* 32: 667-75.

Gopalan, C. and Chatterjee, M. 1985, Use of Growth Charts for Promotion of Child Nutrition, New Delhi, *Nutrition Foundation of India,* pp. 1-120.

Grant, J. 1984, State of the World's Children 1984, Oxford, Oxford University Press, pp. 1-60.
1987, State of the World's Children 1987, Oxford, Oxford University Press, pp. 64-79.

Griffiths, M. 1985, Growth Monitoring of Pre-school Children, Geneva, World Federation of Public Health Associations.

Hendrata, L. 1988, Growth Monitoring and Promotion, New York, UNICEF.

Jelliffe, D.B. 1966, The Assessment of Nutritional Status of the Community, Oxford, Oxford University Press.

Latham, M.C. 1979, Human Nutrition in Tropical Africa, Rome, Food and Agricultural Organisation of the United Nations, pp. 25-30.

1984, Strategies for the Control of Malnutrition and the Influence of the Nutritional Sciences, *Food and Nutr*, 10: 5-31.

1991, Growth Monitoring and Promotion, in J. Himes ed.: Anthropometric Assessment of Nutritional Status, Wiley-Liss Inc., Chapter 17, pp. 287-99.

Morley, D., 1968, Prevention of Protein-calorie Deficiency Syndrome, *Tr. Roy Soc Trop Med Hyg*, 62:200-08.

1973, Paediatric Priorities in the Developing World, London, Butterworth, pp. 1-250.

1988, Personal Communication.

1992, Personal Communication.

Morley, D. Bicknell, J. and Woodland, M. 1968, Factors Influencing the Growth and Nutritional Status of Infants and Young Children in a Nigerian Village, *Tr. Roy Soc Trop Med Hyg*, 62:164-95.

Pelemeier, N.R . 1985, Mother's Knowledge Related to Child Health and Nutrition in Ghana and Lesotho, *J. Trop Pediat*, 31:131-39.

Rohde, J.E. 1984, Growth Monitoring, *World Health*, May 1984, pp. 17-19.

1985, Community-based Nutrition Programmes, in Waiver M. and Huffman S. eds: Health and Family Planning in Community-based Distribution Programmes.

Stephenson, L.S., Latham, M.C. and Jansen A.A.J. 1983, A Comparison of Growth Standards: Similarities between NCHS, Harvard, Denver and Privileged African Children and Differences with Kenyan Rural Children, Ithaca, New York, Cornell University International Nutrition Monograph Series No. 12, pp. 1-95.

WHO (World Health Organisation), 1978, A Growth Chart for International Use and Child Health Care: Guidelines for Primary Health Care Personnel, Geneva, WHO.

CHAPTER 2

Learning Patterns in Infancy

Infant Speech

How does an infant learn to talk? With what phonetic equipment does a new-born baby come into the world? How is the baby's I.Q. related to his speech? Are there laws of speech development? These are questions of perennial interest to parents, and they pose fascinating problems to the investigator of human development.

There are two aspects to the question of the beginning of human speech. The first deals with the origin of language in prehistoric times; the second concerns the beginning of speech, starting with the birth cry, in the young child. The first aspect is so shrouded in the dimness of antiquity that at present there seems no hope of achieving a satisfactory solution. The second aspect, that of the origin and development of speech and language in childhood, obviously is open to observation.

For the scientific investigation of speech, the first need is a set of accurate symbols for the basic speech sounds, just as in physics and chemistry. Scientific progress depended upon the invention of the periodic table with precisely defined symbols for the elements. The English alphabet is not a precise scientific instrument, for one of its symbols may stand for several different sounds and contrariwise, different combinations of letters may represent the same sound. For example, in the words father, sergeant and hearth the symbols *a*, *e* and *ea*, respectively, all are sounded in the same way, like the *a* in ah.

In the International phonetic Alphabet, invented about 40 years ago, the speech investigator has a precise tool that makes scientific work possible. This alphabet unlike conventional ones, has one, and only one, symbol for each elemental sound. Thus the sound *ah* is always represented by the symbol *a*. The complete alphabet is given in the Table 2.1. In our studies at the Iowa Child

Table 2.1

International Phonetic Alphabet is an indispensable tool in the study of infant speech. In it there is only one symbol for each of the elemental sounds that can be uttered by the human voice. A baby is able to make from one to six such elemental sounds during a single exhalation.

IPA Symbol	*Spellings*	*Examples*
æ	*a*, ai	hat, plaid
θɪ, θ	*a*, ai, au, ay, ea, eh, ei, ey	ate, rain, gauge, ray, steak, eh, veil, obey
ɛ:	*a*, ai, ay, e, ea, ei	dare, chair, prayer, there, wear, their
a	*a*, e, ea	father, sergeant, hearth
b	*b*, bb	bed, hobby
tʃ	ch, tch, te, ti, tu	chief, catch, righteous, question, natural
d	*d*, dd, ed	do, ladder, pulled
ɛ	a, ae, ai, ay, e, ea, ei, eo, ie, oe, u	any, aesthetic, said, says, ebb, leather, heifer, leopard, friend, foetid, bury
i	ae, ay, e, ea, ee, ei, eo, ey, i, ie, oe	Caesar, quay, equal, team, see, deceive, people, key, machine, field, amoeba
f	*f*, ff, gh, ph	feed, muffin, tough, physics
g	*g*, gg, gh, gu, gue	give, egg, ghost, guard, demagogue
h	*h*, wh	hit, who
i	e, ee, *i*, ie, o, u, ui, y	England, been, if, sieve, woman, busy, build, hymn
ai	ai, ay, ei, ey, i, ie, uy, y, ye	aisle, aye, height, eye, ice, tie, buy, sky, lye
dʒ	ch, d, dg, dge, di, g, gg, *j*	Greenwich, graduate, judgment, bridge, soldier, magic, exaggerate, just
k	*c*, cc, cch, ch, ck, cq, cque, cu, gh, *k*, qu	car, account, bacchanal, character, back, acquaint, sacque, biscuit, hough, kill, liquor
l	*l*, ll	live, call
m	chm, gm, lm, m, mb, mm, mn	drachm, paradigm, calm, more, limb, hammer, hymn
n	gn, kn, n, nn, pn	gnat, knife, not, runner, pneumatic
ŋ	n, *ng*, ngue	pink, ring, tongue
ɒ	a, *o*	wander, box
ou, o	au, eau, eo, ew, *o*, oa, oe, oh, *oo*, ou, ow	hautboy, beau, yeoman, sew, note, road, toe, oh, brooch, soul, flow
ɔ	*a*, ah, al, au, aw, o, oa, ou	tall, Utah, talk, fault, raw, order, broad, fought

IPA Symbol	*Spelling*	*Examples*
u	eu, ew, o, oe, *oo*, ou, u, ue, ui	manoeuvre, grew, move, canoe, ooze, troupe, rule, flue, fruit
y	o, *oo*, ou, *u*	wolf, look, should, pull
ɔi	oi, oy	oil, toy
au	*ou*, ough, *ow*	out, bough, brow
p	*p*, pp	pen, stopper
r	*r*, rh, rr	red, rhythm, carrot
s	c, ce, *s*, sc, sch, ss	city, mice, see, scene, schism, loss
ʃ	ce, ch, ci, psh, s, sch, sci, se, *sh*, si, ss, ssi, ti	ocean, machine, special, pshaw, sugar, schist, conscience, nauseous, ship, mansion, tissue, mission, mention
t	ed, ght, *t*, th, tt	talked, bought, toe, thyme, bottom
θ	th	thin
∂	th, the	then, bathe
ʌ	o, oe, oo, ou, *u*	son, does, flood, couple, cup
ju, iu	eau, eu, eue, ew, ieu, iew, *u*, ue, ui, yu, yew, you	beauty, feud, queue, few, adieu, view, use, cue, suit, yule, yew, you
ɜr, ɜ	*er*, ear, ir, or, our, *ur*, yr	term, learn, thirst, worm, courage, hurt, myrtle
v	f, ph, *v*, vv	of, Stephen, visit, flivver
w	o, u, *w*	choir, quiet, well
j	g, i, j, *y*	lorgnette, union, hallelujah, yet
z	s, sc, ss, x, z, zz	has, discern, scissors, Xerxes, zone, dazzle
z	g, s, *si*, z, zi	garage, measure, division, azure, brazier
ə	*a*, ai, e, ei, eo, *i*, ia, *o*, oi, ou, u	alone, mountain, system, mullein, dungeon, easily, parliament, gallop, porpoise, curious, circus
θr, ɔ	ar, *er*, ir, or, our, ur, yr	liar, father, elixir, labor, labour, auger, martyr

Welfare Research Station these symbols were used to record the first sounds, babblings and developing speech of our infant subjects.

A second necessary tool in this work is a manageable unit of observation. This was furnished by what is known as the respiratory unit. When an individual speaks, his sounds and words are uttered on the exhalation phase of breathing. It is abnormal to speak while inhaling. Thus a baby always vocalises while it breaths out. The breath unit readily lends itself to observation. In the case of an infant, the number of sounds carried on a single breath varies from one to about half a dozen. And this number of sounds is ordinarily well within the attention span of even an untrained observer.

These two experimental tools, the international Phonetic Alphabet and the breath unit of observation, have proved invaluable for collecting reliable data on the beginnings and the acquisition of speech. They have permitted systematic observation and statistical treatment of the results.

A question frequently asked about our investigation is, "Where do you get your babies?" Obviously this is the simplest aspect of the whole endeavour, for there are plenty of babies in the world. However, the question does lead directly to the general problem of sampling the population of babies. One good source of subjects is a nursery connected with the obstetrical department of a hospital, and a great deal of our work has been done in this situation.

The home is another natural laboratory for this work. After a baby is taken home from the hospital, it is visited at regular intervals of two weeks or a month throughout infancy. At each visit a sample of the baby's speech, as uttered on a number of breaths, is written down in the International Alphabet. If care is taken to select homes of different socio-economic status, the speech sound samples may reflect a number of variables operating in the home situation, and the data subsequently may be analysed in terms of these variables.

We have studied infants' speech development in several other situations : in orphanages, where retardation in speech is notoriously frequent; in state institutions for the feeble-minded; in schools for the deaf, where the investigation of how children deaf from birth achieve intelligible speech, makes a valuable comparison with the development of speech in the normal infant.

The earliest sounds made by a new-born babe are monosyllabic cries. During the first few days of life the infant most frequently gives voice to eight distinguishable sounds, which represent about a fifth of the sound elements used by adults. These eight include only five of about a dozen vowel sounds listed in the International Phonetic Alphabet, and three consonants of a possible two dozen. Its most frequent cry by far is ae, like the vowel in the word fat; this sound amounts to 90 per cent of an infant's vowel utterances. In one study involving 40 babies under 10 days of age, it was found to be the only vowel used by all the subjects. The other four early vowel sounds are I as in fit, ε as in set, ʌ as in up and u as in food. The three consonants are h, l and the glottal stop, a consonant formed by pressure of the breath behind the closed glottis.

Vowels are usually classified into three groups: front, middle, and back, corresponding to the parts of the mouth and tongue used in their phonation. The sound I, as in fit, is a front vowel. The sound u, as in food, is a back vowel. An infant's vowel repertoire consists mostly of front vowels. In its consonant equipment the opposite is usually true: two of the three consonants it uses are phonated by the back mouth parts, namely h and the glottal stop.

As the infant grows older, non-crying sounds begin to dominate the cries. The soft cooing and utterances that delight parents become more frequent. The child achieves increasing control of the mouth parts for vocalising back vowels and front consonants—the labials, dentals and postdentals. Then begins a long period of meaningless babbling. Babbling has a real function in speech development; it is a practice period for control of the sound elements of language. The baby seems to be trying out new vowel and consonant combinations in a bewildering array. He repeats these sounds over and over again on varying pitches, with varying intensities and cadences. He mouths them, gets the kinesthetic feel of them with lips, tongue and cheeks, and unconsciously and endlessly practices them. Significantly, after a year of this, meaningful words—at first mere approximations of words—begin to appear upon the background of infantile babbling.

Meaningful words appear towards the end of the first year or the beginning of the second year of life. At first they constitute a very small proportion of the infant's vocalisation, but during the later part of the second year they become prominent. A word usually passes through an interesting transformation. At first it is a crude approximation. In nurseries the world over, the baby lies in a crib and babbles meaningless sounds such as "mamama" or "adadada." Under the coaching of parents, these babblings are abbreviated to "mama" and to "daddy." This is the way one child learned the word milk: at first it was "meme," then "mik mik" and finally milk. Pillow is often pronounced "pido." In the case of another child, the more difficult word please evolved from "be" through the series "ble," "pez" "pwez" to please. Sometimes the first words exhibit an onomatopoeic character. Thus a watch is a "tick tick"; a dog a "bow wow"; and a cow a "moo moo".

There are no fundamental group differences in the inherent phonetic equipment of human beings. In the first 10 days of life, boys and girls, white children and Negroes make pretty much the same sounds. But by the time they begin to form word patterns, some sex differences do appear. For instance, at a year and a half, girls exceed boys in the ability to use consonants at the beginning, in the middle and at the end of a word. The number of consonants used by girls in the initial position is 8.7 as against 7.7 for boys. For the medial position, the mean for girls is 7.9 and for boys 6.9. In the final position, girls use 2.9 consonants while boys use 2.4.

The average eight-month-old child is unable to use words. At 10 months he probably will have one word; at 12 months, about three words. At a year and a half, his vocabulary may be 20 words. During the next three months it will jump to over 100, and at two years it may contain as many as 250 words.

The ultimate language problem for the growing child is to relate words into meaningful sentences. His first sentence may be a single word; for instance, he will use the word "do" to obtain many of his demands. From a single word grows a variety of longer sentences. The average child's first sentence appears soon after the 15th month. At two years the average length of his sentences is 1.7 words. At five it has expanded to 4.6 words. The 10 words most often used in constructing the first sentence are; "I", "is", "it", "you", "that", "do", "a", "this", "not" and "the." Nouns and verbs at first are used more frequently than adjectives and connectives.

Now the question of primary scientific interest is: Does infant speech exhibit any degree of orderliness in its development; in other words, are there any discernible natural laws governing the emergence of speech patterns ? To an untrained observer, infantile babbling seems to be simply an amorphous mass of sound, incoherent, unintelligible, chaotic, at times monotonously repetitive, at other times in a marvellously complex state of flux. On the face of it, there seem to be hardly any regularities in it.

Yet it has been found to be quite orderly, and its investigation has yielded a number of statistical laws.

To understand this statistical analysis, a few definitions of terms used by workers in this field will help. The elemental speech sounds are called phonemes. For present purposes a phoneme will be designated as a phoneme type. The vowel in the word "hat" is a phoneme type, as is each of the consonants in the word. The term type, then, refers to the speech sounds listed in the International Phonetic Alphabet. Another term employed is frequency, which refers to the number of times a type occurs.

Suppose we have painstakingly visited about 100 babies in their homes twice each month from birth to two and a half years of age. At each visit all the sounds that the child utters on, say, 30 breaths have been recorded. Then our data will consist of sounds on 30 breaths for each of the 60 visits during the 30 months of the period studied. For statistical convenience, instead of analysing the progress of the 100 infants month by month, let us consolidate the data into two month intervals or age levels. This will give us 15 age levels with which to work.

If we now average the number of phoneme types or kinds of sound, uttered by the 100 babies at each of the 15 two-month age levels, we will find that the mean number increases from age level to age level. The number rises at a regular rate, which is defined by the following mathematical equation:

$$N=7.53\ A^{.471}$$

where N stands for the number of types and A for the age.

This equation tells us that the number of phoneme types equals 7.53 times the age raised to .471 power, and that a curve plotted from this equation will be a parabola.

The curve affords a picture of the nature of speech development during infancy. It shows that infants during the first two months of life use on the average about seven and a half sounds. At the end of two and a half years, the average infant uses about 27 sounds. Now there are about three dozen phonemes in the International Alphabet. The curve thus tells us that on an average the baby of two and a half years vocalises only about two-thirds of the sounds he will later use, so that the achievement of a full complement of the phonetic elements is still a matter of further development.

The curve also indicates that progress is not made in equal increments. If the increments were equal, the curve would be a straight line. It is, however, a decelerating curve, which means that although the baby continues to increase his mastery of new sounds, he does so at a steadily declining rate. This matter of rate is important to parents. The average parents are tremendously concerned to know whether their child is "keeping up," or why the youngster next door is "ahead of" their child. The equation, then, is a precise formulation of a concern vital to every parent and, as we shall see later, may be used to establish a fairly accurate answer to a parent's questions about his child's progress.

In the acquisition of new sounds, infant girls show a superiority to boys. In the first year there are no sex differences in development, but thereafter there is an increasing tendency for girls to surpass boys.

When we consider the frequency, or the number of times the phoneme types are used, the situation is reversed. Now the boys advance more rapidly than the girls; in other words, they use fewer different sounds, but they do more talking. For both boys and girls, the frequency rates form accelerating curves, in contrast with the decelerating curves for phoneme types. This means, of course, that the babies use the sounds they have acquired more frequently as they grow.

Thus on the basis of two different criteria of speech development, we see that the early incoherent efforts of infants towards true speech are not as amorphous or as chaotic as everyday observation might suggest.

With the equations thus developed, we can study the differences in speech development of infants in different home environments. A comparison of the speech of babies of working-class families with those whose fathers are doctors, lawyers, teachers or business owners is shown in the chart 2.1. These curves are based on the frequency criterion of speech development. By this criterion the speech development of babies in homes of workers is considerably below that of the professional group. One suggested explanation is that the experience of the worker's child is more manual, while the environment in the professional household is highly verbal.

We have found that low-grade feebleminded children, that is, idiots and imbeciles, in the fourth year of life possess the speech-sound status of year old infants. When these children were examined a year later, they had made no progress whatever. This degree of speech retardation is practically hopeless. A study is now being made of what correlation exists between intelligence and speech development in normal infants.

Chart 2.1

Development of Speech in children of professional families (*solid line*) is somewhat faster than that of those in labourers' families.

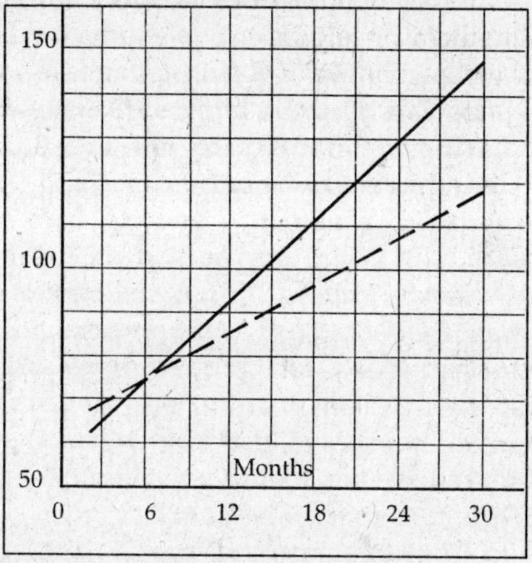

If speech development is really subject to natural laws, it should be possible to diagnose the speech-sound status of any infant and determine whether it is retarded, normal or advanced. Suppose a mother asks us to tell her whether her 18-month-old child is progressing normally in its speech development. The procedure would be to obtain several samples of the child's speech sounds from which to determine its average phoneme frequency. Suppose this value is 100. This would intersect the average curve for all children of 18 months at the 50th percentile, or the median, meaning that the child's development is perfectly normal. In fact, if its value fell between the 25th and 75th percentile lines, the infant's speech-sound status would be considered average. If the value fell between the 75th and 90th percentile curves, the child would be considered above average; above the 90th percentile it might be considered very advanced. If, on the other hand, it fell below the 10th percentile, the infant would be diagnosed as greatly retarded.

It appears that atleast some progress has been achieved in finding the answers to a few of the questions concerning the beginnings and subsequent development of speech in the human being. The next step in this enterprise is to discover remedial measures for babies whose speech seems to show retardation.

Basic Learning Processes

A good place to begin the study of learning related to schooling is the early life of the child, long before he enters elementary school. What happens to the child in the early years does much to determine what happens to him in school and in life. During the early years, his appetite for learning is either whether or dulled, and the foundation is laid for the attitudes that constitute such a large part of the adult personality. In addition, in the early part of life the adaptive behaviour of the infant and child illustrates many forms of learning that play an important role in subsequent development.

A distinction is sometimes made between the terms *growth* and *development*. Growth refers to an increase in the physical dimensions of the body, and particularly in the skeletal and muscular structures. On the other hand, development refers to an increase in specialisation or organisation either of the functions performed by the various bodily organs or of behaviour. Thus while growth takes place in infancy and the body increases in strength, there is also a development of function. By the end of the first year, the legs and arms no longer simply perform unco-ordinated motions, but the legs have become instruments for walking and the arms and hands have become tools for grasping and manipulating objects. This change in the use of the limbs represents development and involves more than a sheer increase in size. The process of development involves differentiation of function (the legs come to do something different from the arms), and the activities involved become part of a co-ordinated system of behaviour.

Many fine text-books have been written for teachers about human growth and development. These include books by Gordon (1969b), Mussen *et al.* (1969) and Stone and Church (1968). This chapter cannot do what these texts do; its purpose is much more limited, to introduce the reader to some of the learning processes that control development.

Let us begin by considering the child at birth. The newborn child, that is, the *neonate*, is born with a nervous system in which many basic structures do not yet function or do not function with full effectiveness. The *neonate* has difficulty in regulating his temperature. The structures related to crawling, walking and otherwise moving about in the environment have not yet reached a level of development where they can function at all and many of the fibres of the brain have not acquired the sheath of myelin that insulates them from other fibres and permits them to function as independent units within a system. The neonate is not a simplified adult with a brain lacking traces of experience with the world. The infant is a very different creature from the adult, not just in the experience he has stored but in the equipment he has functioning in his brain.

Hutt *et al.* (1969) have brought together the information available on the behaviour of the child shortly after birth. Unfortunately, there are problems related to the study of infants at birth because the circumstances of birth and often the drugs given to the mother, may have a disturbing effect on the infant's behaviour. Study of the behaviour of the *neonate* is somewhat analogous to study of the behaviour of an adult immediately after an automobile accident in which his entire nervous system was badly shaken. Sometimes as long as three days or a week may pass before the behaviour of the infant ceases to show the traumatic effects of delivery.

The human *neonate* has a limited repertoire of behaviour, which does not suddenly appear at birth but has emerged during the period of gestation. Some responses to touch have been recorded in embryos only eight to ten weeks old. The hand will show signs of closing on objects before the embryo is fifteen weeks old, the response of withdrawing the leg appears at about the same time, and sucking behaviour occurs at about twenty-four weeks. Babies have been born with calluses on the thumb from thumb sucking before birth.

The determination of the responses that the infant can make to particular stimuli is not the simple matter it might appear to be on the surface, for the response of an infant depends very much on the state it happens to be in. In a broad sense, one can say that the infant has two states, sleeping and waking, and that he spends about 70 per cent of his time in the sleeping state.

This is a gross oversimplification of what happens for the infant may be in any state between the two and may remain so; for long stretches of time, much as an adult may spend the early hours of the morning in a twilight stage in which he is half awake and half asleep. Hutt *et al.* adopt a system of five states, varying from a state in which the eyes are closed, the breathing is regular and there are no movements except occasional startle responses to a state of maximum activity in which the infant is crying. The intermediate states are the state of having the eyes closed but with irregularities of breathing and heart rate and with small muscle movements, the state of having the eyes open but with no gross movements, and the state in which the eyes are open and gross movements occur. The states are claimed to be distinct conditions, and each represents a characteristic cluster of behaviours that tend to go together. A baby may spend a few minutes in moving from one state to another but does not stay long in a condition between one state and another, though he may stay for long periods of time in one state. The state in which the infant happens to be depends on an interaction of internal circumstances and external conditions. The temperature of the environment is one of the most important condition determining state.

Noise has the opposite effect on an infant than it has on an adult, in whom it produces an aroused and awakened state. In the infant, moderate amounts of auditory stimulation tend to produce a state of sleep. Surrounding the infant with blankets and clothes tends to decrease the activity of the baby and to lower the respiratory rate and the pulse. Internal conditions also affect the state of the infant, including the schedule of nursing, and there appears to be a certain degree of cyclic activity built into the very young child. In the study of what the child can do during the first few weeks of life, the common practice is to experiment with him when he is either awake and passive or awake and making gross bodily movements, though some studies have been conducted on sleeping infants and on infants that are in a more active state of fussing. The infant spends about eighteen hours of the twenty-four hour day in sleep. For two to three hours a day the baby is awake and quiet, and for one or two hours a day he is awake and active. For the remaining one to three hours, he is awake and either crying or fussing. The infant may spend an hour or more in one state at a time but only a few minutes in moving from one state to another.

Early in the first few weeks of life, a number of other behaviours occur that are under a high degree of stimulus control. The infant will, for example, fixate with his eyes for short periods on a small bright source of light. Turning of the head in the direction of a sound is also claimed to occur early in life and perhaps shortly after birth, if not at birth. The infant also shows a great many reflexes, some of which are similar to those of the adult and some not. For example, reflexes of the pupil of the eye are the same as in the adult, but reflexes of the foot when the sole is touched lightly are not. This point is raised to indicate that the nervous system of the child has similarities to and differences from the nervous system of the adult.

A particularly interesting response is that termed the *orienting response.* This is a response first discovered by Pavlov, who referred to it as the what-is-it reflex. American psychologists have sometimes called it the *attending response,* a term that loosely describes its functions. The orienting response occurs when a new stimulus is presented and responded to by the infant. The response includes a cessation of on-going activity, dilation of the pupils, dilation of the blood vessels in the forehead, a respiratory pause, and other characteristic responses. In the adult, the orienting response occurs on occasions when the individual says that he is attending to some object or event. The response occurs not only in the typical neonate but even in the embryo only twenty-six weeks old. The early development of the orienting response suggests that the embryo is, in a sense, ready to respond to environmental events at a very early stage of development. Components of the orienting response have been used to determine the stimuli to which very young babies will respond. The newborn infant shows an orienting response to a wide range of stimuli and by the fourth month shows a stronger orienting response to an unfamiliar complex stimulus, such as the face of a stranger, than he does to a familiar complex stimulus such as his mother (see Fitzgerald, 1968).

There are now ways of demonstrating that infants, in the first few weeks of life, retain information about what they see. It can be shown, for example, that an infant fixates on a pattern presented to his field of view. Later, when the same pattern is presented together with another pattern, the infant fixates on the new pattern for a longer time than the original one. This means that the infant has retained information about the original pattern (see Walcher and Peters, 1971).

Despite the fact that the new-born infant behaves, in many ways, as if he were ready to pick up information from the environment, as is evident from his orienting response, his stage of development is still such that he is greatly limited in the information from the environment that he can use. For example, the region of the brain that handles the analysis of visual information appears to be very incompletely developed until about three or four months after birth. Ellingson (1967) points out that up until three or four months of age, the electrical rhythms of that part of the cortex of the brain (the occipital areas) are rudimentary, but after that age the normal rhythms of the older person become well established and the infant begins to show a capability of performing visually related tasks such as grasping at objects he sees.

The facts that the infant is able to fixate on a bright light and is able to respond to a moving light (Wickelgren, 1969) do not imply that there is any analysis made of the information. Even simple attending responses to moving lights are primitive in that they may involve only one eye and do not involve two-eye co-ordination.

This picture of the infant drawn up to this point is that a living creature whose behaviour is controlled to some degree by the stimuli provided by the environment. Stimuli control simple behaviour such as that of sucking, for the baby generally does not suck unless it is appropriately stimulated from within or without. Stimuli also control general states, such as that of sleeping and waking, for sleep can be produced in a wide-awake baby by patting him rhythmically and a loud noise will wake the sleeping infant. On the other hand, some behaviour does not seem to be the result of any particular set of events in the environment. The typical fussing or crying of the infant seems to be quite unrelated to environmental circumstances and to such matters as whether the child does or does not receive much attention. The idea that attending to a baby who is crying, will increase the amount of crying, is probably false, for crying behaviour is triggered by circumstances within the child. Such behaviour can be brought under temporary control by patting the baby and changing his general state to one of sleep, but the control is only temporary.

Before further facts about the behaviour of the infant are presented, let us consider a few terms widely used in contemporary psychology. When a behaviour occurs in the presence of certain stimuli, *i.e.*, in the presence of certain events in the environment, it is said that the behaviour is under *stimulus control*, as described previously. This simply means that the behaviour can be turned on or turned off by the presence or absence of the particular stimuli. Behaviour naturally under stimulus control, that is, simple behaviour that occurs in the presence of a stimulus without any learning first having to take place, is commonly referred to as a *reflex*. The eyeblink of the infant that occurs when a mild puff of air strikes his eyelid is a reflex. A reflex is called a simple behaviour because its major characteristics can be described in simple terms and not because it involves simple physiological processes. Indeed, the processes in a simple reflex response may involve many million nerve cells located in parts of the nervous system both near and far from the physical location of the reflex action.

An event that produces a reflex is called an *unconditioned stimulus*. This term means that the stimulus produces a uniform and predictable response, but it is a response produced without any learning taking place first. A reflex is often described in parallel terms as an *unconditioned response*. The infant shows a great number or unconditioned responses, that is, responses directly under the control of unconditioned stimuli.

A great range of reflex responses that occur in very early infancy have to do with basic biological functions necessary for maintaining life. Thus sucking is necessary for nutrition, the dilation and contraction of the pupil of the eye are necessary for protecting the internal eye, the eyeblink has other eye-protecting functions, salivation is necessary for digestion and preventing the mucous membranes from drying out, coughing removes foreign matter from the throat and bronchial tubes, and so on.

Among the early organised responses, one of the most striking and interesting is smiling. Scott (1967) finds that this response does not occur before the end of the fifth week but that nearly all infants show the response by the third month. Research in this area is made difficult by smiling-like responses that occur during the first few weeks after birth but are more like muscular spasms of the face than they are the familiar smile. In Scott's summary of research, he reaches the conclusion that the response belongs in the category of *primary socialisation* and that it is an inborn social response unique to man. He notes that it is primarily a response to the human face but that any facelike object may elicit it. He suggests that the response is not elicited in the first few weeks because the infant does not have the perceptual skill needed to differentiate faces from other objects. Scott also cites evidence indicating that the association of the smiling response with the presence of a face is not because the presence of a human face has been associated with feeding. He cites an experiment in which babies were fed by individuals wearing masks, but the masks did not acquire particular properties of eliciting smiling responses.

Although the smiling response is unique to man, other species have responses that are related to early socialisation. The dog, for example, has the tail-wagging response, which begins to appear at about the third week after birth and seems to be primarily a social response, though it occurs both in contacts with other dogs and in contacts with human beings. The dog's social contacts with human beings are very similar to the contacts it has with other dogs. The latter involve walking and running together, romping, nipping with the mouth, and so forth. The human primary social response appears to be confined to behaviour towards other human beings.

The smiling response lays the groundwork for further social development. Because the smile of the baby arouses a positive social response in the adult, it forms a basis for future social interactions.

Within a few weeks of birth, many responses, triggered originally only by a particular stimulus, come to be triggered by new stimuli. For example, sucking behaviour is triggered at first only by stimulation of the lips; then it comes to be triggered by the baby being picked up and later by the appearance of the mother. This is a case of *Pavlovian conditioning or classical conditioning,* which most readers of this text will already know something about. As the reflex responses of the baby become triggered by an increasing number of stimuli, Gagné (1970) would say that the baby comes to learn that certain events come to *signal* other kinds of events, as when being picked up comes to be a signal for eating.

Let us depart here briefly from the main trend of the discussion to describe the general nature of classical conditioning. Pavlov demonstrated nearly a hundred years ago that if a reflex is triggered by stimulus *X*, and if stimulus *Y* occurs at about the same time as *X*, then *Y* acquires the property of triggering the reflex. A puff of air produces the typical eyeblink response, but if the puff of air is always accompanied by the sound of a bell, then the bell acquires the power of setting off the eyeblink. The bell has become the *conditioned stimulus* for the eyeblink. The phenomenon is usually demonstrated through the use of some response involving a reflex, but it probably, does not have to involve a reflex. Presumably, a stimulus that accompanies a response (whatever its source) acquires some capability of eliciting the response, and the conditioned reflex is a special case of the phenomenon. The essential characteristic of classical conditioning is that a stimulus occurs at about the same time as a response and acquires the property of eliciting the response. Sometimes this is described as *contiguity learning,* denoting that the stimulus and the response it is to be tied to must be contiguous, that is, must occur at about the same time. Some psychologists have attempted to maintain that all learning is of this character, but most psychologists would probably maintain that this kind of learning is probably only one of several kinds. The issue is highly controversial. One can say that classical conditioning can take place even before birth (see Brackbill, 1967) and that it continues to be an important form of learning throughout life.

An interesting case of conditioning in infancy is that commonly described as *conditioning to the stimulus of time.* This description is confusing because time is not a stimulus in the sense in which a bright light or a bell or pressure on the skin is a stimulus. Let us illustrate the phenomenon with an example. Suppose that a two-month-old child is lying on his back in his crib and that he is in a waking state, showing some random movements of his arms and legs. Now let us suppose that the experimenter arranges for there to be a marked increase in the brightness of the illumination for a ten-second period at the beginning of each minute. Each time the light goes on, the pupils of the baby's eyes promptly contract and then expand again after the added illumination is turned off. After many trials with the increased illumination, the mechanism is turned off. However, a minute after the last time the light was turned up, the pupils of the baby's eyes contract as though there had been an increase in illumination, despite the fact that there was none. The phenomenon represents time conditioning and clearly illustrates that infants have what might be called a time sense. It shows a primitive capability on the part of the infant to show behaviour related to anticipation or expectancy, though we are not saying here that the infant expects or anticipates the presence of the bright light. This kind of conditioning represents a quite complex form of behaviour. Strangely enough, this kind of temporal conditioning of the pupillary reflex does not seem to take place in the adult. The adult probably has a much better time sense than the infant, but it seems to be dependent on other mechanisms. The adult lives in a world in which events occur at particular times, and these events become time signals. Under such conditions, primitive mechanisms probably do not have to function.

Some of the activity of the very young infant is organised to a considerable degree. Sucking and eating behaviour shows such organisation from the start. Fixation of the eyes on bright objects that stand out against the background is another area of organised behaviour. Later, *prehension*, that is, grasping with the hand, shows organisation. Piaget (see Flavell, 1963) takes the position that underlying these behaviours are what he calls *schemata*[1], that is, structures in the nervous system that permit the primitive organisation of behaviour. Thus Piaget speaks of a schema for sucking and a schema for sight. The schema also represents a focus around which subsequent experiences and memories of the experiences become organised. Similar kinds of psychological organisations are proposed by those investigating the development of language. Such research workers, called *psycholinguists,* have proposed that the baby has potential for organising speech sounds he hears, and although they do not refer to the underlying organising structures as schemas, the basic concept is very similar.

Now let us turn to another form of learning in infancy, not primarily related to reflexive behaviour. Let us take as an illustration findings from a study conducted by Sheppard (1969) on his own three-month old infant. The data of interest to us here consist of the leg-kicking movements of the infant. All normal infants kick their legs spontaneously from time to time. Sheppard was able to arrange a device in a special plexiglas crib in which the infant lived so that each kick of the legs tripped a switch and recorded the motion. Sheppard observed how frequently this happened under conditions prevailing before the experiment. He then arranged the equipment so that each leg kick was followed by a flashing light and the playing of a short recording of the mother's voice. The record of the mother's voice had been made during breast feeding, and a short section of this recording was played, monotonously, after each leg kick. When this procedure was followed, the leg kicks began to take place more frequently. Then Sheppard turned off the voice recording and the flashing light, and the leg kicking tended to slip back towards the original rate. The point to note is that the sound of the mother's voice and the flashing light exerted some control over the leg kicking. Perhaps leg kicking is not the most significant response in the world, but the experiment is useful to us here in illustrating some learning phenomena that occur later in more significant contexts.

Before discussing this experiment and its implications at greater length, let us introduce a few terms that will simplify much of our discussion. First, let us consider the leg-kicking form of behaviour. This is an activity in which infants engage. It is not produced by any particular stimulus that one can identify. A baby just kicks from time to time. Such behaviours that are not initially under any kind of stimulus control are sometimes referred to as *emitted behaviours*. The rate at which the leg kick occurred before the mother's voice and flashing light were introduced is the *baseline rate*. The experimenter was able to arrange conditions so that he could increase the rate of kicking above the baseline rate, and he could then cause the rate to decline again.

The combined playing of the mother's voice and the flashing of the light are referred to as a *reinforcer* or a *reinforcing event*. This means that it has the property of increasing the frequency of the particular behaviour that it follows. Sometimes it is said that a reinforcer strengthens a response. In the particular experiment described, it could be said that the reinforcer was contingent on the leg-kicking response or that the leg kick was the contingency reinforced. After the frequency of the leg kick has been increased, through being followed by a reinforcer, the leg kick is then said to be an *operant*. Skinner coined this term because the behaviour operates on the environment to generate consequences (Skinner, 1953).

This form of learning is sometimes called *instrumental conditioning* or *instrumental learning*, because the behaviour involved is the instrument for producing particular events in the environment. The baby learns that the leg kick turns on the mother's voice and flashing light.

Now certain characteristics of reinforcing events must be noted. The reinforcing event just discussed involved a combination of a recording of the mother's voice and a flashing light—and surely the reader must think of this as an odd combination. One can readily understand intuitively that the voice of the mother might be reinforcing, but why the flashing light? The answer to this question is given by Sheppard in his paper. He states that he found by trial and error that a combination of these two events was a strongly reinforcing happening. No doubt he was also influenced by other studies showing that in the case of the very young infant a flashing light does act as a reinforcer. There is also a very large experimental literature in the field of animal psychology showing that a mere increase or decrease in illumination may provide a reinforcement for animal behaviour. The point to be brought out by this is that one discovers reinforcing events, to some extent, by experimentation. Intuition may help one to discover some of the reinforcers of child behaviour, but it cannot be the sole basis for discovering reinforcing events, and sometimes it is not even a sound basis. Sometimes teachers are wrong in the judgment of what is and what is not reinforcing.

Once there was a teacher who thought she could help the work habits of a child by letting him out on the playground for a short time after the completion of each assignment. The reinforcement did the opposite of what it was intended to do. The reason was that the child had learned to avoid the playground because there he was mistreated by other pupils. When the teacher sent the child to the playground, she was punishing him.

Experimenters have found a wide range of unexpected reinforcing events in the case of the very young human infant. Some studies use sound for this purpose, generally a tone about an octave above middle C. Other studies have used a vibrator that provides a rather mild tickle. Still others have used the appearance of a picture of a human face as a reinforcer, or even facelike illuminated signs (Watson, 1969). The kinds of events that have reinforcing properties for infants are varied indeed, and they are also large in number for older children and adults, but probably different in kind.

The Sheppard experiment brings out another phenomenon of considerable importance. Recall the fact that when the reinforcer was withdrawn, the infant began to show a reduced rate of kicking his leg. In technical terms, one would say that the response was becoming extinguished. In time, the operant will return to the baseline rate from which it started. *Extinction* in a set of circumstances in which behaviour that has been acquired through reinforcement is allowed to occur but without the occurrence of the reinforcer.

Extinction may occur also in the case of classically conditioned responses. Let us return to the case of temporal conditioning of the infant exposed to a bright light that flashed on once every minute. The pupillary response of the infant become conditioned so that it occurred at the beginning of each minute, even though there was no increase in illumination, but this response would not continue once every minute for the rest of the child's life. Each time it occurred, it would be less marked, until it would ultimately fade away. This represents extinction of a classically conditioned response.

Many responses that have been extinguished are rapidly relearned when favourable learning conditions are reintroduced. If the leg-kicking activity of the infant is reinforced again, after perhaps only a single reinforcement, he is kicking as rapidly as at the end of the previous set of reinforcements. This is a very important point, for it means that responses that may appear to have been reduced in strength or eliminated may have been just temporarily inhibited. Indeed, many psychologists would take the position that extinction procedures perhaps inhibit a response only temporarily rather than produce any actual reduction in underlying strength. Some psychologists would even go so far as to say that whatever is learned is learned permanently and irreversibly. This is quite a frightening thought, and it may well be not far from the truth.

Operants are brought under the control of reinforcing contingencies by the kind of process that has been described. This kind of process represents a form of learning, just as classical conditioning represents a form of learning. It comes within the definition of learning. In that learning is generally defined as being relatively enduring modification of responses produced by encounters with the environment. In the case of the kicking response, the modification involved an increase in frequency of the response. The events that led up to this change in response frequency are commonly referred to as the acquisition phase of learning. Acquisition and extinction are usually contrasted, because they appear to have opposite results, but extinction is not quite the opposite of acquisition, for during the extinction phase the response learned during acquisition is blocked from appearing rather than eliminated.

In summary, then, one can say that neonates and very young infants already have a repertoire of responses under stimulus control and that, through simple forms of learning, new stimuli in the environment acquire the property of also controlling many of these responses. The mechanisms involved are those of classical conditioning and instrumental conditioning, both of which continue to play a role throughout the remainder of life. These are not the only mechanisms involved, but they are the ones that play roles in the early stages of infant development and perhaps sometimes even before birth. Examples will be discussed later of obvious instances of both of these mechanisms influencing the behaviour of the school-child, even though they tend to become overshadowed by other forms of learning. In addition, the infant has some capacity for learning through mere exposure to events, as is evident from the studies cited earlier.

Some psychologists have attempted to reduce all learning to the categories of instrumental conditioning and classical conditioning, but many suspect that this is a gross oversimplification of human behaviour. Many forms of behaviour that are learned, particularly verbal behaviour, are not readily squeezed into categories, though attempts have been made to do so. Nevertheless, classical conditioning and instrumental conditioning are important categories of learning, and knowledge gained through the study of these forms of learning has provided important keys to the understanding of many forms of behaviour. Of interest is the fact that an understanding of these forms of learning has done much to develop ways of handling behaviour problems, both in and out of school, and has even led to the development of new techniques of psychotherapy.

Schedules of Reinforcement

Laboratory studies of operant conditioning since mid-century have focused to a very great degree on the problem of the effect on behaviour or what are known as *schedules of reinforcement*. Obviously, a person or machine controlling the reinforcement of a living creature may provide a reinforcing event every time a particular class of behaviours occurs or only on certain occasions. When the reinforcement occurs on every occasion, it is commonly described as *continuous reinforcement*. When the reinforcing event occurs only on some occasions when the behaviour occurs, but not on others, the condition is known as *partial reinforcement*. Psychologists long ago established that in laboratory experiments with both animals and human beings, the partial reinforcement situation produces both slower learning and slower extinction. This interesting discovery did not settle all the issues involved, for there are many systems that may be used for scheduling when a reinforcement is to occur and when it is not. The study of the effects of these various systems on learning constitutes a problem to which we must now turn.

The classic work on schedules of reinforcement is that of Ferster and Skinner (1957). Here, as in most other research conducted since that time, the concentration of efforts was on work with animals, partly because automated laboratories permit the collection and collation of vast amounts of data on the topic without consuming much of the experimenter's time. The findings have to do largely with the maintenance of behaviour rather than with the modification of behaviour.

Most of the schedules studied can be classified either as reinforcements occurring after a particular interval or as reinforcements occurring after a particular number of responses. Let us consider first reinforcements after a particular interval. A pigeon learns to peck at a small white disk on the wall of its training box, referred to as a *key*. The experimenter decides to reinforce the animal for a response occurring at the end of each minute, and no other responses are reinforced. This procedure is referred to as a *fixed-interval schedule*. Under these circumstances, the animal shows a typical pattern of behaviour. As the schedule of reinforcement is applied, the pigeon's behaviour settles down into a pattern. After each reinforcement, the pigeon stops pecking at the disk until nearly a minute has elapsed, then it will peck rapidly at the disk until it receives the next reinforcement. Then it stops pecking again for about another fifty seconds. The behaviour of the animal is intermittent. The schedule of reinforcement is not suitable if the experimenter desires to maintain behaviour, for when the reinforcement is withdrawn, extinction takes place rapidly.

Let us now consider a second major category of reinforcement schedule referred to as the *variable-interval schedule*. The reinforcement is set to occur at responses taking place at particular intervals of time, but the intervals are variable. The interval between any two reinforcements may be set by drawing a number at random from a set of numbers representing the various intervals to be represented. Animals trained on a variable-interval schedule of reinforcement show a uniform output of behaviour. The pigeon thus trained to peck at a key continues to peck very uniformly and for long periods. If the intervals between reinforcements are too long, then the behaviour is extinguished. However, the intervals can be *slowly* lengthened until they are so far apart that the animals appear to maintain the pecking behaviour with almost no reinforcements at all. Animals will, of course, give up a particular form of behaviour for reasons other than extinction. One such reason is sheer fatigue.

In contrast with the fixed-interval schedule, the variable interval schedule can produce behaviour quite resistant to extinction, particularly when the intervals are gradually increased.

A third type of schedule is the *fixed-ratio schedule*, in which the reinforcement appears after a particular number of responses. The animal exposed to such a schedule shows a very uniform output of behaviour. The pigeon pecks consistently, and almost with rhythm. The response is also very readily extinguished. The omission of just three or four reinforcements may be sufficient to produce atleast a temporary cessation of the response. Because the nervous system is particularly sensitive to identifying almost any kind of regularity in events, the pigeon is able to identify almost immediately a change in circumstances and adapt its behaviour to the new circumstances. The operant-conditioning psychologist, in discussing this situation, prefers to say only that the behaviour of the pigeon on a fixed-ratio schedule is readily extinguished.

A fourth type of schedule is a *variable-ratio schedule*. Just as in the variable-interval schedule one of the many different systems can be used for determining each time interval, so too in the variable-ratio schedule the number of responses between each reinforced response is varied in some way. The number of responses between two reinforced responses may be derived by drawing a number at random from a selected group of numbers, and it may also be increased as the series goes on in order that the response may become progressively less dependent on the reinforcement. The variable-ratio schedule, once it is turned off, may result in behaviour highly resistant to extinction.

The different effects of different schedules of reinforcement have long been claimed to have implications for education. The main application they have in a school situation would be the maintenance of general habits of behaviour such as orderliness, neatness, and courteousness. In order to maintain such trends in behaviour, or even to improve on them, teachers have long provided reinforcement on a variable-ratio or a variable-interval basis. They have not done this by design, but they have adopted such schedules because their contacts with each pupil, on a personal basis, are necessarily limited, and it is through such contacts that reinforcements are supplied. The typical reinforcer is praise, though nobody knows just how good a reinforcer this is at different educational levels. Social psychologists have long believed that at the age of adolescence praise from the adult is almost worthless but that endorsement by other adolescents has powerful reinforcing properties. Among very young children, praise and warm supportive behaviour on the part of the adult appear to be an effective reinforcer, particularly for the behaviour of girls (see Nickell and Travers, 1963).

Development of New Behaviour

Up to this point, consideration has been given to some of the ways in which a baby's initial repertoire of behaviours is controlled. Through classical conditioning stimuli that did not originally initiate a particular response acquire the property of initiating it. In addition, through the use of reinforcements, some control can be exerted over the frequency with which particular responses occur. By adjustment of the schedule of reinforcements, frequencies of responses above the base rate can be maintained. However, classical conditioning and instrumental conditioning procedures, discussed to this point, tell us almost nothing about the way the infant acquires new ways of responding, as he most evidently does.

One mechanism involved in the development of new responses, not only in infancy but throughout life, is known as *shaping*. Consider the case of a nine-month-old child who has been given a spoon for the first time. The infant holds it awkwardly in his clenched fist and with a little guidance manages to place the spoon in the oatmeal. He lifts the spoon out of the oatmeal, but by the time the spoon reaches his mouth most of the oatmeal has run off it. Very slowly, and over many weeks, he improves his performance, until he has acquired the new skill of bringing the spoonful of oatmeal from the bowl to his mouth without spilling any. The question to be considered here is how the child slowly learns this skill. The skill represents a new response he has learned.

The account given according to operant-conditioning theory of how this skill is acquired is as follows: Whenever the infant, by chance, holds the spoon in such a way that some of the oatmeal reaches his mouth, that way of holding the spoon is reinforced and strengthened. Also, whenever he holds the spoon, by chance, in such a way that the oatmeal slides off the spoon and nothing reaches the mouth, the related responses tend to become extinguished. Because behaviour shows a natural variability, each attempt to take a spoonful of oatmeal varies from the previous one. Features of the variable performance that are effective tend to be reinforced and retained, and features that are not effective tend to drop out.

This process, through which behaviour is slowly modified and new responses and skills are acquired, is known as shaping behaviour. The word *shaping* draws on an analogy between the modification of behaviour and the way in which natural materials are tooled to conform with specifications in a factory or workshop. The emphasis is on the control of behaviour by external means.

One can demonstrate in some situations that new skills can be developed through the well-planned use of reinforcements, but this is far from demonstrating it to be the only means through which new responses can emerge. An alternative proposal, long favoured by many psychologists, including Piaget, is that individuals are inventive of new responses and can generate new behaviour through processes within themselves. There are difficulties in testing this view of human behaviour, which is why many psychologists are reluctant to accept it. Also, it is a view that many did not like to embrace until recent times because it has been difficult to develop mechanical models of how this could happen. Psychologists have been able to develop mechanical mice that can learn as a result of reinforcement, but building a mechanical mouse that can generate new solutions to problems within itself is a much more difficult engineering task to undertake. Nevertheless, it has become possible, in a sense, in recent years, though the mechanical mouse is now a computer. One can programme a large computer so that it can discover solutions for problems that it has not already learned to solve and so that it can store the solutions for use in solving subsequent problems. When the computer discovers the solution to a problem, such as proving a geometrical theorem, it is acquiring a new skill that it can latter use (in proving other theorems). A computer has a great capacity for generating new operations (responses !) that it was not originally programmed to undertake. The computer shows that there is nothing mystical about the idea that the human being may have the capacity for inventing and producing new responses, on his own initiative, without the operation of reinforcement and extinction. These play a role, but other processes are also important.

The clearest examples of new behaviour being generated from sources within the individual involve the development of language. This is a matter that will be discussed in greater detail in later chapters. In the meantime, it is sufficient to point out that a young child experiments with language, putting together combinations of words he has never heard. He does not learn language through the slow shaping of his infant's dabble. He may suddenly say a word or expression without going through any slow process of making closer and closer approximations to the correct form. Language development cannot be understood through any simplistic account involving only reinforcement and extinction. Language is learned, but the process of learning involves the invention of new sentences and sometimes even the invention of grammatical forms. This illustrates how new behaviour can be generated internally, much as the computer can generate new proofs of theorems internally.

In any case, the slow shaping of behaviour is not a very efficient way of generating new behaviour, once the child has reached a stage in which verbal communication is possible for him. In the first year of life, one may slowly shape behaviour related to toilet training, but just a very few years later one may help the same child to produce a new behaviour by simply telling him how to do it. Sometimes one may give the same child a few prompts and then expect him to invent the new behaviour needed to solve a particular problem. Much controversy in education is related to the matter of the extent to which a child should be given an opportunity to generate new behaviour and the extent to which his behaviour should be kept under teacher control or under the control of the educational materials.

Infant Behaviour and Information Analysis

Up to this point, the discussion has focused on very simple forms of behaviour in which, with a few exceptions, the stimulus is a very simple event that produces a rather simple response. The learning processes described have also been at a relatively simple level, with new simple stimuli in one form or another coming to control behaviour. Psychologists have long hopped that the complicated learning undertaken by the older child and adult could be understood in terms of these simple process. Many impressively ingenious attempts to do this have been made by American psychologists, including J.B. Watson's classic works *Behaviourism* (1924) and B.F. Skinner's *Science and Human Behaviour* (1953). These works attracted a large following, partly because of their scientific ingenuity and partly because they offered a promise of providing means of controlling behaviour during the period of development. Perhaps they were embraced also because they gave the impression that behaviour was not really unpredictable, as it often appears to be in daily life. For atleast the first half of the twentieth century, American psychology was dominated by the view that complex learning could be understood in terms of simple conditioning processes, but some psychologists came to doubt the usefulness of this position. Other important processes appear to be involved in learning in early childhood that are not usefully described in the terms of the traditional language of psychology derived from physiology, such as *stimulus* and *response*. The infant soon ceases to be an organism whose behaviour can be readily described in terms of the relationship of simple stimuli to simple responses. Rather, the infant comes to resemble more an information processing system in which there are inputs of information and outputs that may be either adjustive behaviours or outputs of information.

Consider an infant who is the subject of an experiment. The infant has learned to lie still when a certain kind of light display is shown above his head, but when another kind of light display is turned on he kicks his legs. The baby is receiving information that determines whether he will be in one state or in the other. In order for the baby to respond to the information provided, he must have some kind of information analyser that will decide whether he is faced with the one input of light or the other, one situation or another.

Now let us consider the case of the infant who fixates on a point of light. He does this in the first few weeks after birth but very soon begins to show discriminations in what he fixates on. Thomas (1965) gave infants aged two to fourteen weeks the opportunity of fixating on patterns of different complexity. He found that there was a very strong tendency for the infants to fixate on the more complex of the patterns presented. Now consider what this means. The finding carries with it the implication that the infant has a capability of discriminating between less complex and more complex patterns. Of course, he has no capability of saying to himself "This pattern is more complex than that one" or "I prefer to look at the more complex pattern." The infant does have the inborn capacity to make the discrimination and hence, the mechanisms necessary for responding to the dimension of complexity. This means that the infant has some capacity to make an analysis of incoming information and that the analysis results in some displays being stared at longer than other displays. The visual behaviour is not just a random scanning of the visual world. Data from other sources also suggest (see review by Travers, 1967) that, if a great range of complexity of visual displays is shown to an infant, the infant will probably choose to fixate most frequently on one of medium complexity. A study providing evidence related to the later point has been undertaken by Haith *et al.* (1969), who were able to show that limb movements and sucking behaviour were related to the level of complexity of a visual display and that the greatest activity in this respect occurred when the displays were of medium complexity in terms of the range of complexity provided. The displays had high attention-attraction qualities in that they involved the presentation of a light that moved in a pattern of varying degrees of complexity. Complexity also is a factor at all ages in determining attention-attraction properties, a fact that can be used in attracting the attention of older children.

Kagan (1970) has made an analysis of the processes involved in the development and control of attention in infants and points out that attending behaviour moves through a number of stages. In the earliest stage, it is determined by quite crude properties of the stimulus itself. In the case of visual stimuli, the extent to which the object shows contrasts of illumination is crucial. An object that contains black lines on a white surface, or bright white lines on a black background, has high attention-attracting properties. The reason for this is that when a bright line or a bright spot moves across the retina it turns the light-sensitive cells on and off as it moves over them, and the infant has a tendency to attend to those events that produce a high rate of change in his sensory system. An object that presents soft contrasts of shading does not have the property of producing the same marked on-off states in the retinal cells and does not have the same property of eliciting an orienting response. Because boundaries and edges are of greatest importance in producing contrast, objects that have sharply defined and contrasting edges are the ones that attract attention best. However, there is also evidence that as the number of edges is increased an optimum point for attracting and holding attention is reached. If the number of boundaries is increased still further, attention to the object declines. It seems that there is an optimum amount of turning on and off the cells in the retina. The very young child avoids overstimulation, as does the adult. Even the adult can become overwhelmed with the amount of contrast and variation in the environment and may want to withdraw. Combinations of flashing lights and blaring music may become unbearable.

As the infant grows, new processes are involved in the attention process. The infant who repeatedly is exposed to and attends to, a particular pattern retains information about that object or pattern. That information is retained can be readily demonstrated, for the infants reaction to the same repeatedly presented pattern changes. The data suggest that the infant is capable of taking in and storing information that has some degree of regularity to it and is presented on repeated occasions. The internal representation of the object is referred to by many workers as a schema, meaning only that there is an internal representation of the object. This internalisation of information must be considered to be entirely *automatic* (a term originally used by Clark Hull in relation to learning); that is, it has nothing to do with whether the infant decides to attend or not to attend to the object involved. Kagan (1970) takes the position that schemas represent records of information in the nervous system and do not have action components tied to them. Piaget (see Flavell, 1963) has taken the opposite position and suggests that every schema has components that lead to action. Kagan would say that after the infant has had considerable experience with his mother's face a schema containing information about the face is set up. But Piaget would suggest that a schema has action components and includes a tendency to look at and direct attention towards the face.

The formation of schemas in relation to common objects playing a significant role in the life of the infant is said by Kagan to take place during the age of about two to four month. After that time, the schemas become elaborated, other schemas are formed, and some interrelationships among schemas are developed. In addition, a new process emerges.

Towards the end of the first year, an infant will respond particularly to objects for which he has developed a schema, but he will also be particularly attentive towards those that have been modified in some way. He will explore the change if he is able to do so. A mother who presents herself to her one-year-old with a Band-Aid on her face is likely to have it pulled off. Objects that show some deviation from their presentation in the past arouse and prolong the attending response to an unusual degree. Kagan takes the position that in the third stage the child shows evidence of forming hypotheses about the change and sets about testing the hypotheses. If the child cannot test his hypotheses, or has no hypotheses, then he is likely to withdraw from the situation.

Kagan (1970) proposes that all three factors involved in early perception—high contrast, internalisation of information, and hypothesis testing—are processes that dominate attention through the school years. He points out that the books used in the lower grades are illustrated with bright colours and show high contrast. New objects are presented enough times to develop internalisation of the information, and variations of objects are selected for presentation that are within the child's grasp (that is, the variations are selected so that the child is able to formulate hypotheses about the nature of the variation).

Let us now further consider inborn information analysis mechanisms. An infant aged one year is placed on the floor on a porch raised about eighteen inches above ground level. The porch has no rail around it, and the infant crawls to the edge of the porch, looks over the edge, and withdraws. The infant then moves to another part of the porch, approaches the edge again, and once again withdraws. This is repeated many times. In such a case, the infant is confronted with a very complex situation. From what the infant sees in this complex situation, he is able to abstract important information that results in a withdrawal response. We know, from other data, that the information to which the infant is responding is that of the drop from the porch to the ground and that he is able to abstract this important information from the vast wealth of information confronting him as he looks over the edge. The infant is not just responding to depth cues; he is able to analyse the total mass of information presented to him and is able to analyse out from this mass of data a small amount of information of particular importance. The response of the infant is an *adjustive response*, that is, an avoidance of danger response, as is seen in his withdrawal from the edge.

Infants avoid attempting to move over places where there is a sharp drop in elevation, as do members of a number of other species from turtles to rats (see the review of research on this problem by Walk and Gibson, 1961). The phenomenon is known as the *visual-cliff phenomenon*. Gibson and Walk (1960) have explored this behaviour with young infants, using an arrangement in which the visual cliff consisted of a small ravine, perhaps two feet deep at the deep end and a few feet across. The ravine was covered with a piece of plexiglas that could easily support the weight of a one-year old infant. An infant was placed on one side of the ravine, and the experimenter was on the other. The experimenter attempted to encourage the infant to cross the ravine on the plexiglas. Under these conditions, the infant would advance until he reached the edge of the visual cliff, but he would not cross over it even through he might place his hand on it and could see that it provided him support. The infant would skirt along the edge of the cliff, never resting his weight on the plexiglas, and could eventually reach the experimenter by going around the visual cliff.

The visual-cliff phenomenon appears to be a clear-cut case of the nervous system having built-in mechanisms for extracting certain kinds of information from the environment. In this case, the mechanism helps the infant to survive. Many such inborn information analysis mechanisms have been identified in animals. For example, frogs have visual analyser mechanisms that permit them to identify and catch with their tongues small moving objects that have certain characteristics, including that of size. It is not just that the frog has a response triggered by a particular stimulus. Such a simplistic interpretation fails to recognise the fact that the eyes of the frog are exposed to an enormous quantity of information from which it can extract some small amount of highly significant information. The information analysis mechanism in the nervous system has to be fairly complex in that the information extraction process is complex. The complexity of the process is evident when one considers that it would be quite difficult to develop a mechanical or electronic device that would scan the surroundings and indicate when a small fly was in range of an artificial tongue.

Another very interesting example of inborn information analysis mechanism is found in the case of some birds that can orient themselves to the stars. Presumably, in these birds the direction of migratory behaviour is controlled by this kind of mechanism. The nervous equipment of these birds has to be able to identify the position of particular stars and to discriminate them from other stars, and then there must be a mechanism to orient the birds towards the stars. The phenomenon has been demonstrated by bringing birds into a planetarium with stars displayed on the ceiling. The birds orient themselves in relation to particular stars and as the display of stars is moved, change their orientation. Ornithologists suspect that many different mechanisms exist through which birds manifest appropriate migratory behaviour. Some birds, for example, orient themselves to magnetic fields (see Mathews, 1968).

We are only just beginning to understand the inborn information analysis systems of human beings. Indeed, until recently the assumption was made that there were no such mechanisms. The discovery of the visual-cliff avoidance response occurred because such a mechanism had been well established in many other species and finally somebody had the curiosity to determine whether a similar mechanism existed in the case of young human beings. It did exist, and the way was opened up for the search for other innate information analysis systems. Some evidence was soon found to suggest their existence and that they might be much more extensive than had previously been thought. An example of such discoveries is found in the work of Bower (1966a, b) on what is referred to as *size constancy*. Let us consider this work briefly.

The child of elementary school age, or older knows perfectly well that an object seen in the distance is the same object as when it is seen close up. He is not fooled by the fact that the distant object makes a very much smaller image on his retina than does the same object close up. A man does not look smaller when he is forty feet away than when he is twenty feet away, despite the fact that the man far away produces an image on the retina half the height of the image when he is close. This is the phenomenon of size constancy. Psychologists long believed that size constancy was entirely a learned form of behaviour. It certainly makes a lot of sense that the infant should slowly come to recognise that his mother is the same person whether she is seen across the room or beside the crib. He should also soon learn that the bottle is the same, whether it is seen close to his mouth or at a distance of several feet. There are numerous opportunities for the infant to learn early in infancy that objects are the same regardless of whether they are near or far. Bower (1966a,b) investigated the extent to which young infants were able to recognise particular objects regardless of distance. The infants were aged two to twenty weeks, and the technique used for studying such matters in infants is operant conditioning. The usual form of the technique is roughly along the following lines. The infant first has to learn to discriminate between a large square piece of board and a much smaller square piece of board held at the same distance. One can do this by teaching him that when the large square appears he can obtain milk by turning his head. He also learns that when a small square is shown he cannot obtain milk by turning his head. After he has learned this task, then he is shown the large square object, but at such a distance that it produces on the retina an image the same size as that produced by the small square. Now the crucial question is how does the baby respond? Does he respond as if it were the small square, which would indicate a lack of size constancy, or does he show through his behaviour that he recognises it to be the same object as the one shown close to him? The answer is fairly clear. He responds to the large square held at a distance not as though it were the small square but as though it were the large square held at a distance. The evidence indicates that the infant already recognises the phenomenon of size constancy, but it seems unlikely that the infant has managed to master this difficult skill through learning during the course of his short life since birth. He has had some opportunity for such learning, because he has seen his mother and also numerous different objects both near and far, but size constancy should be quite a difficult matter to master. It seems much more likely that the infant has some inborn capability for interpreting information related to this phenomenon in appropriate ways. We know, from the visual-cliff phenomenon, that the nervous system has a built-in mechanism for judging distances, and such a mechanism would be an important component of the size constancy phenomenon. Undoubtedly, there are some aspects of size and shape constancy that are learned. Consider some of the complex constancy phenomena related to the one considered. One recognises a round object, such as a plate, as being round, even when one views the object obliquely and has an oval image projected on the retina. The rim of a cup "looks" round even when it is viewed across the table. A person who learns to draw and who wants to draw a cup viewed obliquely, has to learn to see it as it really is. The child in elementary school typically draws a cup by drawing first the sides of the cup and then a circle on top of them to represent the rim. He doesn't draw a picture that much resembles the image projected on his retina, but he draws a conceptualisation of the cup.

There is still another phenomenon related to depth and size constancy that illustrates very clearly a built-in mechanism for information analysis. In order to understand this mechanism, the reader must be introduced to a case of visual perception in which an adult is placed in a position of obtaining visual information in a form probably very similar to that presented to the infant. The only case, so far, in which this can be done is with adults who have been blind all their lives but are able to gain sight for the first time through a corneal graft operation. The first person to recognise the psychological importance of the reports of these postoperative patients was a German ophthalmologist, von Senden (translated 1960), who wrote a book about the entire topic based on his study of his own surgical cases.

Von Senden operated on his patients in order to give them vision and this he did successfully, but for a long time after they could see they did not have useful vision. Such a patient, after the eye had healed, could be presented with a common object, held up in front of him and he would not be able to identify it. The necessary machinery in the nervous system for object recognition had not developed, and the patient could not undertake the simplest visual task such as telling the difference between a square and a triangle despite the fact he was able to do this easily through touch. However, the visual mechanism did operate at a very primitive level, for he was able to say that an object was held in front of him. It would seem that his native equipment related to vision did make it possible for him to see objects as distinct objects, even though the characteristics of the objects could not be identified. These individuals, with their naive and untrained visual apparatus, did not see the world as just a disorganised confusion. The primitive analyser mechanisms permitted them to recognise the fact that there were distinct objects in the environment and that there were many distinct objects, but the analyser mechanism still had to develop before it would permit them to be able to look at an object and identify its relevant characteristics. A primitive kind of object identification is an inherent capability of man's nervous system, but the analysis of object characteristics is learned.

Von Senden also conducted studies to find out something about how his patients developed the capability of recognising objects. He found that the development of this capability was extremely slow. For example, a patient might take daily training on learning to discriminate a triangle from a square, but even after three months of training he might be able to make the discrimination only by counting the corners. Immediate identification still was not possible.

The implication of von Senden's work is that the nervous system has a crude innate capacity to perceive that there is some kind of organisation in the world, that is, that the world consists of things. However, the attachment of meaning to the things requires a long period of learning that involves the development of more sophisticated information analysis systems. Hebb (1966), who did all the pioneer thinking on this matter, came to the conclusion that one of the major tasks faced by the child or by any growing organism is the development of a system of information analysers that will identify the detailed characteristics of objects so that the objects, crudely perceived as objects by the basic inherent nervous machinery, can be given meaning and significance. Hebb called this process of developing analyser mechanisms *early learning*. It is a very slow process and perhaps the most significant learning process that takes place during the first two years of life.

A very important information system that plays a significant role in the performance of most skills involving movement is the cerebellum—a mass of tissue that is a distinct organ lying at the rear of the brain. When the child begins to walk, as he does at about the age of twelve to fifteen months, he can do this because the nervous system is able to keep track of a great amount of information concerning where his legs are at any particular time, the position of other parts of his body and his orientation with respect to the gravitational field. The cerebellum appears to be an organ that collates all this information and makes adjustments permitting the individual to stay right side up to the world. It seems fairly clear that children do not *learn* to walk, though learning may refine the crude walking act, and hence children must be endowed with the nervous machinery required to keep track of all the information that has to be kept track of, if walking is to take place. The cerebellum functions very much like a computer designed to control a complex programme of activity in which information about many components must be used to make adjustments in the activity of other components (see Eccles *et al.*, 1967).

Although the information analysis systems related to walking are innate rather than learned, information-handling systems have to be acquired through learning so that many learned skills can be adequately performed and controlled.

An area of great significance related to the existence of innate analyser mechanisms is the development of speech. Before the child begins to speak he learns to identify a great many speech sound. Some of the sounds he hears he may suddenly produce himself, as when the child who has not said the word before suddenly says "Bye-bye," a word he has heard others say hundreds of time. The child shows substantial evidence of being able to isolate the sounds of speech and later produce them. For those of us who have heard the sounds of our native language all our lives, there is nothing remarkable about this because we have the illusion that each spoken word is generally said fairly distinctly. Such is not the case at all. Studies of speech show that one sound slurs into another sound and what appears to be distinct sound elements in particular words are overlapping components that cannot be separated in terms of the sound waves they involve. The adult hears words as being separated one from another, but such a separation is strictly an illusion. The sound of speech, as it is recorded, shows no breaks between words. In typical speech, several words are spoken as a continuous stream of sound and then there is a short break followed by another unbroken stream. We learn the illusion that there are breaks between words and that each word consists of a set of separate and distinct sound elements. The young infant appears to have some capacity for making this kind of analysis of sound elements in language. If he did not have some innate capacity to do this, it is doubtful whether he would achieve the extraordinary mastery of language he does during the first two years of his life. Some psychologists also take the view that the child may have some innate ability for discovering the basic structure of language.

Organisation of Information

The theme of the previous section of this chapter has been that the infant has an innate capacity for extracting and using some of the information about the world around him. In addition, the infant has some capacity for organising information, even at this early stage. He does not simply store many small items of information about the environment, pigeonholing each in a separate little compartment of memory. Piaget (see Piaget and Inhelder, 1969) has long stressed that much of the information that the infant acquires is related to such basic functions as feeding, excretion and social responding. He suggests that children have a capacity to organise the experiences they have around these functions and that the nervous system may have an inherent capacity for doing this. As the perceptual systems develop, and as the nervous system develops, they show an ever increasing capacity to extract, organise, and store information about the environment. A considerable amount of space in subsequent chapters is devoted to a discussion of the expanding capacity of the growing child to handle information about the world around him.

Facilitators and Inhibitors of Intellectual Development in Infancy

In many parts of the world, the education of the child begins shortly after birth, when the child is brought to facilities where he is largely reared. The Kibbutzim in Israel were some of the first to develop on any systematic scale this form of institutionalised child rearing, though some groups of American Indians had developed small-scale communal nurseries. The reader interested in a thoroughly readable psychological analysis of child rearing in the Kibbutzim is referred to Rabin's (1965) excellent study of the matter. The Union of Soviet Socialist Republics has also developed a system for providing child-rearing facilities through infancy and beyond (see Cole and Maltzman, 1969) in order that women might be released from individual child-rearing duties. These kinds of activities have raised questions about the best environment for the rearing of children and whether systematic education can profitably start in infancy. These are questions that are also being raised by those concerned with the problems of poverty in the United States, where one proposed step towards solving the problems involves establishing child-care centres. These child-care centres supposedly have the purpose of releasing the mother for productive work outside the home, and they also have potential for stimulating intellectual development in the young children assigned to them.

There can be no doubt that children born in poverty have considerable difficulty in mastering the school curriculum. They are at a disadvantage when they enter school and this disadvantage tends to increase, rather than diminish, as they advance through the grades. Two major factors appear to be responsible for this initial and increasing scholastic deficiency. One is nutrition, and the other is the deprived intellectual environment in which children raised in poverty find themselves.

If anyone doubts the significant effect that nutrition can have on the development of intelligence, he should read the excellent summary of the evidence provided by Green *et al.* (1973). These authors began with the well-known facts that the children of disadvantaged groups achieve less than middle-class children and that these children fall further and further behind as they go through school. These authors go on to point out that the child born in poverty is at a disadvantage even before birth. The mother is likely to be malnourished and also probably lacks adequate prenatal care. When born, the child of a malnourished mother weighs less than the average and his brain is somewhat shrunken within the skull, indicating that cell multiplication has not proceeded to an optimum extent. An undue proportion of the children of the disadvantaged are born prematurely, which often brings with it mental retardation. Children born prematurely achieve somewhat lower intelligence test scores than children born at full term. Even without the effect of prematurely, low birth weight is associated with a depression in intelligence test scores. The frequency of children being born with a weight below that normally expected is actually on the increase among nonwhites, a fact that should arouse the consciences of all.

The children of the poor also have less well developed thymus glands and suffer from the fact that their mothers often have vitamin-deficient diets. There is some evidence that merely giving mothers a vitamin supplement during pregnancy increases the intelligence quotients of their children measured at the age of four years. In addition, malnutrition during infancy appears to have serious effects on the brain. These effects are probably permanent and cannot be remedied by later improved conditions.

Thus when the children of the disadvantaged grow up, they in turn provide unfavourable circumstances for the next generation.

The circumstances of growth in a state of poverty are unfavourable not only nutritionally but also in terms of intellectual stimulation. Bosco (1970) has pointed out that the problem of such a child is not so much understimulation as chaotic stimulation. When a large family lives in very cramped and crowded quarters, conditions are inevitably as stimulating as those of a busy city street, but the infant is not able to learn much from being exposed to such chaos. Living in a room with many other people, most of whom are too busy or too tired to give the infant the kind of attention he needs, provides very inferior circumstances for intellectual development. What the infant needs is a much simpler environment from which he can extract information necessary for his development. For example, in order to begin to differentiate the sounds of speech, he needs to be spoken to by someone who will repeat the same words again and again. The infant can then slowly begin to differentiate the component sounds within these words. This does not mean that the infant will begin to understand what those words mean; the differentiation of speech sounds has to come before any meaning can possibly be ascribed to words. In addition, when the child is a little older, there is little dialogue between him and other members of the crowded community. He is sporadically talked to and given commands such as "Stop that"! or "Put it down!" but there is little of the give and take in the conversation of child and parent living under more propitious circumstances. The culture of the underprivileged does not provide for the intellectual development of the child through such conversation.

A number of studies have been undertaken in which underprivileged infants were exposed to an "enriched" environment, but the difficulty in such studies is determining the effect that the "enrichment" has on the baby. Babies have a rather limited repertoire of things they do. For this reason, infants given an enriched environment may have to be followed up for some years to determine whether advantages have been gained.

An interesting study of the effect of attempting to improve the environment of the infant is provided by Gordon (1969a). In this study, mothers of babies in poor rural communities in Florida were given instruction in how to provide an intellectually stimulating environment for their infants during the first and second years of life. The babies were studied at the end of the first and second years to determine how they compared in their behaviour with a control group of children who had not received the special stimulation. The mothers were instructed to play certain games with their children involving such varied activities as holding out objects for the very young infant to attempt to grasp, giving the names of objects in the case of the older child, and engaging in simple verbal interactions with the child.

The main findings of the Gordon study were that the children of mothers given training in the programme showed enhanced development at the end of the first year of the programme as compared with a group of control children. The enhancement was also shown at the end of the second year, provided the mothers kept up the programme. Such programmes generally seem to show that they produce intellectual advantage. The results also suggest that through such enhancement some of the disadvantages of an impoverished environment can be offset. That such infant training can be provided in the home by women who have somewhat less than a high school education is a matter of considerable significance. Apparently, infant education does not have to be provided by a well-trained professional staff.

Outputs of the Infant

Outputs of the infant in the first few months of life are very limited. Most of them represent little more than random behaviour, that is, behaviour with almost no organisation or structure. A few exceptions to this have already been mentioned and include feeding, excretion, the orienting response, fixation of the eyes on particular objects, and following of a light with one or both eyes. Crying behaviour represents one form of co-ordinated response shown from birth, but the function of crying is not really understood. At one time, the unlikely theory was propounded that crying provided essential exercise for the lungs, but the passage of time has not provided any great crop of more plausible theories. Smiling behaviour also emerges in the first two months of life. Vocalisation in the first three months is very limited in the range of sounds produced. Lenneberg (1967), in his discussion of the development of language, describes the early sounds of the baby as "squealing-gurgling" sounds but also notes that some of the cooing is vowel-like in character. A point of interest to note is that these early sounds are produced by completely deaf babies as well as by those who can hear. By six months, the cooing has changed to a babbling, but the noises have greater structure to them and resemble single syllable sounds. By eight months, the baby begins to repeat certain sounds, as when he lies in his crib and says "ma-ma-ma-ma." The intonation of the infant at this stage may be influenced by such states as frustration and fear. The development of speech at more advanced levels will not be discussed here, and what has been said has been introduced only to indicate the limited nature of the behavioural outputs of the young infant. Behavioural outputs are extremely limited until the infant has developed the necessary mechanisms in his nervous system for the analysis of inputs. Indeed, one can make the generalisation that the machinery for the analysis of inputs must generally precede the production of corresponding outputs. Thus the production of speech lags behind speech comprehension.

Since the work of Arnold Gesell early in the century, attempts have been made to describe the development of the motor responses and other responses of the infant. One of the more interesting attempts to do this, in recent years, has been that of Bruner (1969), whose study of motor development focuses on responses related to feeding and sucking. The baby starts out with complete and complex responses related to feeding, these responses being organised within a schema, according to Piaget's terminology. The responses include two forms of sucking, the orientation of the head and the lips to the nipple, and a holding action with the hands. The baby arrives in the world equipped with a complete programme of responses that take place when he is both hungry and presented with a nipple or a nipple-like object. Bruner points out that in the first few months of life the baby cannot perform this act and some other act at the same time. If he is distracted by some visual object, then he will orient his eyes towards the visual display but will stop sucking. Later, he will become capable of looking at an object and producing the feeding response at the same time. The repertoire of hand and arm responses increases rapidly. In the first month, the baby can grasp firmly if the palm of his hand is touched. Then the grasping action becomes extended so that when the back of his hand is touched the baby will turn his wrist and grasp at whatever is touching it. Later, the baby shows swiping movements that become slowly more refined and he eventually becomes able to grasp objects, but the use of vision as a guide for the grasping hand has to be learned.

The infant appears to have initially, gross patterns of movement, which he can perform as complete acts. These become broken down into components, called *modules*, and he learns to combine the modules into various instrumental acts. An analogy is a computer programme for, say, calculating logarithms. Such a programme consists of many sub-programmes involving addition, subtraction, multiplication, and square-root extraction. One could cut up the logarithm programme and put some of the components together in such a way that tasks other than calculating logarithms could be performed. The infant has a complete programme for holding its mother's breast, involving raising the arms touching, flexing the fingers, and so on. Later, the infant learns to control these components separately and combine them in different ways for performing other acts. In addition, the infant learns to *substitute* one response for another.

A particularly important kind of output that has great significance for the development of information analysis systems in the nervous system is known as exploratory behaviour.

Within the first few months of life, the infant ceases to be just a passive recipient of whatever information the environment happens to provide. A few months after birth, the infant is an active explorer of the environment and manages, through his own efforts, to reach sources of information to which he would otherwise not have had access. By the age of four months, he may grasp at a small wooden cube and manage to bring it to his mouth. The grasping of the object he sees enables the infant to co-ordinate the information derived from vision with the information derived from touch. That such a co-ordination of the two sources of information needs to be learned is very evident from the von Senden data on patients recovering from corneal grafts, who could see but had no way of knowing what the objects they saw would be like if touched. Inputs of information through the various perceptual systems have to be co-ordinated, and this co-ordination occurs largely through the explorations the infant makes of his own accord. Because the activities of the hands of the infant are highly related to feeding from the bottle or breast, it is hardly surprising that almost every object touched tends to be moved in the direction of the mouth. Such a tendency will persist for a long time, indeed, until the infant reaches the point where it becomes displaced by a tendency to view with the eyes any new object that is grasped.

Most of those who have observed the young infant emphasise the significance of exploratory behaviour. Piaget does, and claims that it is vital for normal intellectual development—as undoubtedly it is. An important point to note is that exploratory behaviour is not just a set of random movements but a highly co-ordinated activity that has the effect of increasing the information input to the child.

Basic Learning Processes

In this chapter, we have reviewed some of the basic learning processes that begin to operate early in life and represent important learning mechanisms. An understanding of these processes permits the teacher to gain some control over some aspects of learning. How the teacher gains this control is a matter to be expanded on in subsequent chapters. Although these processes permeate all learning in later years of the child's life, they cannot be considered to represent a complete inventory of all learning mechanisms. An example of a learning process that emerges later, and could not be considered in relation to the life of the infant, is that involving reasoning. The mature person solves many problems in his daily life through the application of reasoning and solving a problem is a form of learning. The solution of a problem gives him a new skill, that is, the skill involved in solving the problem. Problem solving by means of reasoning involves the generation of a new form of responding, and it is one of the mechanisms that permits the production of new responses.

Reference

1. Piaget uses schemata for the plural of schema. Many American authors use schemas for the plural. In each case, that author's preference has been used in this book.

CHAPTER 3

Developing Intelligence in the Preadolescent Child

Introduction

This has been called the century of the child. Indeed, much thought and concern have been expressed about children in this period by parents, educators, theologians, and social and political scientists.

Evidence of interest in the scientific community is seen in the burgeoning of research on child development and behaviour. In the early years of this century, there was concern with tests measuring intelligence; there was, in addition, increased interest in the study of the emotional growth and personality of children. Since 1950, there has been particular interest in cognition and learning. Within the past decade another dimension has been added to these areas of research in the development of children, namely a focus on the development of their ethical judgment.

Scientists as well as many other person have been asking questions related to the development of ethical judgment in children. What are the values held by children at different ages? Whence do they come? Can ethical development be nurtured by outside influences or is this solely the product of family forces? Whose responsibility is it to help children in their quest for values? The growing body of educational materials, including this curriculum unit, which focus on aiding the ethical development of children, reflects the attempt to put to use in educational efforts the results of this research.

The questions which the scientists have asked about the development of ethical judgment in children are asked also by parents and teachers of children. They want to know as much as possible about the nature of children and how their ethical development is nurtured. They want to learn about their own role in this development as parents and teachers. Teachers particularly want to know more about what constitutes a nurturing teacher-child interaction in the school setting for it is an important and often deeply moving relationship.

It is the intent of this chapter to provide parents and teachers with some of the ideas judged valid today regarding these matters, particularly as they relate to the preadolescent child of nine to twelve years of age with whom this curriculum unit is intended to be used.

In attempting to focus our exploration around one age group, we are immediately confronted with a problem. One of the striking lessons coming from research on child development in the past two decades is that children, and all persons for that matter, are not identical nor even very similar, even when they are of the same sex and chronological age. The individuality of every one of us stems from the fact that we have dissimilar heredities; that already at birth we have acquired different constitutional endowments; that from birth onward, our experiences are not only different, but even when they are similar we do not react identically. We are what we are because of the many variables which influence us from conception onward through life. Some of these are physical forces, others emotional and social, and others cultural and economic. Some of these are of greater effect than others because of their nature, and because of the idiosyncrasies of each individual human being in his greater or lesser vulnerability at critical periods in his life.

This individuality of development is well illustrated by the vast differences in pubertal development within a peer group. In the preadolescent grouping an increasing number of females are beginning to menstruate, while others are small-sized and physically immature, resembling those of younger chronological age. Thus while it might be appropriate for the mother of one ten year old to outfit her daughter with that cherished status symbol, a training bra, it would be quite inappropriate for another ten year old who has not developed at the same pace. Some children of this age group are well aware of the opposite sex and already pair off for movies or parties. This early start is permitted or even encouraged by some parents, especially those in suburbia, where early social maturation seems to be a status symbol. Many children however are far from ready for such activity and are more comfortable in groups comprised of members of their own sex.

In addition to differences in physical maturation, children of this age group may also be at different levels of psychological maturation. There is no specific correlation between physical maturation and intelligence and such generalisations should be avoided. The fallacy of assuming that the similarity of chronological age and sex implies a level or type of physical, emotional or mental development has time and again tripped up educators and behavioural scientists as well as parents. Users of this curriculum unit will become increasingly aware of this fact as they encounter an unbelievably wide variety of responses to the materials from the children.

Were this the whole story it would be impossible for us to make a statement descriptive of children who represent a particular age group. The uniqueness of each child in an age group defies any effort to describe, even in general terms, distinguishing characteristics of most of the children within a particular age range. It is not the whole story however. Not only do children of the same age and sex differ from each other, but children in the same general phase of development differ from those in other developmental phases. Because phases of development to have some relationship to age we are able to describe in general terms and in the form of an inventory, those behavioural traits which distinguish preadolescent children from those younger and from those already adolescent.

Almost invariably, for instance, preadolescent girls will be more advanced than their masculine counterparts in every aspect. This accounts for the girls, as a rule, being taller than the boys. It is a temporary phenomenon, however, and soon the boys will spurt ahead in growth. We are able therefore to describe some characteristics of the preadolescent which distinguish him from older and younger groupings. In doing so we need to remain alert to the spectrum of differences also present within the preadolescent years.

A second problem confronts us as we attempt to focus on the preadolescent. This age range of children has received the least attention in the voluminous literature concerning the years from infancy to adolescence, mainly because this group does not easily reveal itself. Unlike the younger child who shows his feelings openly so that we can understand how he feels, or the adolescent who tells us what he feels in no uncertain terms, the preadolescent is betwixt and between. He is no longer candid, but he is not yet forthrightly his own man. Despite all the weighing, testing and measuring of the preadolescent, parents, teachers and researchers have still much to learn about him. As with parents and teachers of earlier generations we have to move with what we think we know, keeping ever alert for new insights and understandings.

Pre-Teens: Nine to Twelve Years Old

This is not the place to describe in detail the physical growth and health aspects of the preadolescent boy and girl. It is relevant, however, to comment about physical characteristics and health as they relate to their behaviour. In general, preadolescents are quite healthy so that medical contacts and hospitalisation are infrequent. Yet often they complain about their body functions and ailments; minor illnesses may be exaggerated, reflecting emotional turmoil in themselves or in the family. Where the family has shown a preoccupation with health matters the behaviour may be duplicated by the preadolescent. Illnesses may be used as excuses to avoid entering group activities, attending school, or meeting other responsibilities. The preadolescent's idea of his body image is still unclear, but a major change in this will come in adolescence. For the most part he does not have any special concern about his body unless he matures early or is physically different from his peers because of illness, disability, obesity, or some other idiosyncrasy.

Preadolescent children show greater skill in motor performance and co-ordination than do younger children. By the use of their energy, hands, and bodies they experience themselves as initiating and generating changes, thus providing themselves with a sense of achievement and accomplishment as well as a tangible sign of growth. At this age children want to be identified with the strong, and they strive for superiority by competition, testing strength or skills. They enjoy their prowess which gains them recognition from peers of adults. A "good batting average" in baseball is not only important as proof of prowess, but for gaining recognition. Susy's baking efforts serve not only to show her skills but to gain family recognition. The increased motor performance also invites more risk-taking, as when bicycle riding is embellished with a flair. "Look, Mom, no hands," aptly describes it. Concomitantly, the number of children having accidents in this age group is high; some seem particularly prone to injury. Normally the sense organs are highly developed so that perception is acute, facilitating performance in games and athletics.

Children at every phase of development may be viewed as facing certain task. At the preadolescent level these include the further establishment of identity and sex role. In working at these tasks various roles are played. Some are elaborations of those used before, some are more refined and changed by experience, others are new roles. The boy may begin to relish being father's helper in carpentry or home repair jobs. The girl may have an interest in baking, cooking, rearranging furniture, or redecorating her room. Problems which face children at such an age, and consequently their parents and teachers, are extensions of those met earlier, plus new ones stemming from experiences in school and in the wider community.

In addition to the further establishment of identity and sex role, tasks at the preadolescent level include working out a further separation from parents and home, establishing a new and closer kinship with one's peer group and relationship with an ever-larger adult world, and the development of a sense of industry as the child attempts to acquire information, new skills, and techniques in learning. There is always an ambivalence in the child's attitude towards working at these tasks. He may have an interest in learning the skills necessary to play a musical instrument, but alongwith the desire to acquire musical skill there is also likely to be a pull against practice. Such conflicts reveal, however, a growing self-evaluation ability as in the child's admission "I sure don't like to practice." This ambivalence is also seen in his attitude towards school and his self-evaluative ability shows itself in statements, "I could have done better" or "Mary gets better marks than I do."

Part of establishing identity is to feel one's individuality. This may be expressed in the tendency to acquire collections in the form of picture cards of baseball players or music groups, bottle caps, popsicle sticks, stones or shells, stamps or coins.

These collections represent property which is subject to one's own government. A survey of fourth graders concerning their three greatest interests in order of importance gave the following results:

1. Possession of objects,
2. "The good life,"
3. Pets,
4. Vocation,
5. Travel,
6. Relatives,
7. Money,
8. School,
9. Education.

In terms of vocation interests, preadolescents still maintain unrealistic choices, with little understanding often of what it means to be a scientist, aeroplane pilot, engineer or doctor.

The drive for identity and individuality are also apparent in the school situation and is sometimes reflected by resentment at having "to do it the teacher's way." Since the right to individuality is at stake, the perceptive teacher would do well to show flexibility. In teaching it is better to allow the expression of individuality than to demand rigorous adherence to established methods. It is really less important that Danny draw the map or do the chart by prescribed rule than it is to maintain his interest or enthusiasm for the task. Too often the problems which a child has in learning have their inception in unreasonable insistence by the teacher that rigid rules be followed leaving little room for individuality.

Preadolescence is an age which is highly discerning about what is "fair" or "unfair," "just" or "unjust" and in which particular sensitivity to injustices towards one's own self develops. As the child strives to establish the individuality of his organism within the environment, he is ever alert to what is "just" or " unjust". His attitude towards aggression, for instance, is in terms of what he thinks the situation demands to preserve some semblance of justice. If parents and teachers were more sensitive to the values important to children, they would better understand what often seems to adults to be socially unacceptable behaviour in particular situations.

It is time for working out feelings as to who is worthy of trust. There is a testing of parents and a testing of teachers, sometimes deviously as in the following example: A teacher told the members of her fifth grade class that they had a choice of attending chorus or not. On the first day those who chose not to attend were given a long copy assignment by the teacher. This persuaded all but George to change their minds and attend chorus. But George was adamant and remained alone in the class to quietly read while the teacher went about her business. As George put it, "It's not that I don't like the chorus, but if they wanted everybody to go they should have said so!" It was his way of trying to see if adults really mean what they say. In using this curriculum unit, most teachers will undoubtedly experience "testing" by the children in their attempt to discover if they are really free to express their views. An adult unable to accept a wide range of responses, some of which may be in sharp contrast to his own views, should not attempt to use these materials.

In the process of separating themselves from parents and home, which will have further acceleration in adolescence, children are likely to have some difficulty in dealing with new loyalties with peers or adults other than their parents. They may try to find reasons or a rationale to bolster the separation from parents. One unconscious technique is to fancy the parents as unloving, faultfinding, and as trying to rid themselves of the child. The child responds with hostility as if he were retaliating against real rather than imagined hostility. This reaction may be called a normal paranoia since it provides justification for the child, and later for the adolescent, to leave home without regret and without guilt feeling.

The school child may show some of his hostility to teachers as well. Some of the resentment against leaving home and going to school may also be expressed when the child is urged or forced to attend church or fellowship school.

The child of nine to twelve years has come a long way in his development of intelligence, his use of the intellect, and his ability to apply himself industriously to the problems of learning. While every child does not become an avid learner in this stage of development, generally there is a heightened curiosity, particularly about natural phenomena and the sciences. This in turn helps a child become aware of the things around him. He gives some thought to his own beginnings as an individual, his birth, as well as the origin of other things in his environment. He thinks about creation, not in a narrow theological sense, but as an evolutionary concept. He is concerned about the effects of war, the atom bomb, and the possibilities of nuclear destruction. He enjoys science fiction and uses some of these themes in play and in written compositions.

His reading habits, according to a Chicago survey, show that boys seek out more information about the physical sciences and sports while girls lean towards the social sciences, biography, and mathematics. More reference reading is in science than in any other field. However, these children are not necessarily insatiable readers. Another survey showed that on an average they watch television twenty hours weekly but devote only one hour a week to reading. An ingenious way of discovering how children really spend their time and where their real interests lie is to encourage them to keep log books about themselves and their daily activities. The "Dear Diary" or "me" approach appeals to them and can provide authentic data.

The "why" questions are again in the ascendancy but on a more sophisticated level than that of earlier years. Scientific concepts can be understood at this age if adequately presented. These preadolescents can also understand concepts of human behaviour when they are consciously incorporated into the educational framework rather than left to chance acquisition. This period can be very productive intellectually if the educational system, especially its teachers, understands the nature of the child's learning processes, his ability to learn, and his skill in applying various techniques in teaching content as well as setting models of adult behaviour. We shall return to a consideration of the child's learning process and to methods of teaching later in this chapter. In addition they are described more fully in a separate section. It is sufficient to point out for the moment that the materials for helping children develop their ethical judgment which appear in this guide utilise much of what has been discovered about learning processes and teaching methods in the last decade.

One of the reasons that the preadolescent years are an opportune time for a wide enrichment of thought stems from the fact that children at this age level become more able to discriminate between myth and fact, fiction and truth, actuality and fantasy. The period may be characterised as one in which the children are moving from fantasy towards adult logic. While they have reached a plateau where they are beginning to reason from concrete experiences, it is not to be expected that logical thinking on a mature or sustained level has been really mastered. Elements of magic and mystery still vie with objective thinking and conceptualisation. Omens and incantations against evil are still part of the armour; "Never step on a crack, or you'll break your mother's back."

Religious education holds a special place in emancipating children's reasoning and thinking powers from the hold of primitive magic and fantasy. Much of the fantasy employed to deal with real events is a distortion of religious experience and belief. Thus in a quarrel one may accuse another, "You lied and God will punish you." The concept of God is important to all children because they have guilt, fear and panic reactions about the super being of God regardless of whether they come from religious or non-religious families, believers or agnostics. Children who come to liberal religious groups from more orthodox or fundamentalist religious sects may have developed ideas of an anthropomorphic God responsible from everything that happens. They talk about God and the powerful forces which guide our destiny and punish us for our wrong doing. They may express confusion over how a God can be all-loving yet revengeful. God is sometimes seen unfair, just as teachers, parents, and even peers can be unfair.

Children of this age pray, but the extent depends on their rearing and earlier experience in religious groups where prayer was traditionally practiced and emphasised. When children of this age pray, they tend to be more altruistic and more self-critical than they were at an earlier age. In their prayers they may admit guilt and express a desire to be better persons. They pray for protection in danger, recovery from illness, better grades in school. Their prayers seem to hold a semi-magical power about which the children may have misgivings, but they may still pray just to be on the safe side. The more self-assured children begin at this age to question the value of prayers and the role of God in answering them.

Religious education can contribute positively in developing and providing a sound intellectual foundation. Literature such as the Hindu epics, the Gita and the Bible may have appeal for its facts about history, sociology, and psychology. Children of this age enjoy learning how people lived, dressed, acted, and what their customs were centuries ago. They are interested in historical figures, have heroes, and enjoy reading about the lives of such heroes. Religious literature, properly used and interpreted, can shed understanding on ethical and moral problems which can be applied to present-day situations. Thus religious literature can become a basic instrument by which to nourish intellectual development. Further, its value as literature, particularly in its mythology and poetry, is another area of intellectual stimulation for which these children are ready. The informed teacher can help differentiate between myth and reality, not denying the value, function, and even the beauty of mythology.

Teachers need factual information and must use facts accurately in order to keep the interest and credibility of the children. When teachers do not have answers to children's questions, some of which are very philosophical, they need not hesitate to admit it. It is reassuring to children to know that they are not alone in not having all the answers; that most people, even scholars, lack knowledge in certain areas. Where teachers document their point of view, or their interpretations of history, they show children how to use evidence.

Educators, like child development researchers, are becoming increasingly familiar with the research of Piaget and other so-called cognitive psychologists. These investigators have formulated ideas about learning which are influencing curriculum development in secular as well as religious education. According to Piaget the early elementary school years (five to seven years of age) hold the beginning of what he calls the phase of intuitive thought. During these years the child begins to respond to situations as if he intuitively knew the relation, in terms of cause and effect, for instance, of the various factors involved in a situation. The child seems to have an intuitive understanding of some things which make it possible for him to act upon a situation so as to influence it towards resolutions which he desires.

He is not yet able to enunciate concepts which describe the relationships or explain his own actions; however he seems to have an intuitive kind of knowledge which he is not yet able to articulate. "He behaves," says Piaget, "as if he intuitively knew what life is about, and this marks the real beginning of cognition."

It is exceedingly important to point out that the child's capacity for intuitive thought during the early elementary years and on through the preadolescent years operates only as he is dealing with concrete situations and problems. He must have concrete situations with which to work where he can feel, taste, smell, see, and hear. Because of this limitation the lesson materials which appear in this curriculum until always begin with concrete experiences called learning activities. The child is not yet able to engage in abstract thinking where the sense impressions and evoked feelings of concrete situations are absent.

By the preadolescent years children are better able to express their intuitive understanding in words. They are more likely to employ speech for expressing their understandings than they were earlier when acting them out was their standard response. Thus Jim can voice his sentiments about teammates who yell abuse at fellow players for making errors. "After all, the kids feel bad enough. You don't have to hurt their feelings that way. It doesn't make you a better player." Or he can be self-judgmental and proclaim, "I'll never be able to run bases." Or he can formally explain a particular idiosyncrasy as, "I like my room messy. That's what makes it my room."

While these children seem to have come far in concrete reasoning and thinking, adults must remember that their reasoning ability is still limited and has not reached the full dimensions of logical thinking which can incorporate diverse factors and extenuating circumstances. Logic will develop more in adolescence and hopefully will fully exist in adulthood. But now the concrete logical thinking is of the either/or, black or white variety. Sibling or peer rivalry is highly subjective and one-sided. "It's Betty's fault. She started it." "I had to get the game, so I don't have to let Billy use it."

Parents are expected to be Olympian gods of justice, fairness, and arbitration. Similarly, teachers are judged by stern, one-dimensional standards and are measured accordingly. If teachers understand the processes in this stage of cognitive development they can conduct themselves so as to promote trust, values, and adherence to principles. But when a teacher is unaware of this stage in cognitive thinking an impulsive decision can damage much that has been carefully built in terms of principles and ethical judgments.

Such was the case when a gym teacher punished an entire class because a few of the children continued to talk when he had asked for silence. In retribution he ordered the entire class to write 100 words about this transgression. Upon their return to their homeroom the children reported this punitive assignment to their well-liked and respected homeroom teacher. Rather impulsively she chose to defend her colleague on the ground that if the majority of them did not influence the few who had transgressed they all should suffer the consequences. Such a concept was well beyond the cognitive stage of this group in terms of multi-dimensional conceptualisation, and their outrage at the unfair distribution of punishment was increased by knowledge of the fact that adults supported each other without regard to fairness, right or wrong. It was injustice heaped on injustice.

Bruce's essay dramatically synthesised the betrayal: "You cannot force a person to think something is right if their mind tells them it's wrong. The mind is the most important thing to me and you can't change it by making me do it with words." In this refrain the composition went on and on to the exact number of 100 words. Understandably it stirred much thought in the conscientious teacher.

This growing, undeveloped ability for concrete reasoning should be kept in mind when using the materials in this guide with preadolescent children. While the learning activities are designed to bolster earlier experiences by providing a concrete experience from which the children can verbalise their intuitive understanding, there will be some disparity in the ability of various children to do this. Most of them will be unable to articulate concepts as complex as the one offered by the teacher in the example above.

In play the preadolescent child is better organised than he was earlier and is often highly imaginative and ingenious. He is also quite concerned about the rules. Before children are nine or ten, they follow rules, seeing them as something made for them by others; however, once children reach that age, although they continue to consider rules important, they no longer regard them as sacred, untouchable, lasting forever, or emanating from adults. It is quite in order for Patty to declare, "Let's play casino another way. The one with the least cards wins." In contrast to the pre-school child where every suggested alteration of a rule is like a transgression, this age group looks upon rules as being arrived at and followed by mutual consent.

Rules, which first seem to be externally introduced gradually come to be made by the child and his group for themselves and are altered as the group feels the need for change. Nevertheless, arbitrary and individual changing of the rules is not acceptable to the group; such action considered unfair and even dishonest. A consensus for changing the rules is demanded by the preadolescent child who is even more insistent on this as he becomes an adolescent.

This changing point of view on rules by the preadolescent is one reason for the value of a curriculum unit on decision making at this age. As these children begin to realise that rules need to change as situations change, they need help and experience in discovering what is important in a situation for which they are to imagine and create adequate rules. An essential segment suggests ways of helping children to become imaginative and creative decision makers.

Leadership qualities are often clearly demonstrated in this age and it may be predicted that when present in preadolescence leadership qualities will remain throughout adolescence and into adult life. Children possessing these qualities seem to have the ability to originate things to do which appeal to others. They are inventive and imaginative, but especially they seem able to present their proposals and ideas in such a way as to harmonise with the group and create a unifying rather than a divisive spirit.

Preadolescents strive to acquire status in peer groups and much of this is done through achievement. They strive for this status through establishing social groups where they can become a force among forces. It is not so much a seeking of power over others as a desire to be allied with power and identified with the strong. Socialisation is a highly important aspect of life at this age. Fear of failure ranks high with the preadolescent and the worst that can happen is failure to become immersed in the life his own age group.

Children of this age show greater interest and concern about sex, frequently engaging in solitary or interpersonal sexual activities. Sexual activity may be precipitated by the stimulation of others, or by upsetting experiences such as failing to learn in school, faulty peer group relationships, anxiety about health, grief, or mourning. A child who is upset and chronically anxious is predisposed to more masturbation. Although he may do this less overtly than he did when he was much younger, it is still a very prominent sexual activity. But now he is prone to have guilt feelings about masturbation and begins to feel that these acts are subject to adult or societal disapproval.

The preadolescent is interested, concerned about , and more or less knowledgeable about the facts of life as related to birth and death. He becomes fascinated with the act of procreation, but is shy about asking questions of parents of other adults lest he be accused of either being ignorant and childish, or unduly interested in an activity which should not interest him until later. An older sibling's love attachment to the opposite sex may be a matter for teasing and even chagrin that this could happen to his sister or brother. Good-naturedly he may tease that "Mary loves Johnny."

School children think in fantasy about sex matters and when some of these items are taboo, they repress their thoughts. Where there is an extreme repression of sexual fantasies, repression may extend into other areas of behaviour, particularly learning. Both sexes are interested in the sex development and behaviour of the other, some children may attempt to examine the genitals of children younger than themselves. The children are overstimulated by parents who exhibit themselves, who talk excessively about sex behaviour, and who are preoccupied with sex instruction.

Sexual identification and role are important at this age and often confusing. Boys are encouraged to do male things and wish to do them, but are not always clear as to what they are. Fathers can be particularly helpful in setting a model. The girl's role has become more ambiguous in today's society since the formerly male prerogatives of business, industry, and athletics are now acceptable for the female image. The boy at this age wishes to be identified as male; however, the girl is not so sure that she wishes to be female. It is also noteworthy that peers approve more of male behaviour in boys than of female behaviour in girls.

If this seems to give boys the edge, there is some compensation for girls in the fact that parents seem to demand more of boys and put more pressure on them to conform to established standards of learning. Similarly in school the behaviour of boys is generally more unacceptable socially than is that of girls and boys seem to get into more trouble. Subconsciously teachers expect to have more disciplinary problems with boys which may or may not in itself be a factor. At any rate the distaff side perceives itself as more accepted and even more valued than boys.

Parents continue to hold positions of importance with preadolescents, but increasingly are equated with peers and other adults as models of behaviour or appearance. Frequently they are compared disadvantageously with the first realisations that father is not athletically heroic and that mother is "fatter than my teacher." Disapproval of parents' behaviour may also be voiced to mother as, "You're always cleaning," or about father, "He always gets the newspaper first." Although they are no longer idols as they were in earlier childhood, parents are still loved and respected, even though the preadolescent does not necessarily feel that his parents understand him.

There is a struggle at this age to break or question old authority bonds and to discover a new basis of authority which includes a measure of self-determination. The earlier unquestioning acceptance of parental authority is now vulnerable to exploratory confrontations with it. In the face of a parent's order to be home by six" he may get as surprise retort from the child, "What right have you to make me?" This is not necessarily outright rebellion or rude defiance but a testing of the basis for authority. Teachers are also viewed as external authorities centered exclusively outside the child. The agencies of church and school can provide a negative denying experience or a constructive power-expanding one, depending on the competence and understanding of the teachers and staff of these organisations. Children respond more favourably in a democratic classroom where they feel they have a "voice" or collectively exert an influence on the teacher. The implication is that methods of teaching can be highly instrumental for learning or the reverse.

As the child perceives other people's interests and needs he can make independent judgments about their social behaviour. Thus he has the ability to relate the parts to the whole and the capacity to develop a basis for justice as well as standards about being governed by others or himself.

This developmental level is a step forward from the moral values of the younger child which were generalised as they were learned. Earlier moral laws had absolute values that were attached to real things and existed as an indivisible part of an object. For example, the command "don't touch the stove" became a property of the stove. Therefore, a stove was something not to be touched. Father and obedience to father were viewed as one; disobedience was an infringement of adult authority rather than violation of inner moral obligation or conscience. Naughty words were bad because they violated adult-imposed taboos. Reproof and punishment were expected as a natural consequence of behaviour; the concept of immanent justice, whereby a misdemeanour is promptly and automatically punished, was held to be true.

While the child of nine to twelve continue to have some feeling of immanent justice, much of this has been replaced by what Piaget calls the concept of distributive justice whereby punishment must be "fair" and compensate exactly and in proportion to the damage done or the wrong inflicted. Since he can now relate the parts to the whole he has ability to make a more objective judgment although theoretical implications and refinements of the process are still beyond him. Nevertheless, moral structures are taking more reasoned shape. The child knows that if he fails to do his homework he can be deprived of television or some other privilege because his parents expect him to finish his tasks, because he has responsibility for it in school, because television is a privilege which he must earn, etc. These are the parts which form the structure upon which he was judged and disciplined. This is not to say that he blandly accepts the punishment. On the contrary it is at this point that his sense of distributive justice and the exact weighing of its "fairness" becomes most at issue. "Let the punishment fit the crime," is the battle cry of the preadolescents at this new level of conscious and moral judgment.

Guilt makes a child seek atonement which he achieves by obsessive-compulsive behaviour, by rituals and other means of self-punishment. Children develop their own taboos about thoughts and acts, with compulsions which serve as penance. One may wish his sister dead, but with quick guilt he may involuntarily make himself say two times over, "I didn't mean it. I didn't mean it." Or for example one will not permit himself to touch or view certain objects, using the prohibitions as a magical protection while at the same time it stops him from looking at and doing things which he assumes are "bad."

Some of the tics and habit spasms seen in this age group are the result of tension. Occasionally the tension is related to anxiety and guilt feelings, or to parental pressures in regard to eating, cleanliness, appearance, school achievement, or to peer difficulties. These body movements are not consciously performed, although children are aware of them. Sometimes they seem to annoy the child, yet at the same time they give him some feeling of relief of tension. Calling attention to these behaviour patterns and remonstrance by parents or teachers do little to alleviate or end them. On the contrary criticism may prolong them.

Lying, stealing, and cheating are common problems in preadolescence and have a variety of causes behind them. Sometimes children cheat and steal because they have witnessed such acts in their parents or in other adults. In play and fantasy, the school-age child uses the rules and values of his elders. Parents are sometimes surprised when they see themselves in their children's unfairness, dishonesty, and cheating. It does not escape notice when the parent understates the age of the child to get a reduced-rate ticket of admission. The parent may realise a monetary gain at the loss of the child's trust in honesty and ethical values. Parents have considerable influence in shaping moral judgments by serving as models, by explicit teaching, and by establishing a kind of home life where certain forms of moral evaluation can develop.

In both secular and religious schools children should be able to learn how to turn for guidance to multiple authorities rather than to parents alone. They already look to their peers, and while this influence can be good, it can also be misleading as when group cheating is engaged in because "everybody does it." Occasionally children steal in order to win the attention and respect of peers. Such prowess gains greater respect and success in school on occasion, not only from peers but even from some parents. At the time of the inception of such habits, parents and teachers should constructively intervene. An object which unexplainably appears and obviously does not belong to the child or his family should be discussed. The child should be helped to fully understand his act and helped to take appropriate steps to return the object without demeaning him or subjecting him to extremes of belabouring and punishment.

By preadolescence children have fashioned still further their consciences. Conscience now can provide self-approval and feeling good about oneself for "good" acts in counterpoint to feeling shame and guilt for "bad" actions. Motives and consequences for acts are considered and these are judged less by the degree of disobedience involved and more by implications of their acts. Conscience finds its anchoring points in mutual respect and awareness collective obedience. If parents and teachers provide consistency in their response to undesirable behaviour, the child's expectance of consequence from such acts will be reinforced.

Children of this age have values although they may be unclear as to how they acquired them or how to acquire new ones. Greater clarity exists about those values which were handed down, the products of adult decisions, than about those they are asked to make themselves each day. Yet the child should be encouraged to act on his own, not constrained by love or duty alone to act as expected by parents or other authority figures. At this age children try to wriggle out of decision making and to keep their options open. They should be induced to express themselves fully and then build on what they have expressed. The personal experience a child has had will make a big difference in his approach to decision making. If parents and teachers show respect for his ability to make decisions and help him accomplish them, the child will be further encouraged to do so. The role of these adults is to help clarify values so that children may learn how to "wrest their own values from the available array," and to help them create their own values in their own time.

We say that the sense of morality has become internalised as the child consciously and unconsciously incorporates the value, standards, and expectations of his elders. Where there has been a lack of such guidance in the family, moral and ethical development is seriously interferred with. By preadolescence, children should not steal because they cannot distinguish between what is their property and what belongs to others. In those families where there has been no clear differentiation of ownership among its members, however, and the older child continues not to distinguish what belongs to other from what he takes as his own, this concept may not develop. Taking things as if they were his own, with the view that all family possessions belong equally to all its members, is best prevented by providing young children with some possessions which are clearly their own and separate from those of others. Private ownership like privacy in activities is the right of young children, but in preadolescence and adolescence children are even more demanding of it.

Role and Responsibilities of Parents

Just as the child faces certain developmental tasks in preadolescence, so too the parents have tasks which go hand in hand with the child's development. They include understanding and helping the child to establish his identity and sex role, to further separate himself from themselves, to establish ties with his peer groups, and to develop his skills, learning, and sense of industry. While the mother's role continues to have some primacy, the father is equally significant in setting models of adult behaviour and sex role. Both parents are involved in helping the child emancipate himself from the close ties with family and to facilitate learning and new experience. Other adults, such as teachers, also have roles akin to those of the parents. In their respective areas they help the child adapt and cope with the stresses of his life.

Most of the child's time away from home is occupied by school attendance. In the arena of the school he daily faces each of the tasks mentioned, whether he is involved in learning or in playing. Although he may continue to have mixed feelings about going to school, and about leaving home, by nine years of age he has overcome the earlier anxiety of separation from his parents who in turn will have become more accustomed to having other adults share some of the responsibility in the educational disciplining of the child. Hopefully mothers will already have some interests outside the home so that they are not involved with their children to the point that they inadvertently create a separation problem.

Preadolescents are more perceptive about parent-child relationships than parents realise. They often feel overprotected and "babied" but can be understanding and rather tolerant of it. Eleven-year-old Jean comments, "Parents think they'll just handle everything themselves and protect their children. But when the children grow up they'll have to handle their own things."

Parents should be aware of the thought capacities of the preadolescent because he is somewhat amenable to reasoning and can begin to make value judgments of his own. But there is another side to the preadolescent too. Well-meaning parents are often "up a tree," because while their youngster understand what is wanted of them, they will not allow themselves to be shaped like putty. Children may enter into transactions with parents, but they manage to reserve their contractual rights to the letter. Nevertheless parents are influential because these children emulate their elders. If parents are honest, socially responsible, and non-aggressive there is a good chance that their children will act likewise. This is not, of course, automatic. Sometimes children may imitate another adult to whom they are drawn. Parental consistency in imposing standards and discipline on their children best guarantees effectiveness. Vacillation by parents does not help to establish a firm basis of moral values.

Sex identification is a major concern of preadolescents and it is important for parents to help them find this identification in the appropriate sex and in appropriate ways. Fathers particularly need to provide identification with the male image. Adequacy with peer groups is of maximum importance for these children and parents should encourage and help provide every opportunity to play work, and group with their fellows. At this age it is from peers that they derive the necessary support to resolve their fears, guilts, and anxieties by "doing what others do." At this age it is in schools, secular or religious, that they may find supportive and leavening influences.

Role of Teachers

Teachers in church schools like those in secular schools have specific tasks related to the preadolescent at this juncture of his development. These include the facilitation of learning, reasoning, communication, and experiencing among children. In addition, however, the religious teacher more than his secular counterpart has a special responsibility in terms of developing moral ethical, and value judgment among children.

The goal of religious education in present society is a challenging one. Religious education must build a link between man's past and his present. It must find a way of giving perspective to the future. It must explore the ethical, philosophical, and spiritual foundations of man in greater depth than can be hoped for from secular schools and yet relate them significantly to the real world of today and the real problems confronting each human being. Concurrently the religious education teacher has also to provide a positive pattern of social behaviour which the child can use as a model. As he makes decisions in the presence of children they will learn from observation how he faces problems and deals with them ethically and morally. It goes without saying that he will be establishing himself as a model many times without being consciously aware of it. Similarly, the child will not be aware that he is modelling himself after the teacher.

Finally, the teacher should help the child develop a greater awareness of himself, and reinforce his self-identification and independence. At this age, organisation of the child's self and his self-picture are still being developed. By understanding this the teacher can help the preadolescent shape a healthy self-image leading to growth and development. Studies have shown that changes in self-image are an inevitable outcome of learning conditions in every classroom, whether or not the teacher is aware of it or aiming for it. A good self-image or a distorted and self-defeating one can be deliberately induced by particular teaching methods. Because the behaviour of the teacher is interpreted by the child in personal ways, it can lead either to personal growth or stultification. Hence knowledge of one's self, style, personal, and emotional reactions is essential for the teacher and demands sensitiveness in relation to the child.

Teachers are human beings and it is not expected that they be more than that. Children may make them heroes, paragons of virtue, or contrariwise find them deficient and inadequate. Very often children identify their church or fellowship school teachers with their academic teachers. Since the latter are frequently considered by preadolescents as people who annoy, punish, criticise, and demand much of their time for lessons and homework, it is natural for children to view their church or fellowship school teachers in the same light. Inevitably by the manner of procedure the teacher will be automatically stressing the similarities and the differences between himself and the regular school teacher, just as he will be differentiating between the aims and objectives of the church or fellowship school and the regular school.

The most important personal characteristics that a teacher can have are the ability to love children, to appreciate them as individuals, and to get satisfaction from relationships with them. If these are inherent in the teacher there is little doubt of success. Children are quick to perceive the presence or absence of such qualities and to judge whether they are simulated or if they are indeed attributes of the teacher.

Children have strong feelings of anger, resentment, joy, and guilt. They also have values in terms of what they are for and of what they are against, although they are unaware to a large extent of the motivation for these values. The teacher should not be surprised at some of the feelings expressed, particularly those which seem cruel, envious, rivalrous, or filled with hatred and suspicion. Neither should the teacher be surprised with his reactions of disgust, hatred, and guilt when he listens to some of these things. What counts is how he deals with these expressions and the feelings involved, whether they appear in the pupils or in himself. The yardstick is the same as for parents in coping with the expressed or acted-out feelings of children. The crucial element is to maintain a positive and constructive relationship, one of trust and helpful support that will lead to constructive emotional growth.

The skillful teacher knows how to guide children to express themselves fully. Questioning them directly may lead to silence rather than to spontaneous discussion of feelings and actions. As a topic is raised it is best to let talk begin freely. Some direction can be given from time to time to keep the talk within the boundaries of time and subject. When appropriate, direct queries can be made of the child to express himself further along certain lines.

The ability to be a good listener is a paramount quality in a teacher. A good listener is one who demonstrates a willingness to listen without being judgmental. Children are hesitant to talk of personal experiences in a group, or even privately, unless they are sure that they will not evoke reactions of disgust or disapproval. Often in a group there is atleast one child who is more verbal and less constrained than the others who sets off the discussion. With encouragement and expertise the teacher can use a verbally free child as the springboard to involve the others.

The teacher must try not to impose his values or judgments on anything the child talks about in terms of his own experiences or reactions to stories in the text. Children need to create their own values and can do so if the teacher is helpful in bringing out materials which clarify values and the processes in making value judgments.

Teachers should be prepared for the feedback in the classroom discussion by way of return on subsequent Sundays to discuss materials previously evaluated. The children may have mulled over ideas from a class session during the week or talked to others including parents. They may come with new ideas or want to amend ideas previously expressed, or to state different values and judgments. The reason for this is that meaningful learning involves more than intellectual processes. It also involves emotions and feelings, not the least of which is guilt. As matters have been discussed which involve basic human values and actions, race relations, bigotry, cruelty, antisocial acts, and the relationship of these directly to the child, his family, school, and community, the discussion doubtlessly triggers self-examination and with it a feeling of guilt. This plays a part in the need to return to a topic and re-express one's opinions. Guilt may drive a person back to previously discussed events in order to express emotions which will relieve guilt.

Another feedback which a teacher may expect is that from parents. Parents often question their children about what they have learned. They may be disturbed at what they hear of the child's point of view and his set of values; they may try to trace its origin by analysing their own role. If their own values are at variance with the child's and they disapprove, they may look towards the teacher as the one who influenced their child not to their liking. Sometimes a parent projects his own shortcomings onto the teacher. Today with such inflammatory subjects as race relations, war, international relations, and family living patterns, it is not unusual for children to raise questions about current events and to express judgments that are so searching and clear in their honesty that the ambivalent parent, or the compromising one, is made exceedingly uncomfortable. They may go so far as to remove the child from class or strongly suggests to the teacher that he changes his manner of teaching and possibly his point of view.

Needless to say the teacher's responsibility is to keep faith with the children and with his own values and beyond that to attempt to help the parents to look within themselves and re-evaluate their own ethical thinking and judgment.

If all this seems a heavy and exceptional responsibility for the teacher whose religious and ethical considerations have motivated this activity, there is no denying that only exceptional people dedicate themselves to such a task. It is their way of serving conscience and mankind. The reward is to know and to feel that they do a work with children that may help children face this troubled world as decent, ethical human beings and perhaps in time to change it in meaningful ways. This is reward enough.

CHAPTER 4

Growing Child and Challenge of Policy Formulation

Introduction

Policy formulation for growth promotion is an essential element of health policy development in every country but is of particular significance in developing countries where malnutrition in children under 5 years is highly prevalent. The aim of any health policy should be to improve health status of the population, thus contributing to human development. The Alma-Ata Declaration and the Human Development Report 1990 reaffirm health as a basic human right (WHO 1978; UNDP 1990). Likewise, the Convention of the Rights of the Child, presented at the World's Children Summit, identified growth as a fundamental right of every child (UNICEF 1990).

In the past, policy formulation in health has been approached with a narrow view and dealt within an unorganised manner. There is a growing consensus that health policy development should be undertaken using a systemic approach based on societal values and goals for human development, political commitment to these goals, sound scientific evidence, resource availability, and cultural acceptability.

As we will discuss in detail later, health policies cannot be formulated in an isolated manner; they are influenced by various sectors in society and should be linked to the broad development strategy of the country, the resources made available for human development (instead of defence and other spending) and to policies in other key areas such as status of women, population policies, education, and agriculture to name a few.

A Conceptual Framework for the Health System

A conceptual framework for the health system is presented in Fig. 4.1. The health service organisation evolves within an external environment. A determining factor in this environment is the political system and the political commitment to human development. Cultural and societal values will shape the health goals to be achieved.

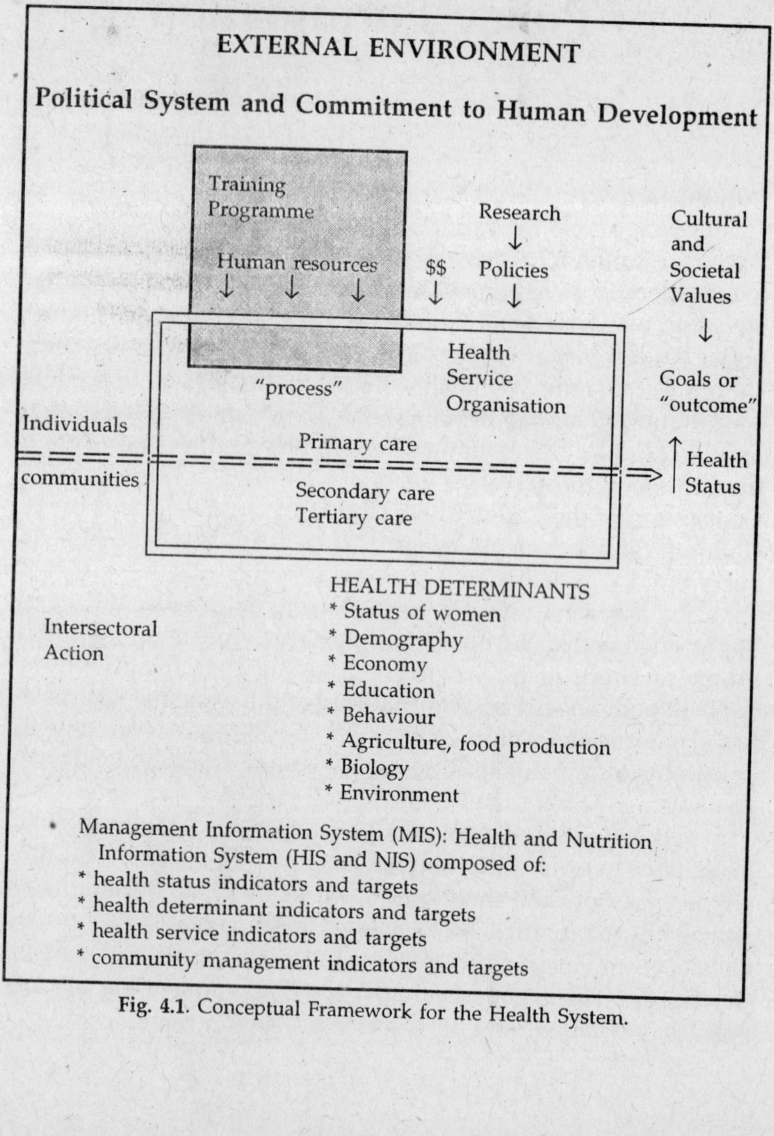

Fig. 4.1. Conceptual Framework for the Health System.

The health service organisation is but one of the determinants of health and generally accounts for only a small proportion of the improvement of the health status of a population. However, it can play a key role by stimulating intersectoral action and may, therefore, impact on other more powerful health determinants listed in the figure.

In an ideal setting the health service organisation contributes to the improvement of health status by collaborating with communities and individuals through a process of primary health care with referrals as needed to secondary and tertiary care levels. Although it is desirable that it be guided by policies based on scientific research, this is most often not the case. Well-trained and motivated human resources should be its most important input. Another fundamental input is an adequate level of financing.

The management information system (MIS) should monitor the impact of the health service organisation on health status and its environment (including other health determinants), track progress of outputs (PHC programmes, intersectoral action, secondary and tertiary care), and inputs (staffing, expenditures and revenues, supplies and drugs). It should, therefore, include indicators and targets for health status, health determinants and health services.

Policy Development for Health

As a first step towards health policy development, societies need to reach decisions regarding human development targets, *i.e.*, improvement in education level and life expectancy, reduction in infant and under-five mortality, and in prevalence of malnutrition. The importance of political commitment to these targets cannot be overemphasised.

The next step in this process should be an exercise in priority setting. The burden of disease is assessed overall and then for each specific condition (health problem, disease entity) by combining severity and frequency.

The *efficacy* of the intervention for each health problem should be evaluated under optimal conditions (laboratory or controlled environment); the *effectiveness*, or practical efficacy, should then be tested under real life field conditions.

Next, both the proportionate and marginal costs of the intervention are measured. Proportionate costs reflect the proportion of all health expenditures attributable to this specific intervention, whereas marginal costs indicate the additional costs incurred when adding this intervention to an already functioning health system. Opportunity costs (such as time of mothers, cost of travel to health facility, etc.) caused by the use of the intervention should also be taken into account, although they are often more difficult to measure.

Combining effectiveness and cost information will lead to an assessment of cost-effectiveness (for example, case of malnutrition averted per dollar invested for a particular growth promotion intervention), a key tool for comparing the "performance" of different interventions. In this regard, Jamison and Mosley are leading an interesting initiative on the part of the World Bank. They have recently published an article entitled : Disease Control Priorities in Developing Countries, Health Policy Responses to Epidemiological Change (Jamison and Mosley 1991).

Costs have not always been measured systematically for growth promotion interventions. UNICEF has only recently taken an interest in obtaining realistic assessments of its financial contribution and that of ministries of health to growth promotion activities. However, this quantitative approach is not sufficient. Interventions should be culturally, socially, and politically acceptable and must involve communities throughout the decision-making process. Although this may initially lead to a different ranking of priorities by communities and health professionals, the communication between these two parties will result in a more comprehensive understanding of the health problems and to effective decision-making.

When integrating interventions into health programmes, it is important to take into account their inter-relationships. One should then study the various strategic options (programme alternatives) and the optimal timing before finalising the programme work plan. Traditionally, policy formulation is envisioned at the global and national levels (*i.e.*, ministries of health, UNICEF, WHO). Yet, adaptations of these policies, specific policy formulation, and health planning should occur at every level of the health system. At the national level, the Health Policy and Planning Unit of the Ministry of Health should be responsible for carrying out strategic planning; identifying national health objectives; and developing a general healthy public policy package, policies for the health services, and specific intersectoral health policies. It must also provide national guidelines for primary health care programmes.

Repeating the planning cycle at the district level, district health management teams (DHMTs) should elaborate health profiles (community diagnoses) and develop action plans in collaboration with other sectors and district authorities, to ensure an integrated approach to health development and the required political commitment.

Operations are carried at the subdistrict or health centre level and at the community level. These levels are key to ensure both community mobilisation and quality delivery of services, yet they have not received sufficient attention expect perhaps in the Americas. The Pan American Health Organisation has done a considerable amount of work on these levels which are referred to as Local Health Systems (Sistemas Locales de Salud or SILOS) (PAHO 1989). The planning cycle should involve community leaders in local health policy development and in ensuring that health receives the priority it deserves.

As mentioned earlier, the health service organisation must be supported by a strong management information system (MIS). Information collected at one level must be used for planning at that level before it is passed on to a higher level. Likewise, higher levels must report on information aggregated from lower levels to provide comparative performances between similar units of the system.

Each level should be linked with the next level up and down with an appropriate amount of "bottom-up" and "top-down" planning respectively. The various levels of policy development and planning process are presented in Fig. 4.2 in order of importance, emphasising the key roles of the family, community, and health centre level. Decision-making must be decentralised with equity and must be effective so that each level is accountable and has the ability to manage both human and financial resources.

This planning process may appear idealistic, but it is essential if one wants to maximise community involvement, effectiveness, and efficiency.

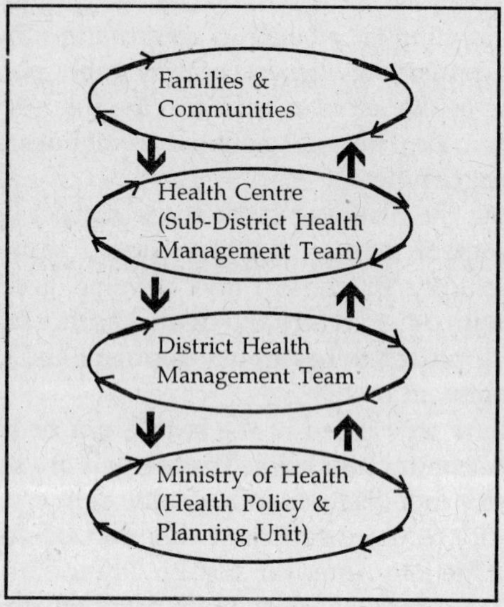

Fig. 4.2. Policy development and planning process for health.The planning cycle (with its priority setting) should occur at every level of the health system, each arrow in the cycle representing one of its four stages: observation, deduction, decision, and action. There should be an appropriate mix of "bottom-up" and "top-down" planning (as indicated by vertical arrow) together with a strong management information system.

Research and Scientific Evidence for Sound Policy Formulation

There is considerable debate about the effectiveness of growth monitoring in improving child growth. This is in good part due to the lack of properly executed studies with rigorous designs. Policy should be based on solid scientific evidence of the effectiveness of the interventions proposed.

Different *types of design* will provide different levels of strength of evidence, from "speculative" to "firm." These are in increasing order of strength of evidence :

* Case reports
* Case series, case studies of programmes or projects
* Ecological studies (comparisons of aggregate risk)
* Cross-sectional surveys

* Case-control studies
* Cohort studies
* Randomised clinical and randomised community controlled trails (RCTs)

However, the type of design is not a substitute for the quality of the design and the rigor of execution. A poorly designed and executed randomised controlled trail may be worth less than a case report!

The quality of evidence on the effectiveness of interventions can be assessed by the following grades (Spitzer 1979):

* I Evidence obtained from atleast one properly randomised controlled trail.
* II-1 Evidence obtained from well-designed cohort or case-control analytic studies, preferably from more than one centre or research group.
* II-2 Evidence obtained from comparisons between times or places with or without the intervention. Dramatic results in uncontrolled experiments (such as the result of the introduction of penicillin in the 1940s) could also be regarded as this type of evidence.
* III Opinions of respected authorities, based on clinical experience, descriptive studies, or report of expert committees.

This attempt at quantifying the evidence has proved invaluable in making rational decisions in the allocation of scarce resources.

Let us take a familiar, yet controversial example of a global intervention that could perhaps have benefited from more rigorous scientific assessment before wide-scale implementation : that of oral rehydration therapy using oral rehydration solutions (ORS) packages versus cereal-based oral rehydration therapy (ORT). As part of a strategy to decrease mortality from diarrheal diseases, UNICEF promoted the utilisation of ORS pre-made packages. It was only several years later that evidence concerning the equal or superior efficacy of home-prepared, cereal-based ORT came to light. Cereal-based ORT would appear to have greater effectiveness than ORS from packages: availability at the time of the diarrheal episode is not an issue because almost every household has cereal and some salt; the prepared diluted "porridge" is very close to traditional remedies in many societies (*e.g.*, "atmit" in Ethiopia) and would appear to be much more acceptable by mothers. It is also less expensive as it does not require manufacturing or an extensive distribution network.

Although the promotion of ORS packages has saved countless lives, a small fraction of the investment could have been used to examine the most cost-effective strategies in different situations; this would have probably led to significant cost savings and slightly improved child survival in many countries.

Recognising the importance of research, UNICEF and other international agencies have been gradually increasing their share of budget for research and development (R&D), as has been recommended by the commission of Health Research for Development (Commission of Health Research for Development 1990).

Evidence for Effectiveness of GMP

Some confusion persists as to what are the interventions in growth monitoring. Growth monitoring can be seen as having three main functions:

* As an educational tool for mothers.
* As a screening tool to identify those children at risk for malnutrition.
* As a tool for nutritional surveillance (for example, as part of an early warning system for famine).

In the first, growth monitoring is an intervention. In the second and third, it is not an intervention in itself but is part of a management information system; it, therefore, cannot be evaluated without its accompanying growth promotion intervention. The debate about the effectiveness of GMP is in part due to this confusion. It is also due to the paucity of properly designed epidemiological studies to evaluate the growth promotion interventions.

This is particularly important as the field of growth monitoring and promotion is an extremely complex subject with numerous confounding factors. Furthermore, the presence of strong effect modifiers such as literacy may explain positive and negative results in better-and less-educated population, respectively.

As is often the case for the introduction of new technologies in health, growth monitoring and promotion programmes were probably introduced on a large scale in many countries without sufficient prior field testing.

We will not review here the scientific evidence concerning the effectiveness of GMP as this has been done by Ruel (Ruel, in press) and in other papers presented at this Colloquium. Most of the papers on the subject are in the form of project or programme evaluations or cross-sectional survey (quality of evidence II-2 or III). We are aware of only one cohort study (quality of evidence II-1) (Briend and Bari 1989) and one randomised, community-controlled trial (quality of evidence I) (George *et al.* 1992), but randomisation was partial and involved only six pairs of communities. It should be noted that the scope and success of some large programmes, such as that of Tanzania (Ljungqvist 1992), probably respresent quality of evidence II-2.

Furthermore, most of the research has focused on evaluating growth monitoring activities, with very little emphasis on growth promotion interventions. The other issues that need to be addressed, assuming that one had an effective intervention in the first place, are:

* Was it given in sufficient quantity (duration of frequency of mothers' participation)?
* Was it delivered to a sufficient proportion of the target population? (Overall PHC coverage and percentage of those attending receiving meaningful intervention.)

Evidence presented by Gerein (Gerein 1991) would suggest that these are often problem areas. In such situation, one would run the risk of committing a type-II error (*i.e.*, assuming no effect of intervention when an effect actually exists). Last, many researchers conduct hypothesis testing when in fact the lack of declared *a priori* hypothesis and the design limitations would suggest restricting oneself to hypothesis generating. It is, therefore, not surprising to see the degree of confusion concerning the effectiveness of growth monitoring and promotion.

Having accepted the premise that potential growth promotion interventions should be scientifically tested before they are implemented on a wide scale, we should, by the same logic, test current growth promotion interventions before abandoning them.

The foregoing comments urge strongly for an increase in research and development (R&D) funding for growth monitoring and promotion and in particular for other carefully executed randomised trails. Randomised trails are the standard design by which we evaluate new drugs; should we not, therefore, use the same criteria for growth promotion interventions?

Management and Implementation

Policies that are not implemented are useless. Formulated policies should therefore, be carried through to the implementation stage. Accordingly, there is a need for dynamic management of the programmes to ensure operations of high quality.

The motivating of personnel should be one of the prime concerns of health managers. Supervision not only increases motivation of staff but is also required for quality assurance. Likewise, in-service training can be a powerful motivating factor and can lead to much improved performance if it is applied and carried out in the context of the work setting.

As health professionals, we often do not make full use of the available body of knowledge in the field of management. The service industry relies more and more on strategies for continuous quality improvement (CQI), on process control (variance control), and operations research and can be an example for health services.

Inter-sectoral Growth Promotion Policies

As mentioned earlier, the commitment of government is crucial to the success of any health care intervention. Government leaders must be motivated to act on and be accountable for human development. Governments, under the guidance of their ministries of health, need to decide on an optimal growth promotion policy package based on the cost-effectiveness and appropriateness of individual interventions, well integrated into existing programmes.

As health professionals, we need to be constantly reminded that most of the improvement in the growth of children can be attributed to health determinants other than health services. It is, therefore, paramount that a national policy for growth promotion not be limited to the health services, as is often the case. We will present here some other key areas of intervention. The list is meant to be illustrative but not exhaustive.

Economic, Employment-Generating, Equity-Producing, and Poverty-Alleviating Policies

The relationship between poor growth and poverty is evident to all; it bears a direct relationship through food security and is linked indirectly through the higher frequency and severity of infectious diseases. Policies that will address these issues could potentially have a major impact on the growth of children.

Education

We have noted earlier the potency of literacy as an effect modifier for growth promotion interventions. Just as in other aspects of health status, the education of girls is one of the most powerful health determinants. Another important aspect of intersectoral collaboration is the development of specific health and nutrition curricula in schools and for literacy programmes. The role of nonformal education of adults through the media, extension services, and health services should not be underestimated. Child-to-child programmes can also play an important role in growth promotion.

The Status of Women

The status of women affects child growth through a multiplicity of causal pathways: a woman's high workload and caloric expenditure during pregnancy may lead to insufficient weight gain and subsequent low birth weight; when she is not pregnant, this same workload may prevent her from having sufficient time for child feeding. Her economic situation may not allow her to provide sufficient food. In many countries, men eat first, thus preventing the mother from giving priority to the growing child. Policies improving the status of women, *i.e.*, those that ensure gender equity, can have a beneficial impact on growth promotion.

Population Policies/Family Planning Programmes

The Impact of child spacing and family size on growth promotion is well-known and need not be discussed further. Among other things, it influences the care of children already born and a woman's health, employment, and economic opportunities.

Agricultural and Environmental Policies

Agricultural policies impact directly no food security and on employment, especially of the rural poor. Food security is an important determinant of growth in children in many developing countries. Agricultural policies should include atleast the following:

* Land tenure and agrarian reforms
* Market type and pricing policies
* Farm input systems (*i.e.*, improved seeds, tools, and traction, credit)
* Post-harvest systems (storage, distribution, marketing)

In his paper, "A Policy Agenda for Famine Prevention in Africa," Joachim von Braun demonstrates the importance of the lack of the foregoing policies, above and beyond the effect of droughts (von Braun 1991).

Food aid can be life-saving in a famine situation but it may have a detrimental effect on local agriculture through loss of revenue by depressing food prices. Food aid programmes should be implemented judiciously and their effects monitored closely.

Water and Sanitation Policies

Although one rarely thinks of water and sanitation policies as having an effect on growth promotion, these can improve growth through a decrease in infectious diseases in children and by saving considerable time for mothers who would then be better able to care for their children.

Health Services Policies

We have assumed universal adoption of Primary Health Care. In practice, however, curative services in urban areas still get a large share of health resources. Redirected health service policies could lead to better infection control, family planning and health and nutrition education thus improving growth.

Healthy Public Policies

Healthy public policies deserve our attention. As an example, smoking is on rapid increase in developing countries. It has a powerful deleterious effect on birth weight. Tobacco farming displaces other more nutritious crops. Finally, parental smoking predisposes to acute respiratory infections in children, thus contributing to reduced growth. Curbing tobacco production and smoking through an integrated approach including a ban on advertising and introducing taxation could lead to small but important improvements in growth.

Conclusion

We have barely begun our work on policy formulation for growth promotion. Much scientific research needs to be done to understand better the role of growth monitoring in the implementation of growth promotion programmes and the cost-effectiveness of various growth promotion strategies. Ministries of health, funding agencies, and other organisations need to increase their share of budgets allocated to research and development.

We must convince our political leaders of the fundamental right of every child to growth and hold them accountable for results. Our approach to growth promotion must be broad, integrated, and intersectoral. It should not be limited to interventions in the health services, as has been the case in the past. In particular, our approach should focus on educating girls and empowering women.

Can international agencies, national governments, health workers, and communities rise to the challenge of tackling growth promotion in a comprehensive manner?

References

Berg, A. 1987, Malnutrition, What Can be Done? Lessons from the World Bank Experience, The John Hopkins University Press, Baltimore.

Briend, A. and Bari, A. 1989, Critical Assessment of the Use of Growth Monitoring for Identifying High Risk Children in Primary Health Care Programmes, *BMJ*, 298 (6688): 1607-11.

Commission of Health Research for Development, 1990, Health Research, Essential Link to Equity and Development, Oxford.

George, S.M., Latham, M.C., and Abel, R. 1992, Effectiveness of Growth Monitoring in Indian Villages, *Abstract*, FASEB.

Gerein, N. and Ross, D. 1991, Is Growth Monitoring Worthwhile? An Evaluation of its Use in Three Child Health Programmes in Zaire, *Soc Sci Med*, 32(6) 667-75.

Jamison, D.T. and Mosley, H.W. 1991, Disease Control Priorities in Developing Countries, Health Policy Responses to Epidemiological Change, *Amer J Public Health*, 81:15-22.

Ljungqvist, B. 1992, Growth Monitoring in Health and Nutrition Information Systems, Tanzania, Paper presented at the Colloquium on Growth Promotion for Child Development, Nyeri, Kenya, 12-13 May.

PAHO (Pan American Health Organisation, Pan American Sanitary Bureau, Regional Office of the World Health Organisation), 1989. Development and Strengthening of Local Health Systems in the Transformation of National Health Systems, PAHO.

1989, Final reports, Meetings on Local Health Systems and Decentralisation, Argentina, Bolivia, Brazil, Honduras and Uruguay, Health Service Development Programme, Pan American Health Organisation/WHO.

Ruel, M. (in press), Growth Monitoring as an Educational Tool, an Integrating Strategy and a Resource of Information: A Review of Experience. In Beyond Child Survival, Enhancing Child Growth and Nutrition in Developing Countries, P. Pinstrup-Andersen, D. Pelletier, and H. Alderman, eds., Cornell University Press.

Spitzer, W.O. *et al.*, 1979, The Periodic Health Examination, A Report of the Periodic Health Examination Task Force, *Can Med Assoc. J*, 121:1193-1254.

UNICEF (United Nations Children's Fund), 1990, Strategy for Improved Nutrition of Children and Women in Developing Countries, UNICEF.

1990, Convention of the Rights of the Child, World Summit for Children, September.

UNDP (United Nations Development Programme), 1990, The Human Development Report, Oxford.

Von Braun, J. 1991, A Policy Agenda for Famine Prevention in Africa, Food Policy Report, International Food Policy Research Institute, Washington, D.C., October.

WHO (World Health Organisation), 1978, International Conference on Primary Health Care, Alma-Ata, 1978, Primary Health Care: Report of the International Conference on Primary Health Care, Alma-Ata, USSR, 6-12 September 1978, jointly sponsored by the World Health Organisation and the United Nations Children's Fund, Geneva; World Health Organisation.

CHAPTER 5

Learning and Discrimination

It is a well-documented phenomenon that discrimination learning tends to proceed faster when the stimuli involved are physically distinctive. The more similar the stimuli, the slower does learning to respond differentially proceed. This effect is demonstrated in the second study, by Spiker, and it is presumed to be a result of stimulus generalisation.

Another factor which has been shown to influence the acquisition of differential responses to different stimuli is that of stimulus pertaining. If a child has previously been required to respond differentially to stimuli, in a subsequent discrimination situation involving the same stimuli his performance will tend to be facilitated. This effect is particularly evident in situations where the subject has previously been required to learn distinctive names for the stimuli to be discriminated, and the third selection, by Cantor, is pertinent to this set of findings.

It is a well-known phenomenon with infrahuman organisms, largely as a result of the work of Harlow and his colleagues, that with increased experience in discrimination learning problems, subjects solve a series of discrimination tasks more and more quickly. It appears that with increased experience in similar situations, the subject learns to inhibit inappropriate responses, to make responses more skillfully, and to seek and observe crucial aspects of the stimuli in appropriate places. This phenomenon has been attributed to "learning set," which has been variously interpreted as a transfer of training or a generalisation phenomenon. The Shepard study provides an example of the learning set phenomenon as it occurs in children.

One of the important features of the discrimination learning situation is that is enables study of the relative effectiveness of different rewarding and punishing conditions. The Brackbill selection is an example of this type of study. One may investigate, in addition, the effects of delay and magnitude of reward, and the influence of different reinforcement schedules, on the acquisition of a discrimination learning task. Some of these other uses of discrimination tasks are dealt with in later sections of this book.

The psychological variables that may be studied with children in discrimination situations are numerous. Studies of discrimination learning are contributing substantially to the refinement of general behaviour theory. Discrimination learning theory in turn has been most productive of hypotheses that can be adequately tasted with children—indeed, some child psychologists think that many learning theory hypotheses are *best* tested with children.

Discrimination Learning in Children

In Discrimination Learning with infrahuman organisms, two procedures for the presentation of the stimuli to be discriminated are available. In a discrimination problem to be learned in a T-maze or a Lashley jumping apparatus and involving a black and a white stimulus, for example, the "simultaneous" procedure involves the presentation of a black and a white stimulus on each trial with position counterbalanced. The "successive" procedure entails presentation of only one of the discriminative stimuli on each trial. The reinforced responses in the simultaneous situation might be going left to black in a black-left, white-right arrangement and going right to black in a white-left, black-right arrangement. Approach to black, therefore, would consistently result in reinforcement. The reinforced responses in the successive situation might be going right to a black presentation and left to a white presentation.

Spence (7) has described simultaneous discrimination learning as resulting from the strengthening of response to the reinforced component of the stimulus complex until it attains sufficiently greater strength than competing incorrect response tendencies to result in consistently correct choices. Spence (8) has also said that the successive problem can be solved as a patterned discrimination, *i.e.*, by *S*'s approaching certain patterns or combinations of reinforced stimulus components, while response to other patterns is not reinforced. He suggested that on this basis the successive problem should be more difficult than a simultaneous learning problem involving the same stimuli, because the stimulus compounds to be discriminated on each trial are more similar than in the simultaneous problem, and he presented evidence for this proposition from rat studies.

Not all infrahuman studies have supported the contention that simultaneous stimulus presentation produces faster learning than successive presentation. Several studies have suggested that atleast under some experimental circumstances successive provides better performance than simultaneous stimulus presentation (*1, 2, 9*). In general, however, those experimental instances in which successive proved easier than simultaneous learning have involved a different kind of response than those characteristic of the T-maze or typical Lashely jumping situation. When the animal is required to ""Orient towards and approach the stimulus complex (path, door, alley, window) containing the positive stimulus cue (white, form, etc.) ..." (8), simultaneous stimulus presentation tends to result in better discrimination learning than successive. When the animal is required, however, to make a response to a locus removed from the stimulus source (*1,2,9*), it is not unusual for successive to prove either equal to or easier than the simultaneous problem. Furthermore, the relative difficulty of the simultaneous and successive problems has been reported to be influenced greatly by the similarity of the stimuli to be discriminated (*1, 3, 4, 8*).

The studies reported here investigate the relative discrimination learning performances of children under the simultaneous and successive stimulus presentation procedures, varying the nature of the response required and stimulus similarity.

EXPERIMENT 1

Experiment 1 involves a learning situation for children in which the to-be-learned responses are to loci (buttons) removed from the stimulus sources (the windows or apertures).

Method

Apparatus: the apparatus was a black plywood box, 12 inch high by 12 ½ inch deep. The front panels were 25 ¼ inch wide. There were three stimulus apertures each faced with a milk glass window on the upper panel and three response buttons on the lower panel. Distance from the three stimulus apertures to their respective response buttons was 6½ inch. Behind each of the windows were five different coloured bulbs (GE C-6 Series type) set in a metal reflecting unit. Three selector switches, one for each window, were situated at the back of the apparatus where *E* could preselect which colour would appear in each window. Another selector switch enabled *E* to preselect which of the three buttons would be correct on each trial. A jewelled reflector light, located just above the middle button, would be activated when *S* pushed the correct button. A toggle switch activated the entire circuit so that *(a)* the preselected light came on in the three windows, and *(b)* response to the appropriate button would turn out the stimulus light and activate the signal light, while wrong responses would merely turn out the stimulus lights. Thus, correction on the part of the *S* was not possible. The buttons were attached to 1/16 inch metal rods which passed through small holes in the response panel, each rod meeting a microswitch inside.

Subjects and Design : The *S*s were 40 fourth grade children obtained from the Bristol, Rhode Island, Public Schools and randomly assigned to one of four groups. Half of the total number of *S*s were administered a simultaneous discrimination learning problem, and half a successive discrimination problem. Half of the *S*s in each of these groups were run in a "similar-stimulus" condition, and half in a "distinctive-stimulus" condition. For the similar stimulus group, the colours were red, pink, and blue. For the distinctive stimulus group, the colours were red, green, and blue. On the assumption that red and pink are more similar physically than red and green, it was presumed that a greater amount of generalisation would occur for the similar stimulus group, thus retarding learning involving these stimuli.

Procedure: A three-stimulus, three-response procedure was employed for all *S*s. Half of the *S*s were administered the simultaneous procedure, and half the successive stimulus procedure. The manner of stimulus presentation for the simultaneous and successive conditions closely follows procedures used in infrahuman investigations of two-stimulus problems. An *S* under the simultaneous condition was presented with the three stimuli exposed together, one in each aperture. Response to the button under one of these colours was consistently followed by the onset of the reward light, while response to either of the other buttons on that trial was not.

The order of stimulus presentation was the same for all *S*s under the simultaneous conditions, and the successive order was the same for all *S*s in those groups. There were three stimulus arrangements (A : 1, 2, 3; B: 2, 3, 1; C: 3, 1, 2,) possible for the simultaneous groups, and three (A: 1, 1, 1; B: 2, 2, 2; C: 3, 3, 3) for the successive groups. Each of these arrangements occurred in each block of three trials. These three arrangements may be ordered in six different ways (ABC, BAC, BCA, CBA, CAB, ACB). The order in which these six combinations were administered was determined randomly (with the restriction that identical stimulus presentations should not occur on successive trials) to provide a total of 18 trials. The 18-trial block was repeated to produce two cycles or a total of 36 trials, the maximum number administered.

Thus, for both kinds of discrimination, each response button is correct once within each three-trial block, and no position response is ever correct two trials in a row. Furthermore, since the correct response order is the same for both, neither group is provided mnemonic cues for possible response-sequence learning that is not provided for the other.

All *S*s performed individually in a room away from the classroom. The same instructions were given all *S*s, regardless of the condition of stimulus presentation to which they were assigned. When seated at the apparatus, they were informed that they would be shown some lights and that when the lights came on they were to press one of the buttons that they thought correct. In the beginning they would not know which buttons were correct but after a while they would learn which buttons to push and then would not make so many mistakes. They were told that the green signal light would go on when they were correct, but that that light would not go on when wrong.

*S*s were trained until they reached a criterion of nine consecutively correct responses or for a total of 36 trials. A trial is here defined in the conventional manner as the sequence proceeding with the onset of stimuli followed by the execution of one response, offset of the stimuli, and where appropriate onset of the reward light.

Results

The response measure here is the number of correct response in 36 trials with correct responses assumed for those trials for any *S* beyond nine consecutively correct. Figure 5.1 compares the number of correct responses made over 36 trials by the simultaneous and successive groups, disregarding similarity of stimuli. While the two groups perform about equally and at

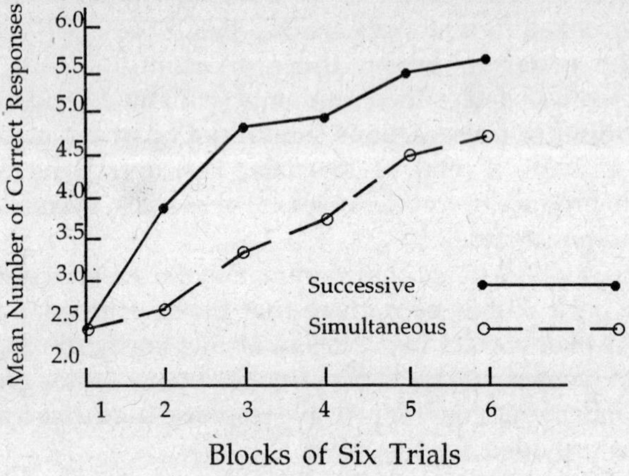

Fig. 5.1. Learning curves for the simultaneous and successive groups of experiment 1, involving response to a locus removed from the stimulus source.

chance level during the first block of six trials, the successive group overtakes the simultaneous and maintains its superiority through the remaining five blocks. Table 5.1 presents the overall means and standard deviations for each of the four groups. An analysis of variance over the number-correct data, including analysis of trials effects, revealed that the superiority of successive over simultaneous training was reliable at the .01 level ($F = 7.39$, $df = 1, 36$). The main effect of stimulus similarity was not different from chance, but the trials by similarity interaction was reliable at the .05 level ($F = 4.04$, $df = 5, 180$), based on a tendency for the learning rate of the distinctive stimulus conditions to be greater than that for the similar stimulus condition. Other than a trials effect significant at the .001 level, the only other reliable effect was the triple interaction ($F = 6.59$, $df = 5, 180$, $p = .001$) based on a tendency for there to be no differences in learning rate for the two successive groups, but a greater learning rate for the simultaneous-distinctive than the simultaneous-similar condition.

Table 5.1

Means and Standard Deviations for the Four Groups of Experiment 1

	Type of Stimulus Presentation				
	Simultaneous		*Successive*		*Total*
	M	*SD*	*M*	*SD*	*M*
Similar (red, pink, blue)	21.2	7.7	27.3	6.1	24.3
Distinctive (red, green, blue)	21.3	7.8	27.5	4.8	24.4
Total	21.3		27.4		

The major finding of this experiment is that under a procedure involving response to buttons removed from the stimulus source, successive stimulus presentation provided reliably better discrimination learning than simultaneous presentation.

EXPERIMENT 2

This experiment was designed to determine the importance of the button-pushing response involved in experiment 1. In the present experiment, all conditions were the same as in the first experiment except that now *Ss* were required only to point toward and touch the correct window on each trial.

Method

Apparatus : The apparatus was the same as that of experiment 1. The buttons, which were removable, were taken from the response panel leaving in their place very small (1/16 inch diameter) holes through which the button rods leading to the microswitches passed.

Subjects and Design: The *S*s were 20 fourth grade children from the Pleasant Street School in Seekonk, Massachusetts. These *S*s had not been subjects in previous experiments and had never seen the apparatus with the buttons attached. All *S*s were administered the red-pink-blue discriminations. Half of the *S*s were administered the stimuli under the simultaneous presentation procedure, and half under the successive procedure.

Procedure : The procedure of discrimination learning was exactly the same as that of experiment 1, expect that response buttons were not available to *S*s. Instead, the *S*s were instructed that they would be shown some lights and that each time the lights were shown they were to point towards and touch the window that they thought correct. If they touched the correct window, they would be told that that was correct, while if they touched the wrong window the *E* would indicate that this was incorrect. Manner of stimulus administration and stimulus order followed exactly the same plan as that of experiment 1. *E* said "Yes" or "Wrong " after each trial.

Results

The learning curves for the simultaneous and successive discrimination learning groups are seen in Fig. 5.2. Here it may be seen that the simultaneous stimulus procedure is clearly superior to that of the successive groups throughout training. The simultaneous group started at chance level within the first three trials of the experiment and by the third block of six trials was performing 100 per cent correctly. The successive presentations group, on the other hand, did not as a group depart from chance performance through the 36 training trials, and only one subject of 10 solved the successive problem by the end of training. A median test of the over-all difference in performance between the groups resulted in a *chi*-square with Yates' correction of 9.8 (*df* =1), which is reliable beyond the .01 level of significance.

It seems quite clear from experiment 2 that, when the children are required to respond directly to the stimulus source, the simultaneous stimulus presentation results in better learning, in contrast to the finding of experiment 1 where

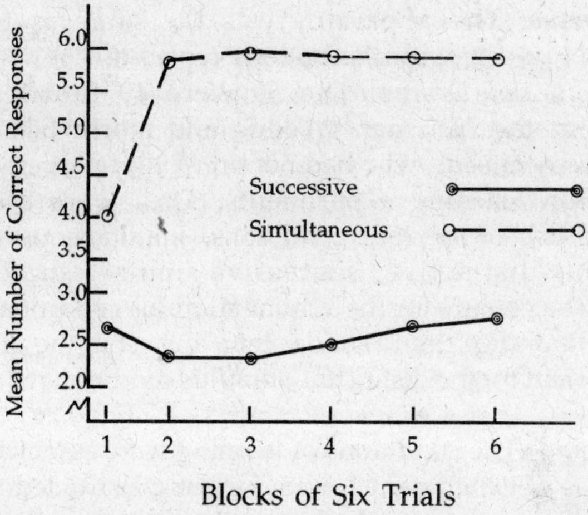

Fig. 5.2. Learning curves for the simultaneous and successive groups of experiment 2, involving response directly to the stimulus source.

*S*s responded to a locus some distance removed from the stimulus source.

EXPERIMENT 3

The next experiment returns to the light-button procedure and investigates the relative ease of discrimination learning under the simultaneous and successive stimulus presentation procedures under two levels of stimulus similarity. The purpose of the present experiment was to test the limit of the successive superiority over simultaneous of experiment 1 by using a condition of extremely high stimulus similarity. It was thought that, at some high level of stimulus similarity, the simultaneous conditions must produce better discrimination than the successive even under the light-button procedure, on the assumption that the psychophysical difference threshold must be smaller for paired comparisons procedures than for methods of single stimuli. Thus, if the stimuli are made highly similar, the problem should be more soluble for simultaneous *S*s than for successive *S*s.

Method

Apparatus: The apparatus was the same as that of experiments 1 and 2, with the buttons replaced.

Subjects and Design: The *S*s were 40 fourth grade children from the Newman Avenue and North Schools in Seekonk, Massachusetts, who had not previously participated in discrimination learning experiments. They were assigned randomly to one of the four conditions: simultaneous-similar, simultaneous-distinctive, successive-similar, successive-distinctive. The colours for the similar stimulus conditions were red, pink, and orange (more similar than any set in the previous two studies), and for the distinctive stimulus condition red, green, and blue.

Procedure : The conditions of learning were essentially the same as those of experiment 1, with *S*s being instructed that on each trial they were to push the button that they thought correct after looking at the lights. Particular caution was used in insuring identical instructions for both the simultaneous and successive presentation groups. All *S*s were trained for a total of 36 trials.

Results

Figure 5.3 shows the mean number of correct responses made in 36 trials by the four experimental groups, and Table 5.2 contains the means and standard deviations on which a factorial analysis of variance was performed. Comparison of the distinctive with the similar stimulus conditions indicates that stimulus similarity has an over-all effect on performance significant at the .001 level ($F = 18.82$, $df = 1, 36$). It may be noted that the mean performance of the distinctive-successive groups is somewhat superior to that of the distinctive-simultaneous groups (as in experiment 1), but for the highly similar stimuli simultaneous presentation provides clearly superior performance to successive. This interaction between type of discrimination and level of stimulus similarity fell just short of significance at the .05 level ($F = 3.92$, $df = 1, 36$), and the difference between simultaneous and successive means under the similar-stimulus conditions yielded a t of 2.33 ($df = 18$, $p = .05$).

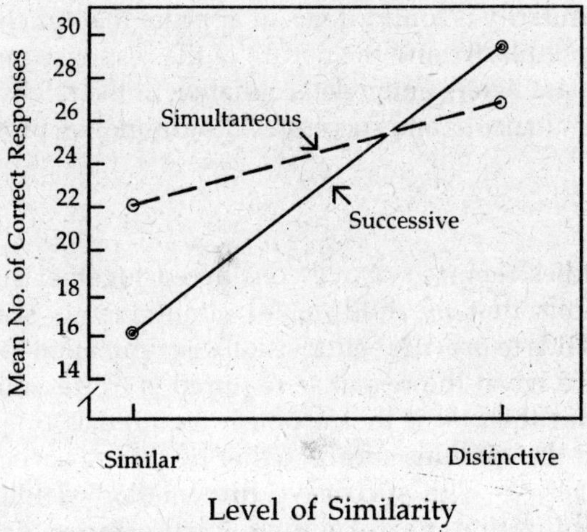

Fig. 5.3. Comparison of mean number of total correct responses from experiment 3 for the simultaneous and successive groups under two levels of stimulus similarity.

Table 5.2

Means and Standard Deviations for the Four Groups of Experiment 3

	Type of Stimulus Presentation				
	Simultaneous		*Successive*		*Total*
	M	*SD*	*M*	*SD*	*M*
Similar (red, pink, orange)	22.9	7.6	15.9	4.9	19.4
Distinctive (red, green, blue)	27.9	7.2	29.3	5.3	28.6
Total	25.4		22.6		

While this experiment did not reliably reproduce the successive over simultaneous superiority of experiment 1, the direction of the difference is the same, and the expected inversion of the simultaneous and successive means with a great increase in stimulus similarity is found. Thus, it appears that for children both stimulus similarity and the nature of the response required are pertinent parameters in the determination of the relative ease of learning simultaneous and successive discrimination problems.

Discussion

The three studies reported above considered together support the propositions that in children *(a)* simultaneous stimulus presentation tends to provide better visual discrimination learning than successive when the response required is to the source of stimulation, but that, *(b)* if the response required is to a locus removed from the stimulus source, either no difference occur or an inversion results with successive presentation yielding the better discrimination performance; furthermore, *(c)* this relationship is affected by degree of stimulus similarity, such that under conditions of high similarity, simultaneous presentation provides better learning than successive while with highly distinctive stimuli this difference may disappear or result in an inversion with successive superior to simultaneous. Thus, conditions which would tend to maximise simultaneous superiority over successive would involve high stimulus similarity and response to the stimulus source, with the obverse conditions tending to yield successive superiority over simultaneous.

Several studies with infrahuman organisms (*1, 2, 4, 8, 9*) have found some of the above phenomena, but few studies have investigated the problem of simultaneous and successive stimulus presentation in humans and fewer still have investigated the interactions of parameters likely to lead to differential learning of the simultaneous and successive problems. Loess and Duncan (*3*) have shown that, under a highly similar stimulus condition or difficult discrimination, simultaneously proved better than successive learning, but when the stimuli were less difficult to discriminate there was no statistical difference between the two procedures and in fact there tended to be superiority of the successive method. Perkins, Banks, and Calvin (*6*) investigated the effect of delay on learning in children. Their situation involved touching and picking up the discriminative stimuli, and simultaneous presentation tended to provide better learning than successive, with no effect whatever resulting from delay (a combination of delayed reaction and delayed reward).

Recently, Murphy and Miller (5) have reported on a study with children using an experimental procedure designed to study the generality of a finding previously obtained with infrahuman primates. Their stimulus presentation procedures involved only the simultaneous method. They found that it is much easier for a child to learn a discrimination problem when he is responding directly to the stimulus source and that the problem becomes very difficult if the task is changed so that the child must now respond to a locus removed from the stimulus source, even if the child has had previous training on the same discrimination problem under the approach-to-stimulus procedure. The results of the present studies would suggest that such results would be most likely in simultaneous discrimination problems and that this phenomenon may not prevail so strikingly under a successive stimulus presentation procedure.

The present experiments suggest that the stimulus similarity continuum warrants more definitive study as it affects simultaneous and successive discrimination in children. They further suggest that other parameters (such as distance from the stimulus source of the response locus) could possibly produce similar behavioural effects and be superimposed upon the stimulus similarity dimension. It is possible also that other experimental manipulations which tend to depress discrimination learning generally such as increasing delay of reward, decreasing age, and large spatial or temporal separation of the stimuli, might have similar effects on performance in the simultaneous and successive problems. Stimulus generalisation may be the pertinent mechanism producing the inversion effects of the present studies and could result in similar findings when produced through other procedures.

Summary and Conclusions

The results of three discrimination learning studies of normal fourth grade children are reported. Comparison of the methods of simultaneous and successive stimulus presentation are made under different levels of stimulus similarity and two types of response, either directly to the stimulus source or to a locus (buttons) removed from the stimulus source. The results of the three studies agree very well with the following propositions:

1. When response is directly to the stimulus source, simultaneous stimulus presentation tends to result in better learning than successive.
2. When the response is to a locus removed from the stimulus source, successive stimulus presentation may result in performance equal to or better than simultaneous.
3. The nature of the response involved in discrimination learning interacts with stimulus similarity, such that in procedures involving response to a locus removed from the stimulus source simultaneous may produce better learning than successive if the stimuli are very highly similar.

It is concluded that the relative ease of simultaneous and successive discrimination learning in children is a joint function of stimulus similarity and the type of response required. It is suggested further that other manipulable conditions undoubtedly interact with the two dealt with here and that possibly stimulus generalisation is the mechanism underlying the effects of each.

Stimulus and Discrimination Learning

Increase in the difficulty of a discrimination task, produced by increase in the similarity of the discriminal stimuli, has been explained in terms of increased generalisation of incorrect approach and inhibitory tendencies. Observations of children in discrimination problems have led this investigator to consider the possibility that increase in stimulus similarity increases task difficulty through the introduction of factors in addition to stimulus generalisation. The present experiment is designed to test for the presence of such additional factors and to attempt to provide a measure of stimulus generalisation that is not contaminated by them.

A successive discrimination task in which one or more of the available responses is always incorrect offers a means of isolating task difficulty contributed by stimulus generalisation and that contributed by other factors. Increase in stimulus generalisation would be expected to increase generalised (intralist) errors, but it would not be expected to increase the frequency of occurrence of responses that are never correct (extralist errors). On the other hand, if increase in stimulus similarity increases the potency of inattention, disinterest, frustration due to failure, etc., one would expect an increase in the frequency of both intralist and extralist errors.

Method

Apparatus: The apparatus was a black box 18 × 24 × 16 inch. Six inches above a 3-button response panel was a 3-inch diameter aperture of flashed opal glass. White geometric figures (square, circle, or triangle) were painted around each of the buttons, each of which was approximately 7 inch from the other two. Two 75 watts projection lamps were mounted 6 inch behind the aperture, each enclosed in a light-proof reflecting container on the front of which a 2×2 inch glass colour filter could be inserted. The *E* could turn on either one of the lamps and predetermine which of the three buttons would break its circuit. For each *S*, one button did not turn out either lamp. If *S* pushed the correct button, the lamp was turned out and a marble automatically delivered to *S*. Incorrect responses resulted in the disconnection of all buttons, thereby preventing more than one response per trial.

Experimental Design: Three experimental groups differed only in the discriminal stimuli presented. The stimuli were obtained by diffusing light through glass colour filters (Corning Glass Works) onto the aperture. Groups HS was presented with a yellow-green (No. 4015) and a green (No. 4308 superimposed on No. 3484). Groups S was presented with the yellow-green and a blue-green (No. 3385 superimposed on No. 4303). Group D received the yellow-green and a deep blue (No. 5330). The stimuli in each pair are readily discriminated by adults with normal colour vision. Within these groups, the position of the disconnected button, which was never correct, was controlled by randomly assigning *S*s to three subgroups.

Subjects: Sixty-five pre-school *S*s from the Iowa Child Welfare Research Station laboratories were randomly assigned to the experimental groups—25 to Group HS, 22 to Groups S and 18 to Group D. The *S*s ranged in age from 4 Yr., 2 mo. to 5 yr.,

8 mo. Some *S*s had previous experience with simultaneous and successive discrimination learning problems, but none had previous experience with the present apparatus.

Procedure: A familiar *E* brought *S* to the experimental room and allowed him to select one of a number of dime-store toys which he would attempt to win. The *E* then demonstrated the two stimulus lights one at a time, instructing *S* that marbles could be obtained by turning out the lights, and that the marbles could be used to buy the selected toy. The appropriate stimuli were presented in a prearranged order that was the same for all *S*s. Each light appeared three times in successive blocks of six presentations, long series of alternations were avoided, and neither light appeared more than three times in succession. Button (position) preferences were verbally discouraged by *E*. All *S*s received atleast 30 stimulus presentations (trials); *S*s who failed to attain 9 correct choices on 10 consecutive trials by Trial 30 were given additional trials until this criterion was attained or until 96 trials had been given. Eleven of the 65 *S*s failed to reach this criterion in 96 trials.

Results

Analysis of the total error scores for the subgroups, which differed only in terms of the position of the disconnected button, revealed no consistent or significant differences among them. Accordingly, the data for these subgroups have been combined within each experimental group. The scores used in subsequent analyses are the number of errors involving the button that was connected (intralist errors) and the number of errors involving the button that was disconnected (extralist errors).

Table 5.3 shows the means of the two types of error for each of the three experimental groups. From inspection, it is apparent that both error types tend to increase in frequency with increase in stimulus similarity, and that the magnitude of the difference between the means of the two error types also increases with increasing stimulus similarity. For each group, the means frequency of intralist errors is greater than that of extralist errors.

Table 5.3

Means of the Two Types of Error

Groups	*N*	*Intralist errors*	*Extralist errors*	*Total errors*
HS	25	21.48	7.44	28.92
S	22	17.64	6.95	24.59
D	18	6.44	3.28	9.72
Combined	65	16.02	6.12	

The statistical significance of these trends was tested by a Lindquist Type I analysis and by further tests of the simple effects. The results of the Type I analysis are presented in Table 5.4. Here it is apparent that the experimental groups differ significantly in terms of mean total errors, and that frequency of intralist errors is significantly greater than the frequency of extralist errors for the combined experimental groups. Furthermore, there is an interaction ($P<.05$) between the stimulus groups and the type of error. The interaction indicates that, with increasing stimulus similarity, there is an increase in the magnitude of the difference between the mean frequencies of the two types of error.

Table 5.4

Analysis of Variance of Number of Errors to Criterion

Source	*df*	*Mean square*	*F*	*P*
Ss:	64			
Stimuli (S)	2	1014.28	6.09	.005
Error (b)	62	166.47		
Within-Ss:	65			
Error type (E)	1	3180.38	32.34	.001
E × S	2	314.50	3.20	.05
Error (w)	62	98.34		
Total	129			

The data were analysed as two simple randomised designs to determine the stimulus effects on the two types of errors separately. For the intralist errors, the stimulus effects were significant at the 1% level ($F = 5.54$; $df = 2, 62$). For extralist errors, the stimulus effects were significant at the 2.5% level ($F = 4.25$; $df = 2,62$). Using the *t* test, comparisons were made of pairs of groups. For the intralist errors, the mean of Group D differs significantly from that of Group HS ($P <.01$) and from that of Group S ($P<.02$). The means of Groups HS and S do not differ significantly. For the extralist errors, also, the Group D mean is significantly lower than the Group HS mean ($P <.01$) and the Group S mean ($P <.02$), but the means for Groups HS and S are not significantly different. Clearly, an increase in stimulus similarity resulted in an increase of errors of both types.

Finally, *t* tests were made of the significance of the differences between means for intralist and extralist errors for the three experimental groups separately. Significantly more intralist errors than extralist errors were made by Groups HS and S ($P<.001$), but the difference for Group D was not statistically significant ($P >.05$).

Discussion

The greater frequency of intralist than of extralist errors presumably reflects the operation of stimulus generalisation, which in the present experiment, is expected to increase intralist errors without directly increasing the number of extralist errors. The interaction between stimulus similarity and type of error is interpreted as the result of an increase in stimulus generalisation with increasing stimulus similarity. This interaction is somewhat more statistically reliable ($P < .01$) when only the extreme groups are considered. It would seem that the interaction provides an index of the amount of generalisation that is not affected by other factors that may be associated with increased stimulus similarity.

The increase in frequency of extralist errors with increasing stimulus similarity is only indirectly due to increased stimulus generalisation. A task made difficult by high generalisation is made even more difficult through loss of interest due to increased number of failures; elicitation of inappropriate responses (orienting away from stimuli, asking to leave the situation, hitting buttons indiscriminately, etc.); and the development of fatigue due to longer experimental sessions.

Qualitative observations suggest that such factors were more frequent among *S*s given highly similar stimuli than among those given distinctive stimuli.

The evidence indicates that errors on a discrimination learning task may provide an overestimate of the direct effects of stimulus generalisation. Children's performance, atleast, appears to be affected by stimulus similarity in a manner that can only partly be attributed directly to stimulus generalisation.

Three groups of pre-school children were given a successive discrimination learning task in which generalised (intralist) or non-generalised (extralist) errors could be made. The conditions for the three groups differed only in the similarity of the discriminal stimuli. The results indicated that increased stimulus similarity resulted in greater numbers of both types of errors and an increased difference between the means of the two types of errors. These results were interpreted as reflecting increased stimulus generalisation as a function of increased stimulus similarity. The increase in extralist error with increased stimulus similarity was interpreted as reflecting the operation of factors in addition to stimulus generalisation, *e.g.*, decrease in interest, motivation or attention, and increase in fatigue.

Pretraining and Discrimination Learning

The prediction that the possession of names for the stimuli in a learning task will enhance performance on that task has been tested in several studies. The enhancement phenomenon has been referred to as the "acquired distinctiveness of cues" (*18, 19*) and "stimulus predifferentiation" (*11, 12, 14*). In general, the experimental paradigm has involved a transfer task situation in which *S*s are required to respond to certain discriminable stimuli. This task is preceded by a pretraining situation in which some of the *S*s are taught names for these same stimuli, the names themselves having no connotations with respect to the nature of the responses in the transfer task. This type of pretraining has been termed "relevant-S." The more recent studies have utilised "irrelevant" pretraining groups, as well as or in place of "no-pretraining" groups, in order to control for warm-up and learning-to-learn effects (*11, 12, 15, 17*). The need for such controls has been demonstrated (*13*). Performances of relevant-S groups on various types of transfer tasks have been shown to be superior to those of irrelevant groups (*11, 12, 15*).

The present experiment is concerned with the relative performances on a transfer task of three groups of children. Two of these involve the conventional relevant-S and irrelevant varieties of pretraining. The third—to be called hereafter the "attention" group—is made to attend to the relevant transfer task stimuli during a pretraining session, but is not given any verbal learning.

It is predicted that the relevant-S group will surpass the irrelevant and attention groups in performance on the transfer task. No prediction is made with respect to the relative performances of the irrelevant and attention groups.

Method

Subjects : The *S*s were 60 children from the State University of Iowa Pre-schools and the Iowa City Parents' Pre-school. There were 10—3 yr.-olds, 38—4 yr.-olds and 12—5yr.-olds. An upper and a lower age group were constituted and *S*s from within each age level were randomly assigned to the three treatment groups.

Procedure: The materials used in the verbal pretraining consisted of photographs of pen and ink sketches of the following: *(a)* a pair of human adult female faces; and *(b)* a pair of human juvenile male faces.

The *S*s in the relevant-S group received relevant-S pretraining in which they learned to associate the names "Jean" and "Peg" with the female faces (Pair A) ; learning was continued until a criterion of 15 consecutive pairs of correct responses was met. The *S*s in the irrelevant groups were given irrelevant pretraining, involving the male faces (Pair B) and the names "Jack" and "Pete." to the same criterion. The stimuli in these verbal learning situations were presented side by side to *S*. The right-left relationship of the pictures were varied in a prearranged and non-alternating fashion. An imitation coin reward was presented to *S* for each correct pair of responses. The *S* was corrected when erroneous responses were given. When the criterion was met, each *S* was allowed to cash in the accumulated coins for one-half of a toy set.

The attention pretraining did not involve verbal learning; rather, the *S*s in the attention group were made to point to various parts of the relevant stimuli (Pair A). The stimuli were presented in a manner comparable to that involved in the relevant-*S* and irrelevant pretraining. Thirty trials were given to each attention group S, however, and a coin reward was given each time *S* pointed to the designated parts of the pictures in what *E* judged to be a "careful" manner. If *S* appeared lax in his pointing responses, the coin reward was withheld and *S* was urged to exercise more care.

All *S*s were treated identically in the transfer task, which was administered immediately following pretraining. The apparatus and procedures of a recently reported study (1) on discrimination learning in pre-school children were utilised, with slight modifications, in the transfer task. The stimuli were two wooden cars, identical in appearance except that each had a different one of the two faces from Pair A mounted on its side. The *S*'s task involved choosing one of the two cars and rolling it down a track. The *S* was led to believe that the car's striking a dummy switch at the end of the track caused a marble dispenser to be activated. Actually, *E* controlled the operation of the dispenser by means of a hidden button. For each S, one of the two cars was arbitrarily designated by *E* as the "correct" stimulus. When this car was chosen by *S* and run down the track, a marble reward was dispensed; when the "incorrect" car was selected, no marble reward was delivered. The choice by *S* of one of the stimuli, followed by the car's run down the track and the subsequent reinforcement or non-reinforcement, constituted a trial. Thirty transfer task trials were given. *S* being instructed to obtain as many marbles as possible. Following trial 30, *S* was allowed to exchange the accumulated marbles for the remainder of the toy set and the experiment was terminated. The response measure was the number of correct choices made in the transfer task.

Result and Discussion

A treatments-by-levels analysis (16) of the pretraining data revealed that the relevant-S and irrelevant groups did not differ significantly from each other in mean number of trials required to meet the criterion. Table 5.5 shows the means and *SD*'s for the subgroups. Table 5.6 presents the over-all means and *SD*'s for the transfer task data.

Table 5.5

Pretraining Results—Number of Trials of Criteria

Age	*Relevant-S*		*Irrelevant*	
	Mean	*SD*	*Mean*	*SD*
L	26.0	10.80	27.3	10.24
U	28.8	14.32	21.8	6.79

Table 5.6

Number of Correct Responses in 30 Transfer Trials

Age	*Relevant-S*		*Irrelevant*		*Attention*	
	Mean	*SD*	*Mean*	*SD*	*Mean*	*SD*
L	23.6	5.97	16.5	5.50	18.0	5.44
U	20.9	7.16	17.2	5.44	17.4	3.98

In order to allow for a treatments × ages × trials analysis, the 30 trials were divided into six blocks of five trials each. A Type III analysis (16) was applied to these data, the results of which are summarised in Table 5.7.

As indicated in Table 5.7, the treatments effect was significant at the .05 level of confidence, as was the treatments × trials interaction. Since on interaction involving age was significant, it was possible to compare the three treatment groups, taken two at a time, disregarding age levels. This was accomplished by the use of three Type I designs (16), the results of which are summarised in Table 5.8.

Table 5.7
Summary of Analysis Applied to Treatments × Ages × Trials Data†

Source	*df*	*MS*	*F*
Between *S*s	59		
Treatments	2	28.10	4.74*
Ages	1	1.88	<1.00
Error *(b)*	54	5.93 ‡	
Within *S*s	300		
Trials	5	4.25	4.01**
Treatments × Trials	10	2.47	2.33*
Error *(w)*	270	1.06‡	
Total	359		

* p<.05.
** p<.01.
†All interactions involving age were non-significant.
‡ On the assumption of homogeneity of variance in the cells, the error terms obtained in this analysis, together with their respective *df*, were utilised in the analysis to be reported subsequently.

Table 5.8
Summary of Analysis Applied to the Data Comparing the Treatments Two at a Time, Disregarding Age Levels

		Mean Squares		
Source	*df*	*Relevant-S vs. Irrelevant*	*Relevant-S vs. Attention*	*Irrelevant vs. Attention*
Between *S*s				
Treatments	1	48.60**	34.51*	1.21
Error *(b)*	54	5.93	5.93	5.93
Within *S*s				
Trials	5	4.53**	4.43**	2.01
Treatments × trials	5	3.65**	.81	2.95*
Error *(w)* 2	270	1.06	1.06	1.06

* p< .05.
** p<.01.

These analysis indicate that the relevant-S group surpassed both the irrelevant and attention groups in mean number of correct choices. The former comparison yielded a difference significant at the .01 level, whereas the latter difference was significant at the .05 level. The irrelevant and attention groups did not differ significantly from each other in terms of treatment effects.

The treatments × trials interaction was significant at the .01 level for the relevant-S vs., irrelevant data and at the .05 level for the irrelevant vs., attention data, indicating that the learning curves differed from each other for the treatment groups involved.

The results indicate that the experience of learning names for a pair of stimuli evidently did facilitate later performance on a task involving those stimuli, as predicted. By the use made of the irrelevant and attention groups, it was shown that the enhancement in performance attributable to the possession of names was greater than that which could be attributed either to the transfer of non-specific reactions or to mere exposure to the relevant stimuli during pretraining.

Summary

Three groups, each consisting of 20—3-to-5-yr.-old children, were given identical treatment in a transfer task situation after having experienced different types of pretraining. The relevant-S group learned during pretraining to associate names with each of the two pictures of faces that subsequently served as stimuli in the transfer task. The irrelevant group was given a comparable amount of paired-associate learning, but with stimuli unrelated to the transfer task. The attention group was not given a verbal learning experience, but rather was merely exposed to the relevant stimuli during pretraining. The transfer task involved a sample discrimination learning situation, the response measure being the number of correct choices made in 30 presentations of the relevant stimuli.

Analysis of the transfer task data revealed that the relevant-S group performed significantly better than did the irrelevant and attention groups. Significant treatments × trials interactions indicated that the learning curves of the relevant-S and irrelevant groups differed, as did the curves for the irrelevant and attention groups.

It was concluded that the result were in agreement with the prediction that the possession of names for the stimuli in a learning task would enhance performance on that task.

References

1. Bitterman, M. E., Tyler, D.W. and Elam, C. B., Simultaneous and Successive Discrimination under Identical Stimulation Conditions, *Amer. J. Psychol.*, 1955, 68, 237-48.
2. Bitterman, M. E., and Wodinsky, J., Simultaneous and Successive Discrimination, *Psychol. Rev.*, 1953, 60, 371-76.
3. Loess, H.B., and Duncan, C. P., Human Discrimination Learning with Simultaneous and Successive Presentation of Stimuli, *J. exp. Psychol.*, 1952, 44, 215-21.
4. MacCaslin, E. F., Successive and Simultaneous Discrimination as a Function of Stimulus Similarity, *Amer. J. Psychol.*, 1954, 67, 308-14.
5. Murphy, J.V., and Miller, R. E., Spatial Contiguity of Cue, Reward, and Response in Discrimination Learning by Children, *J. exp. Psychol.*, 1959, 58, 485-89.
6. Perkins, M. J., Banks, H. P., and Calvin, A. D., The Effect of Delay on Simultaneous and Successive Discrimination in Children, *J. exp. Psychol.*, 1954, 48, 416-18.
7. Spence, K. W., The Nature of Discrimination Learning in Animals, *Psychol. Rev.*, 1936, 43, 427-49.
8. Spence, K. W., The Nature of the Response in Discrimination Learning, *Psychol. Rev.*, 1952, 59, 89-93.
9. Weise, P., and Bitterman, M. E., Response Selection in Discrimination Learning, *Psychol. Rev.*, 1951, 58, 185-95.
10. Cantor, G.N., and Spiker, C. C., Effects of Non-reinforced Trials on Discrimination Learning in Pre-school Children, *J. exp. Psychol.*, 1954, 47, 256-58.
11. Cantor, J. H., Amount of Pretraining as a Factor in Stimulus Pre-differentiation, Unpublished doctor's dissertation, State Univ. of Iowa, 1954.
12. Dysinger, D. W., An Investigation of Stimulus Pre-differentiation in a Choice Discrimination Problem, Unpublished doctor's dissertation, State Univ. of Iowa, 1951.
13. Farber,I. E., Murfin, F.L. Performance Set as a Factor in Transfer of Training, Paper read at Midswest, Psychol, Ass., Chicago, April, 1951
14. Gagné, R. M., and Baker, K.E., Stimulus Pre-differentiation as a Factor in Transfer of Training, *J. exp. Psychol.*, 1950, 40, 439-51.
15. Gerjuoy, I.R., Discrimination Learning as a Function of the Similarity of the Stimulus Names, Unpublished doctor's dissertation, State Univ. of Iowa, 1953.
16. Lindquist, E.F., Design and Analysis of Experiments in Psychology and Education, Boston, Houghton Mifflin, 1953.

17. McAllister, D.E., The Effects of Various Kinds of Relevant Verbal Pretraining on Subsequent Motor Performance, *J. exp. Psychol.*, 1953, 46, 329-36.
18. Miller, N. E. Theory and Experiment Relating Psychoanalytic Displacement to Stimulus-response Generalisation, *J. abnorm. soc. Psychol.*, 1948, 43,155-78.
19. Rossman, I. L., and Goss, A. E., The Acquired Distinctiveness of Cues : The role of Discriminative Verbal Responses in Facilitating the Acquisition of Discriminative Motor Responses, *J. exp. Psychol.*, 1951, 42, 173-82.

CHAPTER 6

Approach to Decision-making Curriculum

PART 1

Creative Ability and Self-Image

Since a curriculum on decision-making deals necessarily with personal feelings and responses, it is important to develop a class climate that supports and encourages the free flow of conversation at this qualitative level. Eventually, if the aims in this course are to be realised, it should be possible for the children to express widely opposing feelings and thoughts within the group and still feel included. Such a group climate has its origin, however, in the children having beginning experiences of acceptance and safety during the initial offerings of their ideas and feelings.

The first class session ought to be spent in an activity through which the children can gradually become acquainted with one-another and with you, and through which you and they can begin to explore each other's feelings and thoughts and learn what is important or of value to each of you.

An activity through which these aims might be achieved involves the creation of a "Me Chart" by each class member and the teacher. A "Me Chart" consists of a large piece of poster board with a picture or symbol placed on it to represent the person making the chart. Around this central figure are placed other pictures or symbols to represent people, things, ideas, feelings, or experiences which are important or of value of that person. One may, for instance, make a stick figure representing himself by pasting toothpicks on the poster board and then surrounding it with pictures from magazines which suggest people and things that are important or of value to him. Both concrete things, a dog, a parent, a record collection, and so forth, or abstract qualities such as love and friendship may be included. The only restriction is that the people or things represented be important to the person making the chart.

To carry out this project a variety of materials should be provided. A large piece of poster board will be needed for each class member. Other materials might include magazines, paste, toothpicks, coloured constructions paper, pipe cleaners, string, poster paints and brushes, buttons, sequins, cotton balls, and anything else that you can imagine to be useful that happens to be readily available. Each of you will have ideas about various kinds of materials which can be used to make the charts. The children will probably add some surprises of their own. The photographs are illustrative of the imagination which children bring to the making of "Me Charts."

This first session should be a relaxed fun Sunday, but the charts are not just busy work. This activity has to do with beginning to work and talk together, encouraging individual initiative and creativity, and thinking about that which is important to each member of the class.

Begin by suggesting to the children that you would like them to participate in an activity through which they can come to know each other better and find out what is important to each of them in their lives. Describe briefly a "Me Chart" and point out the various kinds of materials available with which they can work.

Provide plenty of time for the group to create its charts, perhaps a half hour or until most of the children have finished. When the charts are completed, give each child a chance to show his chart to the class and identify the people and things which are important to him. Be alert to the possibility of conversation that will help you and the children become better acquainted. If, for example, a picture appears on the chart representing a relative or a teacher, ask, "Why is this person important to you?" If a picture representing the latest singing group appears, ask, "What is it about these people and their music that makes you respond to them?" There should be opportunities for many interesting avenues of conversation which will help the children and you begin to become aware of what is important to each person in the class.

Some children seem to be self-conscious when it comes to talking about their "Me Chart." One teacher who has used this activity worked out this problem in the following way. When a child pointed to a guitar on his "Me Chart" and said it was important, but seemed reluctant to say why, the teacher asked the class in general, "Can you think of reasons why a guitar might be important to someone?" Their responses seemed to free the child to talk about why a guitar was important to him.

As the class session ends, hang the charts on the walls of your room. Chances are that in succeeding weeks children will refer to them as they move through this curriculum. And, it may be that towards the end of the course they will want to make another "Me Chart" to indicate some different ideas about who they are and what is important to them after they have had the opportunity to think extensively about values of many kinds.

Before the children leave the classroom at the end of the first session they may be interested in knowing what will be happening in this course throughout the year. Probably you will wish to give them some clues about coming sessions. There are several ways to do this. You might point out that not everyone has the same values, that the same things are not important to everyone; therefore, when we are involved in situations where choices are possible, people have different ideas about which choices are best. The class is going to try to find out how people make decisions, why they make the decisions they do, and whether or not it is possible to know which decisions are the right ones.

Or, you might want to arouse their curiosity by saying, "Next week we're going to take a trip to Mars. And we're going to find out what we would do if our spaceship crashed and we had to live there. So, come with your minds in space gear."

If you decide to use the quarry adventure rather than the Mars trip you'll have to reword your curiosity arouser. You might say, "Next week we're going for a swim in a very dangerous quarry. We're going to find ourselves in some deep water so come and find out if we sink or swim."

Or, you might simply say, "This class is going to be a series of surprises. I may be the teacher, but even I don't know exactly what will happen next. All I really know is that we are going to try to find out how a person learns to make choices in tough situations. The newspapers, the TV, even our own family life are filled with examples of just such problems. Sometimes we are going to pretend we are some of these people having to make a decision; and sometimes we are going to act like a judge and jury deciding whether the best choice was made. In any case, this could be called the Surprise Class, because no one knows how it will turn out. See you next week."

PART 2

Children's Decisions Ability

The material in this part of the curriculum is designed to help boys and girls begin to examine the process of decision-making. They will be confronted with one or two imaginary situations of some complexity. The dilemmas raised are not easily solved, and one who truly becomes involved in the situations becomes aware that profound implications are present in whatever decisions are made. Hopefully, these situations will motivate the members of the class to explore more deeply the steps that need to be taken in order to arrive at more adequate and responsible decisions in any difficult predicament. It is in Part 4 that we will attempt to clarify just what some of these steps are. In the meantime, Part 2 should involve the students in the excitement of decision-making, while suggesting by inference the intricacy of the process.

The following material consists of two situations for which decisions must be made if the problems inherent in the situations are to be solved. One incident describes the crash of a spaceship on Mars and the problems which must be met and resolved. The second situation is the account of a boy who knew his closest friend had gone to a quarry to swim even though it was an exceedingly dangerous place and despite the instructions of his parents that he was not to go there.

Either or both of these situations can be used as the focus for class sessions for two or more meetings. It should be emphasised here, that there is no need to hurry through the course material. You may spend as much time as is profitable for the class discussing either or both of these stories. One, two, four, or even more sessions could conceivably be spent on the material, the time spent to be determined by the length of your sessions and the size and interest of your class. Flexibility is the key word when it comes to scheduling this course in decision-making. Each part or section division is not to be considered a segment of material suitable only for a single session. Some can be expanded several times, while others, because of the special conditions in a particular situation, may be compressed. The word is flexibility.

The Mars trip is described in Section A with detailed suggestions on how it might be used. Section B deals with the quarry adventure, but in somewhat less detail since it is assumed that the suggestions for the Mars trip are applicable to the quarry adventure as well.

Section A—The Mars Trip

There are five parts to the Mars trips story. Each of them outlines the existence of specific conditions that make for difficult problems. Please indicate to the students that the conditions cannot be changed. The special conditions are what make the problem which is to be solved. For example, in the first part additional food simply is not available.

Also, remember that we are aiming not alone at possible solutions to the dilemma presented, but at the values implicit in the solutions being proposed. Therefore, your role as teacher is to keep asking, "Why?" at strategic points. For instance, if someone suggests giving extra food to the elderly scientist in the first part of the story, you may need to ask the reasons motivating the suggestion in order to bring out the value behind the action.

Here is the first part of the situation, with suggestions as to how to proceed:

> 1. Our spaceship has crashed on Mars, and we're in severe trouble because it's going to take quite a length of time to repair the ship in order to return to Earth—perhaps as much as eleven or twelve months. We have a food supply which, if carefully managed, will last a maximum of three or four months. One of our crew is a rather elderly scientist who is the key person for the repair job. He's really the only one who has the know-how to repair the ship and return it to Earth. It is very important that he remain well, energetic, and alert. Should he get more food than the rest of us even though there is already a scarcity for everyone?

To anticipate one possible solution—that of growing more food—you should indicate that under the circumstances it is not possible. For Earth people the Martian vegetation is poisonous. We cannot use it.

A Visual Aid to Decision-making

To aid in the clarification of what is at stake in the granting of equal, extra, or no food to the elderly scientist (and for the additional problem situations which will be raised), two sets of symbols and a playing surface on which to place them are provided in Envelope Number Two accompanying this curriculum guide. The surface looks like this:

<table>
<tr><td rowspan="3">VALUE CHOSEN</td><td rowspan="3">People and/or Things</td><td>More threatened Than Supported</td></tr>
<tr><td>Threatened and Supported</td></tr>
<tr><td>More Supported Than Threatened</td></tr>
</table>

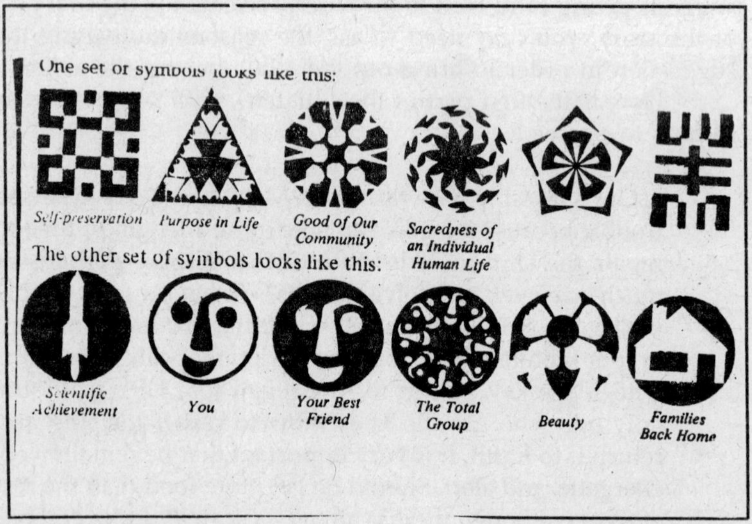

The first set of symbols represents various values that might be important to a person trying to decide what to do in this situation. Each symbol stands for a specific value. The value of each symbol is indicated beneath the sketches of them which appear above. Values are not indicated on the actually symbol in the teaching aids kit, because the symbols will be needed to stand for other values in the quarry situations and for use in a latter part of this curriculum. When using the symbols they should be clearly labelled so that the children can readily see for what values they stand. This can be done by writing the name of the value for which the symbol stands on a small sticker and attaching it to the symbol. There is a form of pressure-sensitive tape which can be written on that would serve this purpose quite well.

As indicated above, the square stands for the value *self-preservation*. The circle represents the *sacredness of an individual human life*. The triangle represents *purpose in life*; and the octagon, the *good of our community*. Two additional shapes are unmarked and you may wish to add even more unlabelled ones. They represent other values which the children might suggest as important in determining what to do in the face of the various problems presented by the Mars trip. These can be thought of as "wild cards"— values that may emerge as the discussion proceeds.

A second set of symbols (also to be labelled by you) is less abstract in shape and represents the various people or things who stand to be more threatened than supported, more supported than threatened, or both threatened and supported, depending on which alternative path of action is taken to solve the situation. This set of figures consists of one representing your own life, *you*; another standing for *your best friend*; another symbolic of the welfare of *the total group*; and others representing such things as *scientific achievement*, *families back home*, and *beauty* or artistic contribution. In this set there are also a couple of unlabelled figures representing other persons or things the children might suggest that must be considered in weighing a specific problem. Additional figures may be added to the set as they are needed to represent other people or things affected by the decisions to be made.

The third part of this visual aid to decision-making is the playing surface which is divided into two major parts with one part divided into three sections. As each phase of the situation is discussed, one or two particular values will probably be the important ones for any one child trying to decide what he would do. For instance, a child might suggest that the scientific purpose of the expedition is of utmost importance. (This assumption is represented most adequately in the first symbol set by the triangle, *purpose in life*). Because of this the child might maintain that it would be better for the elderly scientist to receive extra food rations in the hope that he could get the ship repaired and back to Earth. This would assure certain scientific information getting back to Earth even though all members of the crew might not survive because of having to sacrifice their food.

As this possible solution is presented, the child would place his prime value, *purpose in life,* in the form of a triangle, on the board in the "Value Chosen" square. Then, to complete the implications of the choice, figures from the second set of symbols would be placed in one of the three sections on the other half of the board. Which ones would be more threatened than supported by the choice of this value? Which would be more supported than threatened? Which would be both supported and threatened? At this point some of the unlabelled figures might be given named values to fully elaborate the implications of the person's value choice.

But now let's get specific about how this would be introduced to a class. After the Mars adventure is described and the first problem having to do with the elderly scientist is presented, the class will begin to offer their tentative solutions, and undoubtedly, conflicting ideas will occur. When enough of this discussion has begun to indicate involvement but the absence of a thorough consideration of the implications of the proposed choices, the teacher may bring out the two sets of symbols. The discussion may go something like this:

> *Teacher*: We've had several ideas suggested. Let's see if we can clear up the problem a little by seeing it as well as thinking about it. Different people have suggested different solutions. We choose our solutions on the basis of what we think is most important. We might call these things that

are most important to us: our values. Suppose we were to say that each of these objects stands for something we consider terribly important. For example, this square stands for our own life. We want to keep it, preserve it. This value, then, is *self-preservation*. This one, an octagon, stands for the well-being of our group, our community. In some cases it might mean our family or our nation or our class—but here it stands for our team of scientist-explorers. So this value is the *good of our community*. This triangle might stand for our *purpose in life*; and here's one, a circle, that might stand for the *sacredness of an individual human life*. And here are two that aren't labelled but which you may want to label later on.

Now every value we live by affects people and things in a variety of ways in any one situation. So, to show how that works we have these other figures which represent who or what is affected when we make a decision on the basis of one of these values.

Here's a figure, for example, representing *you*, one's self, your own life. Here's another representing *the total group* and its welfare. Here's one representing the *scientific achievement* which the crew hopes to make. Here's one representing the crew members' *families back home*.

Let's try it out and see how it works. John, you said a little while ago you thought all of us were in this situation together and that either all of us or none of us should survive, so we should all get equal amounts of food. From that, I would say that the value you're operating on is the *good for our community*. That's what you're saying is most important, right? Let's put that value out here (placing octagon on the "Value Chosen" box) where everyone can see what your value is.

Now the question is: "How does that affect the real people and things in the situation? Who or what is being threatened or supported or both threatened and supported by basing your decision on that value? Let's put the things we think are being more threatened than supported in the upper section, the ones being more supported than threatened in the lower section, and the ones being both supported and threatened in the centre section. How about the scientific contribution of the crew? Is it more supported or more threatened or both by the decision? How about your best friend who is a member of the crew? Is he more supported or more threatened or is he both supported and threatened by your decision? How about your own life? Is it more supported or more threatened or both by your decision?

Continue on through the rest of the people and things which are affected by John's decision, and then go through the same process as you and the class look at the consequences of the suggested decisions of other members of the class.

Clearly there is some blurring of lines of classifications between the values and things affected. For instance, *purpose in life* in the first set of symbols seems similar to *scientific achievement* in the second set. We make a somewhat arbitrary division here in order to dramatise the fact that *(a)* decisions imply a choice between values and *(b)* decisions affect specific personalities, goals, things, and ideals. As we continue on through the course, some more precise and sophisticated categories will emerge from the discussions. For the moment the goals is simply to indicate the general nature of the process and its effect.

After the situation involving more or less food for the scientist has been thoroughly explored, go through the same process for the additional problems detailed below which occur on Mars to the space crew:

2. During the crash, one of us is seriously injured. A doctor who is a member of our crew says the injured man is dying and that he can't possibly live for more than two weeks. Should he be given food or should it be kept for those of us who have a better chance to survive?
3. One of us has become overwhelmed with the beauty of the Martian countryside, and the only thing he wants to do is to go off and paint it. He has not the slightest interest in helping to repair the ship. The rest of us feel the need of his help with all the work that has to be done. We meet to make a decision about him. What, if anything, will we want to do?

4. The only woman in our crew, a skilled flight technician, is the wife of the captain. In the course of the journey she has become pregnant and her baby is to be born in four or five weeks. In the meantime she feels unable to do much work of the strenuous nature required for the repair of the ship. When the baby is born both mother and child will require special care and of course, special diet. Another mouth to feed is to be added to a group already in trouble because of food shortages. What, if anything, is to be done?

5. A particular metal is needed for repairing the ship. The metal needed is present on Mars but in very limited quantities. All of it that has been found by the Martians during many years of searching has been moulded into a small statue representing the Martian God. The Martians have placed it on an altar in one of their temples of worship. There's no other place to get the metal without extensive mining which might possibly take years. The Martians say their temple will be desecrated if the metal of the statue is used for our repairs and that their God will be angered and offended. The Martians are a small dwarf-like, although fully human people who would be unable to stop us from taking the metal if we should decide to do so.

Section B—The Quarry Adventure

The following story is intended to be used either as a supplement to the Mars adventure or as a substitute for it. In either case the attempt to visualise the values involved and the people and things affected is suggested as a helpful tool for use by the class.

This time the first set of symbols might be labelled with such terms as *loyalty, fear, obedience,* and *adventure.* Again, some unlabelled symbols will encourage the group to identify some values not already included.

The second set of symbols could be labelled *you, your friend, his parents, your parents,* and *respect for the law.* Here is the story:

1. Your best friend tells you at school on Friday that the next day he is going to sneak off and go swimming in the rock quarry a mile south of your town. He invites you to

go along too. You would like very much to go with him, but you know that it is a very dangerous place to swim. Several children were drowned in the quarry a few summers ago after which town officials urged parents to forbid their children to swim there. Your parents and the parents of your best friend have often forbidden you to go there. Would you go with your best friend or decline? Would you tell his mother of his intention in order to protect the life of your friend?

2. The next day, Saturday, shortly after noon, you meet your friend on his way to the rock quarry to swim. Now you know he wasn't kidding the day before. He is really going to the quarry alone to swim and his life may be in danger. You pass by his house on way to your own home. Would you stop to tell his mother?

3. Around seven o'clock Saturday evening your best friend's mother calls your home to inquire if you know where he is. He had left his home immediately after lunch, telling his parents that he was going to the school playground for a baseball game. When he didn't return home for dinner his father drove to the playground, but found no one there. You know that you friend went to the quarry, but you don't know whether he's just enjoying himself and has perhaps lost track of the time, or whether something has happened to him. Would you tell his mother that you knew he had gone to the quarry early in the afternoon?

4. Assume you told you friend's parents that he had gone to the quarry. They go to find him and discover him there. He had lost track of the time but nothing had happened to him. They withdrew all his privileges for a full month. At school the next week he passes you in the hall, but refuses to speak to you. Some of your mutual friends also seem less than friendly towards you. What would you do?

In the next part of this course we begin to deal with that difficult question: Why don't we all come to the same decision when confronted with the same problem. It is clear that something influences the choices we make. Can we learn what and why and how? We shall give it a try in Part 3.

PART 3

Decisions And Individuality

This part of the curriculum begins with the exploration of the sources of our values which are derived largely from outside influences. It is true that persons seem to be innately the possessors of widely variant temperaments. We appear to be born with a tendency towards, or a receptivity to, a certain intrinsic mode of response to various experiences that arise. But somewhere within the range of limitations of each of us, there is a rather malleable area that can be influenced. It is in this area that values are nurtured, instructed, and transformed. In Part 3 we shall discover how this area is influenced.

> *Section A* : We don't all make the same decisions because our values are different and these influence our decisions.
> *Section B* : Our values tend to originate outside ourselves.
> *Section C* : Our values are different because each of us has been influenced by different important others.
> *Section D* : Our values are different because each of us has been influenced by a different environment.

Each of the sections may take one or more sessions to complete. There should be no compulsion to hurry.

Section A—We Don't All Make the Same Decisions Because Our Values are Different and These Influence Our Decisions

Specific Goal

To discover that one's values are the basis for his decision-making, that what is important (of value) differs from one person to the next, and causes us to make different decisions. And to discover that even with one person, what is most important changes from situation to situation.

Lead Activity

Point out to the children that over that past few meetings they have been trying to make decisions regarding various problems that arose on a trip to Mars and/or a swim in a dangerous quarry. Emphasise that members of the class came up with different decisions and that for the next few class sessions they will be exploring why their decisions were different.

Envelope Number Three accompanying this curriculum guide contains twenty sets of five cards each. Each card in a set contains one of the five numbered statements listed below. The statements are:

1. Avoid trouble.
2. Get something I want.
3. Be helpful to others.
4. Do what important people think is right.
5. Live up to people who trust me.

Each of these statements suggests a value which might be very important to a person in a particular situation. A child or an adult may refrain from doing a particular thing because avoiding trouble is of value to him. Similarly being a person who is helpful to others may be of significant value or importance to particular people in certain situations.

Tell the children you are going to read them a story. At the end of the story they are to individually and without consultations with each other, decide what they would do if they were faced with the situation presented in the story. After they decide what they would do, they are to arrange their set of cards so that the card on top has the statement on it which seems to have most influenced their decision. The remaining cards are to be placed under the top one in a order reflecting their descending influence on the decision which was made in this situation. It is true of course that these statement may not include the value which most influenced the decision of a particular child. The five statements do however reflect a wide range of values and will probably include the determining value for most of the children in your class. The story is:

> Two girls stopped by the public library on way home from school one afternoon to get some books for a homework assignment. Jill had just finished checking out hers when her good friend Linda walked past and said, "Let's go." They left the building and as they rounded the corner,

Linda took room under her coat a large, new, and obviously expensive book on dress designing.

"Where did you get that?" asked Jill.

"From the library," was the reply.

"Didn't you check it out?"

"Nope. They've got lots of books; they'll never miss this one. Anyway, I discovered I didn't have my card with me today."

"Are you going to keep it?"

"May be," said Linda, running off towards her home.

Jill was really bothered by the theft. She thought about it all the way home and when she stopped in the kitchen for a snack her mother noticed something was wrong.

"What's the matter, Jill," she asked.

"Nothing."

"Now I know better than that. What is it? School?"

It took a while, but Jill's mother finally wormed out of her the story of the incident at the library.

"What do you think you should do?" she asked.

"I don't know. Am I supposed to do something?" said Jill.

After the children have individually made their decisions and have ordered their cards, ask each child to read you his ordering according to the number on each card rather than the value statement itself. Write each child's ordering on a chalkboard or on a large sheet of paper as suggested by the tabulation chart which appears below:

John	*Mary*	*Cindy*	*Andy*	*Mike*	*Debby*	*Jan*
4	1	3	5	1	5	1
5	2	4	3	5	1	2
3	5	5	4	2	3	5
1	4	1	2	3	4	4
2	3	2	1	4	2	3

When your tabulation is complete go back to the first child and ask him what he would have done and why, if he had been faced with the situation in the story. Given the fact that John placed card number four at the top of his pile he might say, "Well

I wouldn't have reported my friend to the library, but I would have told him the next day that I thought he should return the book. I'm pretty sure that's what my mother would think I should do and I bet my dad would too. I kind of do whatever they seem to think is best in a situation like that."

Looking back at the tabulation chart you might then say, "Let's see John. You put card number four on top which states, 'Do what important people think is right.' What you're saying is that doing what people who are important to you would want—people such as your father or mother—is pretty important to you. You look to them for clues as to the best thing to do. So in this situation it was important to you to do what important people might think is right."

John of course might revise the particular way you have interpreted his decision and the reasons prompting it. You should be able however, in a minimum amount of time, to understand what he thought he would have done and the value (influencing factors) that determined his action.

Go through the same process for each child in your class if there is time. If your class is large you may want to question only a part of the children.

In all probability you and the children will discover that different decisions as to what should be done, were made, and that behind these decisions were various orderings of values.

Focusing

In order to clarify the significance of the above activity ask the children, "When do we discover from this which tells us something about why different people make different decisions about the same situation?" The children will probably come forth with the ideas that different things were important to different people and that these differences resulted in the variety of decisions.

Key Activity

Tell the children that you are going to read them another story. This story, however, has four parts to it. Each part adds a little bit more of what actually happened in the situation which the total story describes. The children are to decide what they would do after each part of the story and then order their cards as they did for the library book story. The story is:

1. Early one Saturday afternoon a group of boys gathered at the vacant lot on the edge of the golf course. They were sprawled around on the grass trying to decide what to do when Ben arrived.

He stopped in the middle of the lot, nonchallantly pulled a cigarette lighter from his pocket, and snapped it a couple of times. It flamed up as Ben picked up a twig and lit it.

"Where'd you get that, Ben?"

"What you going to do with it?"

"Anybody got a cigarette," Ben asked.

No one had.

"Whose is it, Ben? Did you find it?"

He snapped it off and on a couple of times more as he burned a gum wrapper.

"Let me try it once, Ben."

Ben ignored the request. It was obvious that no one was going to get the lighter without a struggle.

"Forget the old lighter. Let's go down to the pond and fish out some golf balls. We can make some money this afternoon and go to the movie tonight."

The boys started scrambling to their feet, and Ben saw that his audience was about to leave him.

"Hey," he said, "let's build a bonfire. Go get some sticks and stuff and let's build a big one."

A couple of boys hesitated a moment. It seemed like a good idea. But Bob and David, already heading for the pond, turned and shouted, "Come on. Last one there is a..." The words were lost as they were off and running.

It was almost an hour later that the boys heard the sound of fire trucks approaching. Standing in or on the edge of the pond they saw the trucks race past them.

"Look, there's smoke," one of them shouted. "It's over towards the lot."

Minutes later, they were standing by the fire engines watching the hoses being unrolled and the smoke billowing up. The wind was brisk and the fire had a good start. It was threatening a row of houses a little way down the street, and the flames were reaching toward the tops of the trees along the edge of the golf course.

The boys, after their first excitement, were subdued. The first admission of what was on all their minds came from Jim.

"Boy, I'm glad I didn't stay with him."

"Let's say we never even saw him today."

"Wait a minute. We don't know for sure that Ben started the fire!"

"Of course he did. There wasn't anyone else around."

"My mother says he's a very sick boy, and he's going to get in a lot of trouble if he doesn't get help."

"Listen, there's nothing wrong with Ben. He just wanted to have a compfire. I thought about the same thing when we were talking with him, but I just didn't have the guts to go ahead and build it."

"My folks say that Ben gets in trouble because his mother's away all day working, and nobody knows what he's doing."

"Today's Saturday. She doesn't work on Saturday."

The conversation went on as the battle with the fire continued, until someone in the group asked. "What are we going to do?"

Ask the children to decide individually what they would do and arrange their cards as they did for the previous story. This time ask for three volunteers to share the results of their ordering of the cards with the total class. Tabulate the results on a chalkboard or a large sheet of paper as you did before. Ask each of the three children what he decided he would have done and the reasons for his decision.

Leaving the tabulation on the board or paper, add the following additional fact to the story and ask the children to decide what they would do and order their cards.

The additional fact is:

2. Word comes that an old woman was found burned to death in a little cottage on the other side of the hill where the fire has spread.

Tabulate the results of the ordering from the same three children as before, listing them under the tabulation you made for the first part of the story. (See the tabulation chart below.) Again inquire as to what each of the three children would have done and the reasons behind their decisions.

Again leaving the previous tabulation results on the board or paper add another complication to the story. The complication is this:

3. Ben joins the group to watch the fire.

As the children to decide what they would do in this situation and to order their cards. Tabulate the ordering of the three children, and proceed as in previous parts of the story. Then add one additional complication. It is this :

4. A policeman approaches the group and asks if they know anything about the fire.

Ask the children to once again decide what they would do, have them order their cards and then collect the ordering from the three children. Inquire also as to what they decided they would do and ask what influenced them in making their decisions.

By now your tabulation chart should look something like that shown opposite. The tabulations alongside the letter "A" are those the children made for the first part of the story; those alongside "B" are for the second part etc.

Focusing

Focus with the class on the rankings of the three children for the first part of the story. In all probability the rankings will differ from one child to the next. Ask the children, "What do we discover from this which tells us something about why different people make different decisions about the same situation?" As with the library book story the children will probably grasp the fact that different things were important to different people and these resulted in different decisions.

Focus next with the class on the tabulations of the rankings of one of the three children for all four parts of the story. Notice how he has ranked his cards as new facts were added to the story. In all probability the rankings changed. Ask the children,

"What happened to the rankings of the cards as we added new facts to the story?" The children will probably be aware of the change in rankings. In a similar manner examine the rankings of other two children. Ask the children what we discover from this. They will probably grasp the fact that not only do different people make different decisions because different things are important to them, but even for the same person different things become important as situations change which results in a person changing his mind about what he would do in the situation.

Follow-up Question

Can you remember any instances during our trip to Mars or during the quarry adventure when people made very different decisions about what was best because different things were important to them?

	Cindy	Mike	Jan
A	1	3	4
	2	5	5
	3	4	1
	4	2	2
	5	1	3
B	3	1	4
	4	2	5
	5	3	1
	1	4	2
	2	5	3
C	1	4	3
	2	5	5
	4	1	4
	3	2	1
	5	3	2
D	4	2	1
	2	5	5
	1	3	2
	3	1	4
	5	4	3

Section B—Our Values Tend to Originate Outside Ourselves

Specific Goal

To discover that over values tend to originate outside ourselves.

Lead Activity

There are two ways you might approach the following activity, depending on which is the more congenial to you. Either method gets at the same idea—the exterior sources from which we derive values.

First approach: Ask the children to imagine that a group of visitors from various countries of the world is visiting their town. Each of their families has volunteered to entertain one of the visitors as an overnight guest. Each child may decide which one he would like to have in his home. All of them speak English. The nations from which the visitors are coming are: Brazil, Egypt, Pakistan, Norway, Africa-Liberia, Japan, Holland and Algeria.

Give each child a set of the cards contained in Envelope Number Four which accompanies this teacher's guide. The cards in a set are printed with the names of the nations from which visitors are coming. Two blank cards are provided with each set. You may use these if you wish to add the names of two countries of your own choice to each set. Ask each child to order his set of cards by placing on top the card listing the nation from which he would most like to have a visitor, arranging the other cards in a descending order of preference.

Second approach: Ask the children to imagine that each of them has been given the opportunity to visit any one of the countries from which the visitors in the first approach were coming. The visit will be at absolutely no expense to the child or his family. Use the cards found in Envelope Number Four and ask each child to order them by placing on top the card naming the country which he would most like to visit with the other cards arranged in the descending order of preference.

After the children have had a chance to decide their order of preference tabulate the results. Ask first how many had a Brazilian visitor or a visit to Brazil as their first choice. Then inquire how many had an Egyptian visitor or a visit to Egypt as their first choice. After all of the first choice tabulations have been made, collect similar information for the second through eighth place choices. Your tabulation chart should look something like the one shown below.

Country	1	2	3	4	5	6	7	8
Brazil	2	0	4	3	2	4	1	1
Egypt	1	2	2	3	1	2	4	2
Pakistan	4	2	1	0	4	2	0	4
Norway	6	2	5	1	1	1	1	0
Africa-Liberia	0	1	1	5	4	0	4	2
Japan	1	3	2	4	2	1	2	2
Holland	3	6	0	1	2	3	1	1
Algeria	0	1	2	0	1	4	4	5

Explore the significance of the preferences by asking the following questions: Are there some nationalities or nations consistently high or consistently low? (In the tabulation below for example Norway is consistently high while Algeria is consistently low). What might be some reasons for this?

Ask how many of the children have met people from these countries or visited the country itself? While a few children may know personally someone from one or two of the countries or may even have travelled in the countries most of them probably will have had little or no contact with either the people or the countries.

If we have had little or no contact with these people or the countries from which they came, how are we able to show a preference? Where do we get many of our evaluations or attitudes about other people and their countries? List all the potential sources which have influenced our evaluations of foreign countries and their people. The children will probably suggest text-books, newspapers, movies, television, friends, parents, etc.

Key Activity

Give each child a set of the cards contained in Envelope Number Five which accompanies this teacher's guide. On each set of cards are the following statements:

learn to smoke	let your hair grow
get a motor bike	dye your hair
run for student council	drink when asked
join a church youth group	join a school organisation — band, drama, chess, pep club, etc.
get a library card	join a teen centre
start a record collection	get a job
take a modelling course	try drugs
get good grades	

After the children have the cards, read the following situation to them. For the girls in your class the cousin the situation is a girl; for the boys the cousin is a boy. The situation is:

> Your sixteen-year-old cousin has just returned to the United States or Canada (depending on where you live), after spending the last five years in India where his parents have been working for the Peace-Corps. He and his family have moved into your community and he is very anxious to become popular with the teen-agers in the community. He has asked you for your advice on the sort of things he should do.

Ask each child, on an individual basis, to divide his cards into two piles—activities that he would suggest for his cousin to help him become popular with the other teen-agers and those which would hinder his becoming popular or atleast not contribute to it. Point out to the children that of course some of the suggestions on the cards are applicable to boys only while others are applicable only to girls.

Tabulate the choices on a blackboard or a large sheet of paper, discussing their reasons for choosing certain activities and eliminating others.

Ask the children if any of them have actually done these things in order to become popular teen-ager. Since nine to twelve year old children are not yet teen-agers they of course have not tested for themselves the validity of their choices. Ask them how they have arrived at the assumption that doing some of these things would help one become a popular teen-ager. Where did they get their evaluations of these activities? They will probably suggest that they have acquired them from older brothers and sisters, magazines, movies, television, etc.

Focusing

Ask the children to think about both the activity they have just completed and the one in which they could choose which foreign visitor they would have in their home or which country they would visit. Where do we tend to get many of our evaluations and attitudes about other people? About important things to do? The children will probably grasp the fact that many of our ideas about what is important (of value) about other people and what acts are important originated from outside ourselves.

Section C—Our Values are Different Because each of us has been Influenced by Different Important Others

Specific Goal

To discover the influence of important people in our lives on the development of our values.

Lead Activity:

Begin a group conversation aimed at pinpointing both the source and the contents of some of our ideas about what is important that come from the important others who influence our lives. The direction of the conversation is suggested by the following questions:

> *Teacher:* We talked last time about how some of our ideas about what is important come from outside influences. One outside influence is the important people in our lives. Who are some of the people in our lives who have influenced our values or what we think is important? (The children will probably suggest parents, friends, teachers, and relatives.)
>
> What values or ideas about what is important have you acquired from your parents? (Encourage the children to express themselves on this point.)
>
> But some of our values of opinions of what we think is important are not the same as those of our parents. What are some of these differences?
>
> Where do we get these ideas? (Encourage the children to identify the particular source of certain ideas they have about what is of value or important. Press them for as

many direct connections as possible. See if they can connect a certain ideas of what is important to them with the influence of a particular teacher, relative or other person.)

Key Activity

Ask each child to write a brief one-to-two page story about how what is important to him would be different if he had never met one of the people he knows best. There are a number of different kinds of people around whom the story might be focused.

(a) The person might be the child's best friend. How would what is important to the child be different if he had never known this friend?
(b) The person might be one of the child's parents. How would what is important to the child be different if he had never known one of his parents?

A slightly different approach would be to ask each child to write a story about how what is important to him would be different if someone not now close to him had been very close to him throughout his life.

(a) The story might be written from the focus of how what is important the child would be different if the parents of his best friend were his parents.
(b) A method that might be fun for the child would be for him to imagine that a famous contemporary personage were his parent. The child would then focus his story on what would probably be important to him if this person were one of his parents. If you would like to suggest this approach to the children you might clip pictures of famous personalities from magazines prior to the class. Choose people like widely known sports figures, astronauts, politicians, movie stars or TV personalities. Let each child choose one of the people from among your collection or even a famous person for whom you do not have a picture.

When the children have finished the writing of their stories, ask those who are willing to share them with the class.

Focusing:

What is one second-hand source of our ideas of what is important or of value? Why would these differ from person to person? How would these affect the decisions different people make in response to the same situation? The children will probably have discovered that people important in our lives influence the development of our values and these influence our decisions.

Follow-up Questions:

Can you think of any instances during our trip to Mars when one person made different decisions as to what would be best to do because of the influence of an important other?

Supplementary Material for Your Use:

> There is a famous legend about two girls in India who were abandoned in the jungle when they were very young. They were adopted by a wolf mother and raised as her own children. Some years later, when one was about eight and the other much younger, they were found by villagers. What would you guess they were like? What kind of ideas about what is important do you think they had—human or wolf?
>
> Actually, the children behaved as animals. They had no idea of course about language. At night they howled, and they lapped water instead of drinking in the human manner. In addition they crawled around on all fours.
>
> The younger died shortly after being found, but the elder lived until she was about seventeen. For ten years she was given a normal education. She learned how to walk more or less upright and to speak with a vocabulary or forty-eight words. But she never managed to humanise herself completely. Her infancy with the wolves left its indelible mark.

What does this say to us about how and where we get our values?

> In August, 1911, barking dogs awakened workers on a small ranch outside Oroville, a town in northern California in the Mount Lassen foothills. The dogs had cornered a

wild man—a man who turned out to be "the last of the wild Indians."

Ishi was the name given to the man who came out of the Stone Age that morning and entered the twentieth century. He was the last survivor of a tiny tribe whose existence had been unknown. Out of loneliness or fear or despair he finally ventured out of the hills and into contact with "civilised" man. For five year Ishi lived in a University of California museum in San Francisco, re-creating for the professors and the public many of the skills that had kept him alive in the wilderness. He chipped arrowheads and other tools from stone, made fires with a drill, and sewed clothing from skins. But perhaps most interesting of all, he learned about what was then the modern world.

What values do you think changed for Ishi when he came to live in the city?

And how would Ishi have learned the values of civilisation?

Section D—Our Values are Different Because each of us has been Influenced by a Different Environment

Specific Goal

To become aware of the influence of environment in determining what is important to people.

Lead Activity

In this section you are to use the photographic essay depicting life in an urban ghetto which is included in Envelope Number Six which accompanies this guide. Its use is intended to suggest how environment can influence the formation of values. The environmental conditions within which we live, whether they be those of the natural world or manmade, impose certain priorities upon us. Environmental factors such as geography, climate, proximity of other people, hazards, and many others make their demands upon us. The goal of this section is to help children discover some of the ways in which environment influences what is important to people.

The goal is not easily accomplished with children, but its accomplishment is probably even more difficult with adults. The environment in which any one of us lives, and what becomes important to us because of it, becomes so natural to us that it is hard to comprehend why a different environment nurtures quite contrasting values in other people. Witness the difficulty today of middle-class people comprehending a value structure which would cause people in the hard core city ghettos to shout, "Burn baby, burn!" and then act accordingly.

Your task in this activity is to help the children become aware of different environmental features depicted in the photographic essay and how these would influence what is important to the people who live there.

Prior to your class session preview carefully the photographic essay. Try yourself to become aware of as many conditions as possible which would significantly influence what would be important to the people who live there. Unsafe places to play, a lack of privacy, jobless parents, decrepit buildings, and other unfavourable conditions are all factors that could contribute to the development of values. Your own familiarity with the essay will help you to call the children's attention to value-influencing features depicted in the essay which the children might miss. You should give the children every chance to discover them for themselves first. If they consistently miss a feature such as the presence of decrepit buildings, however, you might point to them and ask, "What are these and would they influence what people think is important?" Do not tell them initially why you think decrepit buildings would influence what people think is important. Let them puzzle about it themselves. The goal here is to encourage some imaginative thinking among the students in the hope that they will be able to think on their own in other times and places about the influence of environment.

Have the essay on display in your room as the children arrive. It should be displayed in a manner which makes it easily visible during your class session. Develop a discussion around the essay using the following questions:

1. What is different about this place than the place where you live?
2. What things are the same? What reminds you of your home, neighbourhood, and town?
3. What might worry people who live in this place? What would be some of their problems?

4. What kind of things might become important to people living here?

Key Activity

There are any number of film documentaries available for rental that are of great value in helping children discover the influence of environment on what becomes important to people. Listed below are a number of films, with information about where they are obtainable, their length, and the rental fee as of the time this is being written. These films have been found useful in helping children discover the influence of environment on values. There are no doubt many others, some of which you may know about and which might be more readily accessible to you. In any case, arrange to have a relevant film available for showing.

After the showing of the film develop a discussion around the film using questions similar to those you used with the photographic essay. It is important that you preview the film so that you will be as alert as possible to as many of the conditions it depicts which might influence values.

Recommended films:

Bolivian Boy
15 min. colour. rental. $7.50
Produced by Nicholas Read, Potomac Films.
Distributed by Contemporary Films, 330 W. 42nd St., New York, N.Y. 10036

> Depicts daily activities and customs of a ten-year-old Aymara Indian boy and the pride and wonder he feels for the civilisation of his ancestors, the highland Indians.

Children Adrift
26 min. b/w. rental: $12.50
Prix Jean Vigo, 1958.
Distributed by Contemporary Films (as above)

> A study of a lonely boy in a foreign refugee camp outside Paris. An example of the way universal emotions unite human beings of diverse language, nationality and age.

PART 4

The Enabling and Reinforcing Segment

In Part 2 of this course we looked in a general way at the process of decision-making. A trip to Mars and a swim in a dangerous quarry let us in on some of the complexity of decision-making. In Part 3 we discovered some of the factors which influence the decisions we make. Outside forces including important others and environment were all discovered to be influences in the shaping of the values we hold which in turn influence the decisions we make.

In Part 4 of the curriculum our goal will be to help children develop a process of decision-making. This process includes a number of steps one might take to help him make more imaginative and responsible decisions. These steps suggest various things requiring attention in any situation where one must make a decision. Following these steps does not of course insure that one will make responsible decisions, because the necessary intangibles of sensitivity, perceptiveness, and adequate judgment cannot be guaranteed by following a series of steps. Neither can one ever know all the factors influencing a situation. Sometimes a factor of which one is unaware rises and destroys the decision-making efforts of even the most responsible. It is the conviction of the creators of this curriculum however that conscious awareness of these steps and growing skill in using them will enhance the possibilities for more imaginative and responsible decision-making. The following outline suggests the approach:

Section A : Become aware of the needs and feelings of persons by going behind behaviour to discover motivation.

Section B : Enlarge the "we".

Section C : Evaluate carefully the information we receive.

Section D : Recognise self-deception.

Section E : Order one's values.

Section F : Identify the source of values and evaluate them.

Section G : Explore alternative courses of action and possible consequences.

Section H : Be willing to live with the consequences of one's decision.

CHAPTER 7

Children and Mathematical Concepts

Describing some remarkable experiments which the reader, if he has a subject handy, may perform himself. Among other things they show that in a child the historical development of geometry is reversed. It is a great mistake to suppose that a child acquires the notion of number and other mathematical concepts just from teaching. On the contrary, to a remarkable degree he develops them himself, independently and spontaneously. When adults try to impose mathematical concepts on a child prematurely, his learning is merely verbal; true understanding of them comes only with his mental growth.

This can easily be shown by a simple experiment. A child of five or six may readily be taught by his parents to name the numbers from 1 to 10. If 10 stones are laid in a row, he can count them correctly. But if the stones are rearranged in a more complex pattern or piled up, he no longer can count them with consistent accuracy. Although the child knows the names of the numbers, he has not yet grasped the essential idea of number: namely, that the number of objects in a group remains the same, is "conserved," no matter how they are shuffled or arranged.

On the other hand, a child of six and a half or seven often shows that he has spontaneously formed the concept of number even though he may not yet have been taught to count. Given eight red chips and eight blue chips, he will discover by one-to-one matching that the number of red is the same as the number of blue, and he will realise that the two groups remain equal in number regardless of the shape they take.

The experiment with one-to-one correspondence is very useful for investigating children's development of the number concept. Let us lay down a row of eight red chips, equally spaced about an inch apart, and ask our small subjects to take from a box of blue chips as many chips as there are on the table. Their re-actions will depend on age, and we can distinguish three stages of development. A child of five or younger, on an average, will lay out blue chips to make a row exactly as long as the red row, but he will put the blue chips close together instead of spacing them. He believes the number is the same if the length of the row is the same. At the age of six, on an average, children arrive at the second stage; these children will lay a blue chip opposite each red chip and obtain the correct number. But they have not necessarily acquired the concept of number itself. If we spread the red chips, spacing out the row more loosely, the six-year-olds will think that the longer row now has more chips, though we have not changed the number. At the age of six and a half to seven, on an average, children achieve the third stage: they know that, though we close up or space out one row of chips, the number is still the same as in the other.

In a similar experiment a child is given two receptacles of identical shape and size and is asked to put beads, one at a time, into both receptacles with both hands simultaneously—a blue bead into one box with his right hand and a red bead into the other with his left hand. When he has more or less filled the two receptacles, he is asked how they compare. He is sure that both have the same number of beads. Then he is requested to pour the blue beads into a receptacle of a different size and shape. Here again we see differences in understanding according to age. The smallest children think that the number has changed: if, for instance, the beads fill the new receptacle to a higher level, they think there are more beads in it than in the original one; if to a lower level, they think there are fewer. But children near the age of seven know that the transfer has not changed the number of beads.

In short, children must grasp the principle of conservation of quantity before they can develop the concept of number. Now conservation of quantity of course is not in itself a numerical notion; rather, it is a logical concept. Thus these experiments in child psychology throw some light on the epistemology of the number concept—a subject which has been examined by many mathematicians and logicians.

The mathematicians Henri Poincaré and L.E.J. Brouwer have held that the number concept is a product of primitive intuition, preceding logical notions. The experiments just described deny this thesis, in our opinion. Bertrand Russell, on the other hand, has supported the view that number is a purely logical concept: that the idea of cardinal number derives from the logical notion of category (a number would be a category made up of equivalent categories) while the notion of ordinal number derives from the logical relationships of order. But Russell's theory does not quite fit the psychological processes as we have observed them in small children. Children at the start make no distinction between cardinal and ordinal number, and besides, the concept of cardinal number itself presupposes an order relationship. For instance, a child build a one-to-one correspondence only if he neither forgets any of the elements nor uses the same one twice. The only way of distinguishing one unit from another is to consider it either before or after the other in time or in space, that is, in order of enumeration.

Study of the child's discovery of spatial relationships—what may be called the child's spontaneous geometry—is no less rewarding than the investigation of his number concepts. A child's order of development in geometry seems to reverse the order of historical discovery. Scientific geometry began with the Euclidean system (concerned with figures, angles and so on), developed in the 17th century the so-called projective geometry (dealing with problems of perspective) and finally came in the 19th century to topology (describing spatial relationships in a general qualitative way—for instance, the distinction between open and closed structures, interiority and exteriority, proximity and separation). A child begins with the last: his first geometrical discoveries are topological. At the age of three he readily distinguishes between open and closed figures: if you ask him to copy a square or a triangle, he draws a closed circle; he draws a cross with two separate lines. If you show him a drawing of a large circle with a small circle inside, he is quite capable of reproducing this relationship, and he can also draw a small circle outside or attached to the edge of the large one. All this he can do before he can draw a rectangle or express the Euclidean characteristics (number of sides, angles, etc.) of a figure. Not until considerable time after he has mastered topological relationships does he begin to develop his notions of Euclidean and projective geometry. Then he builds those simultaneously.

Child of three draws this but not rectangle

Curiously enough, this psychological order is much closer to modern geometry's order of deductive or axiomatic construction than the historical order of discovery was. It offers another example of the kinship between psychological construction and the logical construction of science itself.

Let us test our young subjects on projective constructions. First we set up two "fence posts" (little sticks stuck in bases of modelling clay) some 15 inches apart and ask the child to place other posts in a straight line between them. The youngest children (under the age of four) proceed to plant one post next to another, forming a more or less wavy line. Their approach is topological: the elements are joined by the simple relationship of proximity rather than by projection of a line as such. At the next stage, beyond the age of four, the child may form a straight fence if the two end posts parallel the edge of the table, or if there is some other straight line to guide him. If the end posts are diagonally across the table, he may start building the line parallel to the table's edge and then change direction and form a curve to reach the second post. Occasionally a youngster may make a straight line, but he does so only by trial-and-error and not by system.

At the age of seven years, on an average, a child can build a straight fence consistently in any direction across the table, and he will check the straightness of the line by shutting one eye and sighting along it, as a gardener line up bean poles. Here we have the essence of the projective concept; the line is still a topological line, but the child has grasped that the projective relationship depends on the angle of vision, or point of view.

Child of seven straightens a row of "fence posts" by sighting along them

One can proceed to study this with other experiments. For instance, you stand a doll on a table and place before it an object oriented in a certain direction: a pencil lying crosswise, diagonally or lengthwise with respect to the doll's line of vision, or a watch lying flat on the table or standing up. Then you ask the child to draw the doll's view of the object, or, better still, ask him to choose from two or three drawings the one that represents the doll's point of view. Not until the age of about seven or eight can a child deduce correctly the doll's angle of vision.

A similar experiment testing the same point yields the same conclusions. Objectives of different shapes are placed in various positions between a light and a screen, and the child is asked to predict the shape of the shadow the object will cast on the screen.

Ability to co-ordinate different perspectives does not come until the age of 9 or 10. This is illustrated by an experiment I suggested some time ago to my collaborator Dr. Edith Meyer. The experimenter sits at a table opposite the child, and between the child and herself she places a cardboard range of mountains. The two see the range from opposite perspectives. The child is then asked to select from several drawings the ones that picture both his own and the opposite person's views of the mountain range. Naturally the youngest children can pick out only the picture that corresponds to their own view; they imagine that all the points of view are like their own. What is more interesting, if the child changes places with the experimenter and sees the mountains from the other side, he now thinks that his new view is the only correct one; he cannot reconstruct the point of view that was his own just a little while before. This is a clear example of the egocentricity so characteristic of children—the primitive reasoning which prevents them from understanding that there may be more than one point of view.

It takes a considerable evolution for children to come, at around the age of 9 or 10, to the ability to distinguish between and co-ordinate the different possible perspectives. At this stage they can grasp projective space in its concrete or practical from, but naturally not in its theoretical aspects.

At the same time the child forms the concept of projective space, he also constructs Euclidean space; the two kinds of construction are based upon one another. For example, in lining up a straight row of fence posts he may not only use the sighting method but may line up his hands parallel to each other to give him the direction. That is, he is applying the concept of conservation of direction, which is a Euclidean principle. Here is another illustration of the fact that children from mathematical notions on a qualitative or logical basis.

The conservation principle arises in various forms. There is first the conservation of length. If you place a block on another of the same length and then push one block so that its end projects beyond the other, a child under six will suppose that the two block are no longer of equal length. Not until near the age of seven, on an average, does the child understand that what is gained at one end of the block is lost at the other. He arrives at this concept of the conservation of length, be it noted, by a process of logic.

Experiments on a child's discovery of the conservation of distance are especially illuminating. Between two small toy trees standing apart from each other on a table you place a wall formed of a block or a thick piece of cardboard, and you ask the child (in his own language, of course) whether the trees are still the same distance apart. The smallest children think the distance has changed; they are simply unable to add up two parts of a distance to a total distance. Children of five or six believe the distance has been reduced, claiming that the width of the well does not count as distance; in other words, a filled-up space does not have the same value as an empty space. Only near the age of seven do children come to the realisation that intervening objects do not change the distance.

However you test them, you find the same thing true: children do not appreciate the principle of conservation of length or surface until, somewhere around the age of seven, they discover the reversibility that shows the original quantity has remained the same (*e.g.*, the realignment of equal-length blocks, the removal of the wall, and so on). Thus the discovery of logical relationships is a prerequisite to the construction of geometrical concepts, as it is in the formation of the concept of number.

This applies to measurement itself, which is only a derived concept. It is interesting to study how children spontaneously learn to measure. One of my collaborators, Dr. Inhelder, and I have made the following experiment: We show the child a tower of blocks on a table and ask him to build a second tower of the same height on another table (lower or higher than the first) with blocks of a different size. Naturally we provide the child with all the necessary measuring tools. Children's attempts to deal with this problem go through a fascinating evolution. The youngest children build up the second tower to the same visual level as the first, without worrying about the difference in height of the tables. They compare the towers by stepping back and sighting them. At a slightly more advanced stage a child lays a long rod across the top of the two towers to make sure that they are level. Somewhat later he notices that the base of his tower is not at the same level as the model's. He then wants to place his tower next to the model on the same table to compare them. Reminded that the rules of the game forbid him to move his tower, he begins to look around for a measuring standard. Interestingly enough, the first that comes to his mind is his own body. He puts one hand on top of his tower and the other at its base, and then, trying to keep his hands the same distance apart, he moves over to the other tower to compare it. Children of about the age of six often carry out this work in a most assured manner, as if their hands could not change position on the way! Soon they discover that the method is not reliable, and then they resort to reference points on the body. The child will line up his shoulder with the top of his tower, mark the spot opposite the base on his thigh with his hand and walk over to the model to see whether the distance is the same.

Eventually the ideas of an independent measuring tool occurs to the child. His first attempt in this direction is likely to be the building of a third tower next to and the same height as the one he has already erected. Having built it, he moves it over to the first table and matches it against the model; this is allowed by the rules. The child's arrival at this stage presupposes a process of logical reasoning. If we call the model tower A, the second tower C and the movable tower B, the child has reasoned that B=C and B=A, therefore A=C.

Child of six measures the height of a tower of blocks with her body

Later the child replaces the third tower with a rod, but at first the rod must be just the same length as the height of the tower to be measured. He then conceives the idea of using a longer rod marking the tower height on it with his finger. Finally, and this is the beginning of true measurement, he realises that he can use a shorter rod and measure the height of the tower by applying the rod a certain number of times up the side.

The last discovery involves two new operations of logic. The first is the process of division which permits the child to conceive that the whole is composed of a number of parts added together. The second is the displacement, or substitution, which enables him to apply one part upon others and thus to build a system of units. One may therefore say that measurement is a synthesis of division into parts and of substitution, just as number is a synthesis of the inclusion of categories and of serial order. But measurement develops later than the number concept, because it is more difficult to divide a continuous whole into interchangeable units than to enumerate elements which are already separate.

To study measurement in two dimensions, we give the child a large sheet of paper with a pencil dot on it and ask him to put a dot in the same position on another sheet of the same size. He may use rods, strips of paper, strings, rulers or any other measuring tool he needs. The youngest subjects are satisfied to make a visual approximation, using no tools. Later a child applies a measuring tool but he measures only the distance of the point from the side or bottom edge of the paper and is surprised that this single measurement does not give him the correct position. Then he measures the distance of the point from a corner of the paper, trying to keep the same slant (angle) when he applies the ruler to his own sheet. Finally, at about the age of eight or nine, he discovers that he must break up the measurement into two operations: the horizontal distance from a side edge and the perpendicular distance from the bottom or top edge. Similar experiments with a bead in a box show that a child discovers how to make three-dimensional measurements at about the same age.

Measurement in two or three dimension brings up to the central idea of Euclidean space, namely the axes of co-ordinates—a system founded on the horizontality or verticality of physical objects. It may seem that even a baby should grasp these concepts, for after all it can distinguish between the upright and lying-down positions. But actually the representation of vertical and horizontal lines brings up quite another problem from this subjective awareness of postural space. Dr. Inhelder and I have studied it with the following experiments: Using a jar half-filled with coloured water, we ask our young subjects to predict what level the water will take when the jar is tipped one way or another. Not until the age of nine, on an average, does a child grasp the ideas of horizontality and predict correctly. Similar experiments with a plumb line or a toy sailboat with a tall mast demonstrate that comprehension of verticality comes at about the same time. The child's tardiness in acquiring these concepts is not really surprising, for they require not only a grasp of the internal relationships of an object but also reference to external elements (*e.g.*, a table or the floor or walls of the room.)

When a child has discovered how to construct these co-ordinate axes by reference to natural objects, which he does at about the same time that he conceives the co-ordination of perspectives, he has completed his conception of how to represent space. By that time he has developed his fundamental mathematical concepts, which spring spontaneously from his own logical operations.

The experiments I have described, simple as they are, have been surprisingly fruitful and have brought to light many unexpected facts. These facts are illuminating from the psychological and pedagogical points of view; more than that, they teach us a number of lessons about human knowledge in general.

Mathematics for the Slow Learner

For those responsible for the teaching of mathematics to the less well-endowed pupils in the secondary school there are two main problems: what should be taught and how to do it effectively. Unfortunately so much of what we do is traditional that very often we do not even ask these questions or perhaps we sense that there are not ready-made answers. The rapid changes in the teaching of mathematics, especially in primary school, should be making teachers of older children who are slow at learning look afresh at the mathematics curriculum. Perhaps it is time to make a more realistic assessment of the needs of those who will never wish to take an external mathematics examination, feel the need to solve quadratic equations, use a slide rule, compute compound interest or use negative numbers. There are still too many teachers facing large classes of such wide ability that individual guidance is almost impossible. Mixed ability groups offer many advantages in terms of social development, but a pupil whose rate of learning is well below average also needs the help which comes from a careful diagnosis of problems, remedial exercises and a strong personal relationship with the teacher. Social workers, probation officers and employers who struggle with the problems of not only the illiterate but the innumerate would no doubt share this view.

The causes of poor attainment in school are complex and often mystifying. Usually many factors combine to give a low level of learning—physical, intellectual, emotional and social. The most common are slow maturation, poor attendance, environmental deprivation, emotional disturbance, and below average intelligence.

Initial testing of eleven-year-old entrants has revealed that among some there are particular weaknesses in language perception, memory and conceptual thinking. The most common disabilities are:

(a) difficulty in solving problems involving language,
(b) lack of ability to remember basic number facts or tables,
(c) confusion in the meaning of arithmetic signs +, ×, —, ÷,
(d) no understanding of place value,
(e) little evidence of transfer,
(f) problems in counting, with little practical use made of the idea of grouping,
(g) uncertainty of the concept of fractions or area,
(h) an intuitive approach to a problem often resulting in improbable answers,
(i) confused ideas of methods of subtraction, multiplication, and division with impossible answers freely give, and
(j) poor work habits, frequent distraction, short periods of concentration and rapid fatigue.

These are the children we must set out to help by providing a realistic curriculum and methods which can minimise their handicaps to learning.

The Curriculum

It is very unlikely that children with the difficulties listed above will go on to take competitive examinations in mathematics and so our aim must be to provide sufficient knowledge of the subject to give adequate social competence. What standard of arithmetic is needed by most adults in normal circumstances? There has not been much research to answer this question but three surveys by Wilson in America, Moore and Thompson in England, all arrived at very similar conclusions:

(*a*) between 80% and 90% of all arithmetic was concerned with money,
(*b*) most problems were oral and calculated mentally,
(*c*) most problems concerned the addition of small sums of money,
(*d*) very little use was made of subtraction, multiplication and division,
(*e*) little over 5% of all calculations involved capacity or measuring,
(*f*) all need to tell the time, with occasional use of time-tables and
(*g*) some use of simple fractions, generally halves and quarters.

The syllabus for mathematics must therefore concentrate on this minimum core of knowledge. The following basic aims are very similar to those suggested by a number of experienced teachers of slow-learning children.

1. Recognition of number values to 100.
2. Accuracy in counting to 100.
3. Addition and subtraction up to 100.
4. Grouping in twos, fives, tens and fiftys and hundreds.
5. Recognition of coins and their value.
6. Recognition of symbols for denoting money values.
7. Addition of money to £ 20.
8. Training in giving change by 'adding on'.
9. Practical measurement in yards, feet and inches, also meters, centimetres and millimetres, with rulers and tape measure.
10. Familiarity with finding weight, using different types of scales.
11. Experience with simple measurements of capacity using standard measures.

12. An understanding of the common mathematical terms used in everyday language.
13. Training in telling the time, including the use of 24 hour system.
14. Simple budgeting.
15. Understanding pictograms and block graphs, etc.
16. Using a calendar and timetable.
17. Finding position using simple coordinates.
18. Using a simple scale to find distance.
19. Linking time and distance for travelling.
20. Talks on saving, insurance, hire purchase, rent and rates, bargains and the social uses of money.

Some teachers may wish to break this syllabus into sections for different age groups. With many teachers taking the same children at different terms there is the danger of a lack of continuity so that some system of recording what has been understood will greatly aid purposeful teaching.

Perhaps the hardest task of the inexperienced teacher of older slow-learning pupils is to appreciate how little they really understand, unless some familiarity with the writings of Piaget has led to trying some of his experiments; see, for example, Lawrence (1955), Lovell (1961) and Bunt.

Many ten-or eleven-year-olds will find difficulty in grasping the principle of conservation, *e.g.*, that a pound butter remains a pound of butter no matter what its shape, texture, colour or consistency. It is worthwhile for the teacher to repeat some of Piaget's experiments if only to prove the point to himself. Demonstrations in front of the class will arouse considerable interest, discussion, and argument, but the teacher must try to remain neutral, letting the individual child come to understand the concept in his own time. A simple exercise in conservation can be done with Plasticine and a pair of scales. A child balances two pieces of Plasticine on the scales, make sure to balance them each way by changing sides. The pieces are now accepted as the same weight. The question to be discussed is whether, if we change the shape we also change the weight. First stretch out one piece or Plasticine into a long sausage and test whether they are now the same weight. Compress one piece into a tight ball and reweigh. Now make a hole in the middle and compare again. Challenge the class — can you change the weight without adding or taking anything away? Even some eleven-year-olds will be astonished when the two pieces of Plasticine always balance. Those that are quite convinced it is some sort of trick are still at the pre-operational stage. Some who are half-convinced but not sure if the Plasticine is changed to sand will be uncertain. These pupils are at the intuitive stage. Only those who think the whole thing is obvious from the start are at the operational stage and will be sure that changes in the relationship of numbers in a group cannot alter the total. This can be verified by a simple game. Give each child ten counters and ask him to separate them into two piles, with eyes closed, keeping the counters hidden under each hand. Lift one hand and see how many are there and now guess how many under the other hand. Then play in pairs taking turns in guessing how many underneath partner's hand. Only when the child is right every time does he understand the concept of conservation and reversibility for that quantity.

In the secondary school teaching by verbal explanation is still the commonest method. While communication can be made with brighter pupils, the use of lengthy explanations of method is seldom effective with pupils who are handicapped by an inadequate understanding of language. Berstein states (N.F.E.R., 1961):

> In arithmetic they may master mechanical operations involved in additions, subtraction and multiplication, provided they have also mastered their tables, but they will have difficulty in division. However, verbal problems based upon these operations may confuse them. They will have great difficulty in ordering the verbal argument before applying the operations. They will have difficulty in generalising the operation to a wide range of contexts. Their conception of number will be restricted. Although such pupils may pass the primary stage without a great sense of unease, the discrepancy between what they are called upon to do and what they can do widens considerably at the secondary level. The central problem for such children is primarily that of learning how to learn, and to make educational experience happy and contented is not necessarily to solve the problems of learning.

The teacher trained in the formal uses of language continually complains of the limited linguistic skills and vocabulary of his pupils. Often the difficulty of sustaining or eliciting adequate communication appears insurmountable. It seems the child is speaking a different language. Berstein corroborates this belief and isolates it to a particular social class who feel little need for conceptualisation, but whose use of language is implicit, and whose communications are rather by non-verbal signals requiring a close relationship and empathy. The conditions of the normal classroom with an impersonal authoritarian method dependent upon formal language makes effective communication impossible and suggest that the individual teaching method in small groups, although fatiguing to the teacher, offers the best hopes for the close psychological relationship necessary to give a true learning situation. There are a large number of mathematical words in our normal vocabulary and the teacher of slow learners must not assume that the child understands the mathematical concept implicit in the word, or the word for a concept which is understood. In many cases the word will have a restricted meaning or a limited association with some particular object or event. The teacher must be conscious of the need to introduce, expand and clarify the whole range of mathematical terms the children will need. Several lists of words have been prepared but once the teacher is aware of the children's inadequacy in understanding the mathematical vocabulary he will be on his guard against the difficult-worded question and the lengthy explanation involving the use of such words. In the small group situation the teacher will find it far easier to make his meaning clear and develop the children's vocabulary. (See reference list.)

Class Organisation

Faced with the responsibility for developing mathematical language, arithmetical skills, adequate motivation, social competence, reasonable behaviour and individual help the teacher may well decide to find some less-demanding occupation. Certainly there will be little hope of success without the following:

(a) A maximum class size of twenty.
(b) A large selection of apparatus.

(c) Graded work-cards and text books.
(d) Diagnostic tests and individual records.
(e) Duplicating equipment.
(f) Wallcharts, handbooks, films and film strips.

The following suggestions may help the inexperienced teacher to decide how best to plan his teaching. Generally it is best to work on the '3 layer' principle.

1. A foundation of work which is always available, graded and needing the minimum of explanation.
2. An individual programme of graded work-cards or sheets for particular difficulties.
3. A series of mathematical activities, set verbally or on cards.

Class teaching is used when a particular topic involves discussion and demonstration, for example, using a new piece of apparatus. Such a system leaves the teacher free to observe, question and help individual pupils, while allowing them and the maximum opportunities for success. Behaviour problems usually arise where the task set is beyond the capability or understanding of the pupil. A sense of co-operation should be encouraged as some children will already be conditioned to be inconspicuously idle.

The emphasis given to each of these 'layers' will ultimately depend on the characteristics of the class and the personality of the teacher. There is no proof that any particular method is best and it is probable that, as in the teaching of reading to slow learners, the two factors most conducive to learning are the skill and enthusiasm of the teacher and a blend of methods to suit the situation.

Basic Work: The first task of the teacher of a class of pupils who have found little success in arithmetic is to restore lost confidence, to convince them that there are ways of finding answers without just trying to remember them on asking the teacher. This subordination of teaching to learning is helped by having available various types of apparatus, structural apparatus being of prime importance. In deciding which type to choose, there are four main points to consider:

1. Is colour helpful?
2. Is size important? Small blocks can be difficult to handle, while large blocks take up a lot of space.
3. Should the rods be marked? Marking tends to encourage one to one counting.
4. Are there cards or books suitable for pupils who are weak at reading?

Some teachers may decide that more than one type of apparatus will be most useful, but one basic type should be established in the early stages to avoid confusion. Once the purpose of structural apparatus is understood, the children can confidently be left to discover the type they find most useful. Some directed practical activities given orally will help to establish the true meaning of the most common arithmetic operator. For instance, using rods the following methods could be used:

1. *Addition.* Place the rods end to end. Measure with a ten rod. How many tens? How many units?
2. *Equality.* Take a ten rod. Place two rods end to end beneath it to make the same length.
3. *Multiplication.* Take 3 equal rods. Measure with a ten rod. How many tens? How many units?
4. *Subtraction.* Take a ten rod. Find 2 rods equal to ten. Take one away. What is left?
5. *Difference.* *(a)* Take one rod. Put a different rod underneath it. What do you need to make them equal? *(b)* Take 2 rods. Place them end to end. Take 1 rod smaller than the 2 put together. Find what rods you need to make up the difference.
6. *Fractions.* *(a)* Take a 6 rod. Find 2 equal rods to make 6. We say 3 is half of 6. The half can be written as ½. The 1 stands for the whole length, the — stands for cut, split or shared, and the 2 shows how many equal rods.

   (b) Take an 8 rod. Find 4 equal rods to make 8. We say 2 is a quarter of 8. A quarter is written ¼. 1 for the whole length, the — showing it is cut, shared or split and the 4 which shows how many equal pieces (rods). What is a half of 8?

A well-graded series of exercises given practice in writing the number symbols and operation signs will be required. In making a choice of books to be used it is important to take the low reading age of the children into account so that one is not faced with a situation where the arithmetical difficulties have been minimised but the language problem aggravated.

Individual Work

It will soon become apparent that although we have commenced an arithmetic programme which allows each child to explore the world of number, there will be those who have specific difficulties and need extra help or practice. Here is a challenge to the teacher's ingenuity in providing individual activities and exercises which will capture the child's interest. The very fact that the teacher is supplying a special piece of work is often sufficient motivation in itself if the work is at the right level. Here is a description of one of the techniques used by the writer.

(*a*) On quarto-sized paper write out the exercise in pencil leaving space for the pupil's name at the top. Have definite spaces or empty squares for the answers and use the minimum of simple language, the idea being an exercise the pupil can do on his own.

(*b*) Heat-copy using any one of the many types of machine available to give a spirit stencil.

(*c*) Run off a number of copies and file in boxes or cabinet.

(*d*) File the 'master' copy.

The heat-copying stage is useful because it enables the teacher to keep a master-copy and build up a file on each section of the curriculum. Without this system the teacher would be unlikely to have the time to prepare enough particular exercises, or would perhaps feel inhibited about changing a particular exercise because of the work involved in preparing an individual work-card. The great speed with which a copy can be prepared means the teacher can provide exactly what is needed rapidly, give the pupil a sheet for homework, and replace a sheet which is lost or spoilt easily. One advantage over the traditional work-card is that the pupil has only to write the answers on the question sheet in the spaces provided. This considerably increases the quantity of actual arithmetic done compared with a system requiring sums to be copied.

Group Activities

The teacher of a class of less-endowed children will probably find that many of them will also have symptoms of maladjustment and immaturity. They tend to be self-centred and find difficulty in working with others as part of a team. Group work can help to develop self-discipline and good social habits, while providing opportunities for language development and concept growth. The best activities are those that arise out of the normal day's activities. It may be a birthday which prompts an activity connected with calendars, or the football results which begin a study of league tables. A boy may bring in an old gramophone, or a bicycle wheel, both of which can be used as a source of multiple mathematical activities. The teacher should also have a stock of stimulating material which can be brought out piece by piece at suitable intervals. Junior school teachers are well aware of the value of such mathematical project methods, but the teacher of a class of slow learners will need to be ready to give more direction in order to get a new project under way. When recording results, the children should be encouraged to try various methods of communicating their findings, using blocks or matchboxes to make graphs, cut-out paper, drawings, pictograms and models. The transition from the concrete to the abstract has to be patiently encouraged. The boy who is finding how much milk five cows have given may need to have five model cows and the model churns before reaching the abstraction of a set of figures. For very backward pupils R. H. Nicholls' experiments in programming Piaget-type activities would be worth studying by the teacher.

Activity lessons can be planned in three ways.

1. *Directed Activities*
   - *(a)* Teacher chooses activity.
   - *(b)* Demonstration and discussion.
   - *(c)* Teacher isolates particular concepts involved and teaches the vocabulary needed to describe them.

(d) Oral questioning with simple numbers involved.
(e) Cyclostyled exercise.

2. *Partially-directed Activity*
(a) Pupil or teacher promotes the activity.
(b) Teacher suggests approach.
(c) Discussion of material and apparatus needed.
(d) Teacher assists in recording results.

3. *Pupil-directed Activity*
(a) Pupil chooses own activity with teacher's approval.
(b) Organises own material and apparatus.
(c) Records own results.

Number: From the surveys carried out by Wilson, Moore and Thompson, it is clear that, apart from specialist occupations, adults use number very little. House, bus and telephone numbers have to be read and understood in number from only. The sequence of number is needed when using rulers, tape measures, mileometres, as well as finding a particular house in a street. Accurate counting should be encouraged for checking quantities of goods, newspapers sold and as an aid to the shopkeepers' method of giving change. Multiplication is best begun as repeated addition with tables or ready reckoners as aids. The social use of fractions is limited and not common outside of halves and quarters. Boy may need to identify fractions giving sizes of bits and spanners but will not need the four rules of fractions. Much of the drill formerly associated with the learning of number after the initial concepts have been established using structural apparatus can also be carried out using decimal currency.

Hints on Teaching Number

1. Encourage an attitude of equity by asking questions, *e.g.* Does it matter which number comes first in that sum (addition/subtraction)? In number bonds, when one number gets bigger, does the other one always get smaller?

2. When giving number exercises plan them so that the children have to discover something about the answers. *e.g.*, what do you notice?

(a)	1 + 1	=	1 + 2	=	1 + 3	=	1 + 4	= ....
(b)	0 + 0	=	1 + 1	=	2 + 2	=	3 + 3	= ....
(c)	2 − 1	=	3 − 1	=	4 − 1	=	5 − 1	= ....
(d)	3 + 5	=	5 + 3	=	3 + 6	=	6 − 3	= ....

(e)	10 + 1 = 11	*(f)*	10 + 1 =	*(g)*	10	10	10
	9 + 2 =		10 + 11 =		+ 11	+ 21	+ 31
	8 + 3 =		10 + 21 =		—	—	—
	7 + 4 =		10 + 31 =		—	—	—
	6 + ? = 11		10 + 41 =				
	5 + 6 =		10 + 51 =				

The last exercise often shows a lack of understanding of place value. Much of this is due to the confusion caused by the same symbol having different meanings. Some children are helped by writing the previous exercise in two ways :

	1 ten + 0	10	1 ten +0	+ 10	1 ten + 0	10
add	1 ten + 1	+11	2 tens +1	+ 21	3 tens + 1	+31

A few lessons showing the use of an abacus will help to make the system of place values clear. A diagrammatic form of the abacus can be used in remedial exercises.

(a) Write the number

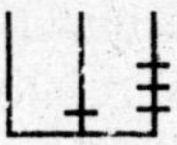 Add 10  Add 20 

_____ _____ _____

(b) Which rod shows the tens? Add a ten bead. Write the new answer.

Certain games are useful in helping children to grasp place value. The teacher can produce a score board divided into hundreds, tens and units in several ways.

(i) 3 compartments each holding only ten blocks. As the right-hand compartment is filled, one block is put into the middle compartment and the right-hand compartment is emptied.

(ii) Use the beads to show the score on a vertical abacus. Also useful is the board-type abacus using coloured tablets of L.G. Sealey which also parallels in concrete form the written layout of addition.

(iii) Simplified Billiards Scoring Frame with units at the top and tens along the bottom.

(iv) Counting Machines: a large variety of these are available. Also bring the children's attention to the counting mechanisms on for example tape recorders, cyclometers.

(v) Games. Some may need modifying *i.e.* Bagatelle, by reducing numbers.

Subtraction: This entails separating a small group from a larger group. The difference may be visual or symbolised by counting and recording. The easiest method for slow learners is by counting on. This has to be taught as some children trying to find how many are needed to make 7 into 12 will start 1 every time. When transferred to money the technique is known as the Italian or shopkeeper's method.

Money: The most essential part of the mathematics scheme is money. The elementary stages which may need re-teaching to slower older children are briefly:

(a) Coin recognition.

(b) Coins to symbols/symbols to coins.

(c) Addition, starting with lower value coins.

(d) Complementary addition to give change.

(e) Adding larger amounts by grouping.

The relevance of money as a symbol of value in the buying of articles is difficult to teach. The worth of objects is such a wide question that it cannot be confined to the narrow boundaries of mathematics. In this sense it is best included as part of a social study course.

Shopping exercises using money give some reality to our arithmetic, especially with self-service, making sure the dummy cartons are the same weight as that shown on the label and the totals are checked on leaving. Most shops will provide posters showing prices of goods but the best way is to price the goods in the shops. Ideally the slower children can run a real shop selling crisps, biscuits or apples. In most schools, however, teacher will need to structure his money learning to give sufficient practice at each stage. Variations of simple shopping exercises would include 'Sales' catalogue ordering, paying fares, going out for a meal, simple budgeting and visiting the post office.

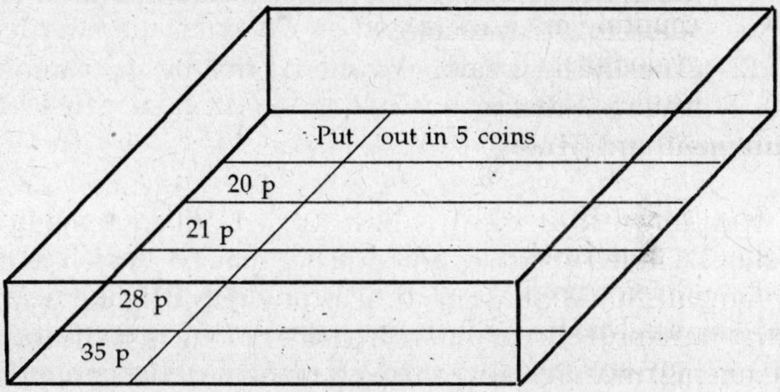

Hints on Teaching Money

1. Shoe-box lids, with exercises requiring the answers in coins, will stop the coins slipping on the floor. The exercise is written on the inside of the lid.

Variations

   (a) Put out a fixed amount using different numbers of coins.
   (b) Make up an amount to a fixed total.
   (c) Pay for stamps or tickets with coins.

2. Money dice, money dominoes and various money games give extra practice.
3. Cyclostyle bills for shopping.
4. Let children make own shopping cards from old mail-order catalogues.
5. Use bags from bank to collect coins for totalling.
6. Make up sets of wage packets. Letter each packet and mark on outside the coins that it should contain. This saves endless arguments about the total when some of the coins are on the floor. Have an answer slip for checking.

7. Either cyclostyle or buy simple ready reckoners.
8. Have a rota for collecting and checking dinner money.
9. Dramatise social situations involving money, *e.g.* the wrong change, making a choice, buying a ticket.
10. Make a survey of class savings, pocket money, starting wages.
11. Show films on shopping, insurance, banking, hire purchase to promote discussion. Film strips on similar subjects are available.
12. Consult the handbooks offered free by the National Savings Scheme.

Measurement and Time

Most work on measurement is best carried out in the school workshops. Graded exercises and practice may be needed in the classroom but should be as practical as possible. Brighter pupils can carry out simple surveying with chains or long tape measures to find missing measurements on diagrams of the school premises. Scale drawing and map work are possible if carefully planned to minimise possible complications. The measurement of area is most easily taught using plastic grids, and grids can also be used for simple work in coordinates. Most classes enjoy an exercise using a cyclostyled grid to find the 'treasure'. This also brings in some useful work on direction which leads to simple angles using a compass and circular protractors. If the teacher is aware of the limitations of his class in computation many interesting topics can be explored without great difficulty.

The true concept of time is only gained by experience and is very undeveloped even at the secondary stage. Ask a class to guess when a minute has passed and the estimate will be wildly out, but this fact can be used advantageously in discussing ways of telling the time, from sand egg-timers and candles to the newly-acquired wristwatch. The smaller intervals of time are easiest to learn. It is relatively easy to count seconds, but difficult to estimate hours. A clock on the classroom wall is essential but so are calendars. If we start with telling the time it is interesting to notice how small a part the numbers play when we look at a clock, and in fact many clocks now leave out the numbers. Check the wristwatches in the classroom, or look at the television clock. Clock time is given in three ways, verbally, as when we say twenty to four, and written, either as 3.40 p.m. or 15.40. The two most important are the verbal statement and the Continental written method. For the poor readers the verbal statement need never be written in full using words. A shorter way is to have a clock face marked with hours in one colour, minutes in another (see diagram). The hour hand should be the colour of the hour number, the minute hand coloured the same as the minute numbers. When the pointer is on the right the number is *past* the hour—when on the left it is *to* the hour. It is written as 25 past 3, ¼ past 4, 10 to 5—in fact as it is said.

Then show the change to putting hours first, then the minutes and dropping the half and quarter past. 3. 25, 4.15. Then comes the problem of minutes to the hour, which has to be changed to minutes past. Here the minutes market on the edge of the clock faces will help. 10 to 5 becomes 4.50.

Changing the dial to a 24-hour clock offers no further difficulties in writing down except the use of the nought as a space filler, *e.g.*, 20.05 but it will take much time to get people to accustom themselves to converting 9 p.m. to 21.00 and many of our slow learners will find this difficult.

The most important work is in the first stage, and exercises should show a clock faces with question on what happens at the time shown, including some on the school timetable.

Children will generally find the use of second and minute timers much easier than telling the time and these should be used in the initial stages. Girls can make up cooking charts and boys time athletic activities while both can time various experiments in the classroom or radio and TV programmes.

We also need to record the days, months and years using the calender, and keeping a record of birthdays, holidays, national and local events. All work written in school should be dated as part of this training and topics on time periodically give. Postmarks can be collected and show the time taken for delivery; lighting-up times and the hours of daylight can be graphed. Some training will be needed in calculating ages and writing dates of birth. Many boys, especially in towns and cities, will be vague about the seasons. For journeys we shall have to consider the relationship between time and distance and for those about to leave school we must study time and earnings.

The Last Year: The advantages of studying mathematics as part of a social study scheme are particularly obvious for pupils in the last year at school where they can become a natural part of many activities. Some knowledge of formal processes is essential, but only as means of solving problems faced in everyday situations. The emphasis should be on making the situation realistic enough to motivate the pupil into finding a solution. This may also be linked with the responsibility for certain jobs involving numbers.

(a) Checking attendances.
(b) Keeping scores for games and checking equipment.
(c) Keeping a mileage record and calculating cost of running a school bus.
(d) Collecting house points and keeping a graph.
(e) Stock taking.

In addition to such practical activities in school, pupils should be given projects which take them outside the school and involve them in experiences requiring numerical activities. Such visits are most useful educationally if done individually or in pairs.

(a) Buying stamps and posting letters.
(b) Buying a postal order.
(c) Accompanying secretary to bank money.
(d) Using a public telephone.

As the visits are extended, pupils will find a need for local maps and guides. The use of maps will lead to a need to understand grids, scales and compass bearings which can easily develop into exercises in navigation and planning road journeys including distance, time and cost problems

School leavers should be trained in social service and, apart from shopping, other arithmetical activities may include laying a new lawn, buying seeds and plants, planning a tea-party for old people, and running a sale.

Many activities will involve pupils in problems which require simplification. When a method has been established by discussion using simple number the calculation of a total involving larger sums of money should proceed by realistic methods emphasising the value of estimation.

Ideally, methods and examples in mathematics would be related to the occupations likely to be followed by the unacademic pupils. However, little valid research has gone into making a detailed study of the mathematics required for everyday occupations. Teachers tend to set exercises based on imagination rather than fact. Anyone watching a carpenter at work on a building site quickly notices how little a ruler is used. A plumber can put in a complete central heating system without a single measurement, except by eye. The gardener spaces out his plants with a handy length of stick, not a tape measure.

The greatest use of mathematics will be in reckoning money. The casual worker may be earning three or four pounds a day shortly after leaving school and yet have little idea of the value of his money. Training in simple budgeting should be started early, with discussions on the rewards of saving and the dangers of over-spending and hire purchase. Classroom saving schemes for visits and outings may help to develop good habits, and records of individual savings can be recorded pictorially.

Games

Initially many pupils will play games without scoring, unable to face the difficulties of calculation. The teacher should modify such games by simpler methods of scoring, gradually increasing the numbers involved. Bagatelle boards or pin tables are always popular. Have a simple version with numbers upto 20, then introduce another with numbers to 50. Attach a small slate and chalk for scoring, or have a simple abacus or adding machine.

Dice games can be useful. A board divided into two parts, marked off in squares, and a cube market with numbers and plus or minus signs is very popular. If the dice shows +2, then 2 counters go on to the squares, while –2 would mean taking 2 counters off. Variations can be introduced and a similar game can be made using decimal currency.

Shove-ha' penny is a game which can involve scoring, and a small skittle board is another test of skill which brings in counting. Billiards or snooker are valuable, especially if the proper scoring board is used. Darts, hoop-la, table tennis, cards including games like summit, all help to exercise pupils in computation as well as developing skill in popular recreations.

References

P. Bell, *Basic Teaching for Slow Learners*, Muller Educational Ltd., 1970.

E. Brideoake and I. D. Groves, *Arithmetic in Action*, University of London Press, 1939.

L. N. A. Bunt, *The Development of the Ideas of Number and Quantity According to Piaget*, Wolters, Groningen, Djakarta, 1939.

W.E. Chambers, *I Do, and I Understand*, Nuffield Maths Project, 1961.

E.M. Churchill, *Counting and Measuring*, Routledge and Kegan Paul, 1961.

L.W. Downes and D. Paling, *Teaching of Arithmetic in Primary Schools*, Oxford University Press, 1958.

D.H. Gale, *The Teaching of Number*, Hulton Press, 1963.

D.H. Gale, *Number Language*, Hulton Press, 1964.

E. Lawrence, *Some Aspects of Piaget's Work*, National Froebel Foundation, 1955.

CHAPTER 8

Learning Skills in Handicapped

Delayed Reaction

The present chapter derives its chief significance from the fact that the child tested did not possess vocal language and probably not gesture language either.

In the work with the delayed reaction on children previously published, five subjects were used: M., 8 years, Hd., L., and H., each 6 years, and F., 2 years. All these children possessed vocal language. M. received 38 trials on delays; Hd., 46 trials; H., 15 trials; L., 41 trials. All of them succeeded with delays as great as 25 minutes. There was some indication that the children first encountered particular difficulty in the intervals from 4-6 secs. The child F. received 507 trials on delays. Her maximal delay was 50 secs. The periods of greatest difficulty were at 5 secs., 7 secs., 10 secs., 15 secs., 30 secs., and 40 secs. Although F. was given 45 trials on the one-minute delay and failed, it is possible that more prolonged training would have enabled her to master the interval.

When the present tests were begun, the writer hoped to secure subjects who would fill in the great gap between the child F. and the older children. Success has not attended these efforts mainly because of a lack of convenient material. One three-year-old child was tested, but the data are of so little value that they will not be presented. The second and fundamental purpose of this study was, however, to study the delayed reaction in a child too young to possess vocal language. This is of particular importance because of Watson's insistence that the delayed reaction, if solved by internal factors other than orientation, must be solved by vocal language.

The Subject Tested

The subject of these tests was the writer's daughter, Thayer, thirteen to sixteen months of age from first to last of the experimentation. She was a normal, healthy child physically—a little slow perhaps on the behaviour side, due to the lack of the constant attention that many children receive. She learned to walk alone rather suddenly at about 15 months; and by 16 months, she could indicate with a little certainty her eyes, ears, nose and mouth. When 13 months old, she could 'throw a kiss' and wave 'bye-bye.' Even before this, as early as the tenth month, she swayed and waved her arms to music. These observations are presented as a sample of her best accomplishments. She had no vocal language. She made many sounds, some of which were in response to definite stimuli; but in no case did she use the sounds spontaneously and in no case did she use them as symbols. Her equipment was not large in the first place, and what there was purely of stimulus-response nature. During the period covered by the experimentation, the following vocal behaviour was present: 'Dăddy' she said whenever a distant door was heard and I was away, or when she heard me coming up the steps. 'Whĭtte' came in response to the striking of the clock or the ringing of the door bell. She could say 'bōōb-bōōb' for the dog; 'dăy-dăy' for the duck; 'm-m-m' for the cow'; a funny noise for the donkey; and 'y-gōb, y-gōb' for the turkey. These were in response to the specific questions, "What does the dog say?" etc. Some of these she got mixed up and later forgot all but the duck, the turkey, and the cow. In addition to these vocal responses there occurred only the more conventional baby noises.

One gesture might possible be termed language, *viz.*, raising her arms to be taken up. It is impossible to say, however, that this was not in response to present stimuli. It is also impossible to say with any certainty whether or not the child used a vocal cry specifically to " to attract attention" to her needs. I have no evidence to indicate that such was the case. Experimentation was purposely stopped before the first signs of language (in the conventional sense) appeared.

Apparatus and Method

The apparatus used in this experiments consists of three boxes placed upon a stand whose top is 6 inches above the floor. Each box is approximately 3 inches deep, 4 inches wide, and 5 inches long. Each is covered by a hinged top. The apparatus was wired for electric lights, but these were never used. Another type of apparatus more nearly approximating that used with children in the previous work was constructed. It, however, proved unsuited to Thayer and was used only with the three-year-old child.

The only features necessary to secure in devising an apparatus for the delayed reaction are these:

1. It must be adapted to the size of the subject and to its mode of response—walking, reaching, swimming or flying,
2. It must provide a means for presenting a stimulus in one of several places,
3. These stimulus positions must be equally accessible to the response, and
4. The stimulus and the method employed should be such as to present no differential cause to the subject during the intervals of delay.

These requirements, although rigid, are simple and can be met for practically all organisms. I am therefore unable to agree with Professor Yerkes when he says that the multiple choice method of studying ideational behaviour is superior to all others in:

1. Applicability to standardisation;
2. Susceptibility to standardisation;
3. Quantitative nature of results; and
4. Intelligibility of data acquired.

Nor can I acquiesce in the claim that "It is already obvious that the method enables us to compare, as has never before been possible, the response to certain standard situations, of human and infra-human, normal and abnormal, mature and immature subjects." Both the multiple choice and the delayed reaction methods are valuable for the study of human and animal behaviour; but they are applicable, I think to very different problems.

In the experiments reported in this chapter, the following method was used. Thayer sat in front of the apparatus and the stimulus object was placed in her hand. A great variety of things were used for stimuli: dolls, keys, rattles, shoe-buttoners, small books, etc. Every effort was made to keep up the child's interest. Occasionally two different stimulus objects were used in the course of the day's work. Such methods are necessary, if a child of this age is even to approximate to the vigour with which a hungry animal attacks its problem. The stimulus object was taken away from the child almost as soon as she received it and was placed in one of the boxes. The lid of the box was left open and Thayer was pushed over (or permitted to lean over) and made to look into the box. Often she tried to reach in and get the stimulus; but in every case, her hand was withdrawn and she was raised back to an upright position. The lid of the box was now closed. Save for a few instances to be mentioned in due time, the subject was distracted during the interval of delay. Distraction took either one of several forms:

1. I might place my hands over her eyes and rock her body back and forth from right to left.
2. She might be stood up, turned around with her back to the apparatus, kept there awhile and then put down.
3. I might cause her to turn her head by speaking to her.

She would remain in this position and imitate animals for me (as described above under vocal habits) as long as anv delays here used required. About 2 secs. before the end of the delay period, her body was straightened around and she sat facing the middle box, *b*, entirely free from contact with me. (She almost never looked back at me; and when she did, she paid no further attention to the problem. I never spoke to her during the delay. These facts together with the child's inability to reach delays of a minute or more, indicate that she was not deriving cues from the experimenter.) Thayer was now left to her own devices until she opened the box containing the stimulus object. In all but a few cases, she began to hunt for the stimulus as soon as she was straightened around. Time was taken with an ordinary watch and was counted from the moment the box lid was closed until the subject made some movement toward one of the boxes. In the records particular attention was given to the orientation at the time of response and to the behaviour during the delay. A reaction was counted wrong if the child opened any box save that containing the stimulus.

Experimental Results

In this experiment there was no period of learning the association between the stimulus object and the three boxes. Seeking for objects that had disappeared was already a part of the subject's behaviour equipment. I noted as early as her eleventh month that if I showed her a toy and then hid it behind something, she would immediately reach or creep toward the spot. I have no doubt, however, that this type of reaction occurred earlier. The present test was more example than this in that the toy might be in either one of *three* different places.

I quote the following from my diary records indicating the results at the very beginning of the work. "Data, 10-23-15. Trial 1. Toys put in middle box and door shut. (All this done by Thayer on her own initiative.) I now put my hands over her eyes and shook her head and whole body playfully but thoroughly. No orientation of upper part of body retained. 13 secs. delay from time she straightened up after closing box until she reached toward *b*. She reacted correctly, straight to middle box."

"Trial 2. Toy put in right box, *a*. 12 secs. delay with distraction above. Reacted correctly."

"Trial 3. Same as no. 2, 13 secs. delay. O.K."

"Trial 4. Thayer preferred right or middle box. I had her put toys in left one, *c*. Distraction by standing her up and turning her to me. 17 secs. O.K."

"Trial 5. Middle box used. Baby tired of test. 14 secs. Distracted as in first trial. Reaction wrong."

In these tests made on the first day, Thayer missed one of five or 20 per cent. The delay ranged from 12-17 secs. Distraction was always used. The same orientation at the moment of release was held for all, *viz.*, orientation to *b*. These long delays were very startling and held out a promise of very rapid development through training. This was the last of October. A longer stage of delay was not successfully reached and consistently maintained until after Christmas. This fact is shown in Table 8.1

Table 8.1

Delay in secs.	*Correct trs.*	*Wrong trs.*	*Per cent correct*
3	3	0	100
4	1	0	100
5	6	0	100
6	3	0	100
7	2	2	50
8	4	2	66
9	4	1	80
10	11	4	73
11	6	2	75
12	6	3	66
13	5	0	100
14	6	8	42
15	13	11	54
16	5	5	50
17	4	3	57
18	2	1	66
19	1	1	50
20	9	15	37
21	1	5	16
22	2	3	40
23	1	0	100
24	2	3	40
25	0	3	0
26	1	1	50
30	3	5	37
35	2	0	100

This table shows the size of the delays and the number of correct and incorrect reactions made. All trials given the subject through December 2 are included. The statement is not chronological. The reason the intervals of delay increase so gradually is that within a few seconds variation, Thayer herself determined when she would begin the reaction. All I could do was to place her facing the apparatus and await results. Table 8.2 groups the delays into five classes which may be called the 5 secs., 10 secs., 15 secs., 20 secs. and 25 secs. intervals. The 10 secs. interval may be regarded as mastered, but no higher intervals. (This is understated, as will be indicated).

Table 8.2

Delays	*Per cent correct*
3-7 secs.	88
8-12 secs.	72
13-17 secs.	55
18-22 secs.	37
32-35 secs.	44

Table 8.3 gives data gathered from January 2 through January 10. An interval of one month had elapsed during which no tests were made. A comparison of Tables 8.2 and 8.3 indicates a marked gain in ability to deal with the 15 secs. and 20 secs. intervals. In Table 8.3 the 15 secs. interval can be regarded as mastered and the 20 secs. interval as practically perfected.

Table 8.3

Delay in secs.	*Right*	*Wrong*	*Per cent right*
5	4	0	
6	0	1	77
7	3	1	
8	2	0	
9	1	0	
10	10	3	82
12	2	0	
15	25	8	75
20	24	10	70
25	2	2	50

The tables just given are valuable in showing just what the child actually did in the work *as a whole*. Her achievements are much obscured, however, by such a presentation, inasmuch as poor incentives and position factors frequently dragged her total percentages down. Here, *e.g.*, is the diary record for the ten tests made November 12. (Data included in Table 8.1) The delays were all above 20 secs., and 7 trials of 10 were successful. Where the word "distracted' is used, Thayer's eyes were covered and her body was shaken back and forth; or she was induced to look up at the ceiling and listen to me count while I waved her arms about. The letters in the last column indicate to which box the reactions were made. In every case the subject was oriented, body and face, to *b* at the moment of reaction. This day's record is better than any that preceded it. Two weeks previously, she had succeeded with intervals between 11 and 19 secs. But during those two weeks that followed, she was largely the victim of position habits. The day following the above diary record, she again fell back into position habits. I kept holding pretty well to 15 and 20 secs. delays with an occasional one at 30 secs. The task was too difficult, however, and she shifted from one position habit to another.

Table 8.4

Box with toy	*Delay*		*Behaviour*
a	20 secs.	distracted	*a*
a	22 "	"	*bca*
c	21 "	"	*abc*
c	20 "	"	*c*
b	35 "	"	*b**
a	22 "	Stood her up	*a*
c	26 "	distracted	*c*
b	20 "	"	*b*
c	22 "	"	*c*
c	24 "	Stood her up	*ac*

* Very slow and 'careful.'

Work was discontinued for a month. By the end of this time, the following changes had occurred in the child:

1. Old position habits were temporarily lost;
2. new interest was taken in the problem;
3. greatly increased control of her own body appeared—shown mostly in walking and balancing; and
4. a stronger aversion to being held during distractions had developed.

Table 8.3 summarises the results for this period. It also understates the subject's behaviour. On January 5, she made the entire day—9 trials—at 15 secs. without error and with no correlation between orientation and direction of response. She now fell into a position habit, but recovered and made 20 secs. delay correctly 5 times in succession, again with no dependence upon orientation.

Thayer's best delays may be recorded as 20-24 secs. The child F. used in the earlier work reached a delay of 50 secs. F.'s record would probably have been higher had she been tested with a method similar to the one here employed, *i.e.*, a method where the satisfaction is derived from the stimulus object and not from an associated food supply. The gap between Thayer and F. would undoubtedly be bridged in a gradual manner by a continuous increase in periods of delay. Greatest interest now centers on children of less than one year of age. How early ontogenetically does this ability to react independently of orientation appear?

It remains to comment upon the position habits and errors that appeared. The frequency with which these stereotyped forms of response interfered with the work and *the fact that the child if permitted would watch the box containing the toy during the interval of delay,* indicate the great importance of kinaesthesis in the response. Position habits occurred with each of the three boxes so that during a particular position habit period Thayer always chose a particular box first. I made no tests where the choice lay between two boxes as opposed to three. This is limited both by the speed with which a baby grows and even more by the necessity of staying within the limits of the child's interest and patience. Table 8.5 analyses all incorrect responses and gives the relative number of times the subject followed the different possible orders. Thus when an error was made, 17 times Thayer first opened *c*, then *b* and then *a*. The table shows that three times more errors were made beginning with box *c* than with any of the others. When the subject opened *c* first, she opened *b* next 45 times out of 66, or 68 per cent of the time. When she opened *a* first, she chose *b* next 15 times out of 20, or 75 per cent of the time. When *b* was opened first, *a* was chosen next 16 times out of 26, or 61 per cent of the time. In other words, when the reaction began at the end of the apparatus the tendency was to take the

Table 8.5

					Total reactions made
Order ~~of~~ response	cba	cab	ca	cb	
No. made	17	13	8	28	66
Order of response	abc	acb	ac	ab	
No. made	6	3	2	11	22
Order of response	bac	bca	bc	ba	
No. made	7	3	7	9	26

boxes in order until the solution was reached. Only six times in all did the subject go to the same box twice in the same trial. These cases are distributed throughout the entire period of experimentation. The following is a record of the order of the boxes chosen :

cccab
bcba
cacb
cacb
bcba
cacacab

Of the 114 errors recorded in Table 8.5, 32 (28 %) occurred when the box containing the toy on the last previous trial was re-selected. Inasmuch, however, as such a mode of response often led to success the percentage is very low. This form of behaviour as well as that of the six instances above given is apparently far less current in the present subject than in Hamilton's dog. The later study made by Hamilton reports the case of a child 26 months old. Out of 38 trials, 60.53 per cent (34.21 plus 26.32) of the reactions involved the type of behaviour given just above as occurring but 6 times during the present work, 264 trials. Since Thayer missed 120 trials (66 plus 22 plus 26 plus 6), her percentage is 5. This extreme difference in behaviour is undoubtedly due to one or both of the following causes: (1) the guiding influence of the absent stimulus in the delayed reaction tests: and (2) the fact that only three boxes were used here as opposed to Hamilton's four. It would be very interesting to determine whether a variation in the number of boxes would result in a corresponding variation in "reaction tendencies". If this were true, the possibility of phyletic correlations would be pushed still farther back than appears in Hamilton's work.

It will be valuable to put beside this work, similar data gathered on rats and raccoons in 1910-1912. The records here given are representative and include only tests made with three boxes on periods of delay. The following indicates the maximal delays attained by the animals whose records are used in this chapter:

Rat No. 9, maximal	delay	10	secs
Rat no. 2,	"	"	1	sec
Dog Blackie,	"	"	5	mins.
Raccoon Bob.	"	"	30-35	secs.

Table 8.6 summarises the errors made by these four animals. It includes for comparative purpose the data for Thayer. The raccoon's records include delays from 1 sec. through 20 secs.; those for the dog, from 1 sec. through 7 secs.; those for rat No. 9, from the third stage of delay (turning light off just as animal was released) through 7 secs.; and those for rat No. 2, from the third stage of delay through 1 sec. I have included the data represented by 'per cent of *B* to *C*' because Hamilton's percentages are based only on those reactions that included all the boxes of his apparatus. The column '3 place errors' includes the trials that involved a testing by the animal of each of the three boxes. By 'persistent errors,' I mean all errors that involve trying any one box more than once each trial. These were all 3 place errors. This column corresponds to reactions belonging to Hamilton's types *D* and *E*.

The only one of Hamilton's human subjects whose percentage in *D* plus *E* rose above 6.45 per cent was a 26-month-old child whose grade was 60.53 per cent. Of the animals below man, the lowest grade (best record) was 22.58 per cent made by a dog. Hamilton's results and my own here presented indicate a marked difference between man and other animals in reactive tendencies, *i.e.*, in forms of kinaesthetic habits. (There is, I think, no clear evidence as yet that the tendencies are instinctive.) Whether this is caused by phyletic factors, or by experimental and environmental conditions is a matter undecided. My infra-human animals are essentially on a par. And so I think are Hamilton's in that practically all of them made their highest percentages in what I here term "persistent errors". (His curves would be quite different, naturally, if *D* and *E* were combined and if *B* and *C* were combined.) Much work is undoubtedly needed to determine how minute a classification of reaction tendencies can be and still be significant for animal ability.

Table 8.6

Animal	*No. of trs.*	*Total no. of errors A*	*3 Place errors B*	*Persistent errors C*	*Per cent of A to C*	*Per cent of B to C*
Thayer	264	120	54	6	5	11
Racoon, Bob	720	209	78	29	13	37
Dog, Blackie	570	127	75	25	19	33
Rat No. 9	565	144	42	13	9	30
Rat No. 2	345	152	69	47	32	60

Theoretical Considerations

There is very little in the way of interpretative comments that I can add to what has already been said in other papers.[1] The delayed reaction problem can be solved at least in two ways:[2] (1) by the maintenance of bodily orientation in whole or in part during the interval of delay or by the chance recovery of the proper orientation just at the moment of release; and (2) by the use of some intra-organic factor which is non-observable by the experimenter. In the first method, the animal always responds in accordance with orientation; in the second, he does not. The cue used in the second method may or may not be retained in the focus or neural activity during the delay. It is highly improbable that such retention occurs under conditions of distraction. What one has, then, is a system of processes or cues which 'stand for' certain differential responses as a result of association. These cues are susceptible to selective re-arousal and subsequent successful functioning in initiating responses. This is the condition which I have previously found in raccoons and in one child, F., 2½ years old. It is the condition here presented by Thayer, ages 13-16 months. This second method of solution which I am describing may be mediated by any type of intra-organic process which can be re-aroused without the presence of the external stimulus, toys as used in the present study. Inasmuch as kinaesthetic factors can be so aroused, and inasmuch as they have been demonstrated to have great importance not only in animal reactions in general but in the delayed reaction in particular (position habits and maintenance of orientation), it is most probable that the intra-organic factors are kinaesthetic in nature. (The genetic relations of sensation, image and imageless thought are discussed in 'The Delayed Reaction,' pages cited.) In certain cases this type of process has its locus in the vocal organs with frequent resulting audible sounds. This we term vocal language as it occurs in normal human adults and in children of a certain development. In other cases the observance of the sounds and their accompanying behaviour does not indicate that the organism uses either the sound or the parallel kinaesthetic as a substitute of the type above described. This is the situation in all animals that indulge in vocalisation. But this intra-organic kinaesthetic factor may arise elsewhere than from the throat. Some part of the general bodily musculature may be the origin. Here when the behaviour is overt, we speak of gesture language. When it is not overt, the delayed reaction method has proved serviceable in detecting it. Language is ideational in function. So also are the cues which function in many responses of raccoons, of children and possibly of dogs (Walton). The resulting conception of these cues is that they are kinaesthetic sensory ideas. This line of reasoning leads one to conclude that a true language non-vocal in character appears phylogenetically and ontogenetically prior to vocal language. Such language, although undoubtedly of great service to the individual in controlling his reactions, is of little social significance.

Stimulus Pretraining and Subsequent Performance

Several Investigators have reported studies of the delayed reaction in children (1, 2, 6, 10, 11, 12, 14), although much remains to be done in discovering the relevant experimental variable and in specifying the theoretical significance of the delayed reaction experiment itself. One of the factors that has been suggested by Hunter (10,11) and by Skalet (14) as influencing the correct performance of children in the delayed reaction experiment, as well as in determining the length of delay that can be tolerated by *S*s without interfering with the correctness of the performance, is the presence of symbolic or linguistic responses to represent the relevant stimulus features. Skalet reported that her child *S*s could tolerate longer delays with stimuli for which the *S*s had names (familiar animal forms) than for stimuli for which the *S*s did not have names (geometrical figures). She concluded that the children's abilities to represent the animal forms with symbolic responses in some way facilitated recall following delay.

Although the writer is unaware of published studies of the relationship between stimulus similarity and the correctness of the delayed reaction or the length of delay that can be tolerated by *S*, this variable undoubtedly relevant. In the extreme case, if identical stimuli were used, *S* would have no basis at all for a correct response following the delay. It is conceivable that the animal forms which Skalet used were less similar than the nonsense figures, and therefore that the better performance with the former is due to stimulus distinctiveness rather than to possession of names.

The present experiment is concerned with a more direct test than Skalet's of the hypothesis that the possession by children of names for the stimuli leads to more correct choice following a delay period. In the present design, half the *S*s are taught different names for two similar stimuli in a pretraining session, while the other half are given discriminative experience with the same stimuli but without learning names for them. All *S*s are then run in a delayed reaction situation involving these stimuli. Since older *S*s, even without pretraining, are more likely than younger *S*s to invent names or other descriptive phrases for the stimuli, the prior learning of names should be relatively more effective for younger *S*s than for older *S*s. Accordingly, each experimental group consisted of a younger and an older subgroup in order to study the interaction between age and type of pretraining.

Method

Apparatus : The primary apparatus consisted of a round wooden disc, 18 in. in diameter, mounted on the shaft of an electric motor. Fastened to the top surface of the disc, one opposite the other, were two identical wooden boxes, 4 in. on each side, with hinged covers. The hinges were placed on the outside of the boxes on the sides toward the center of the disc. The tops of the boxes were covered with a transparent acetate, under which the stimuli could be placed, and a wad of white cotton was put in the bottom of each box to prevent the rattling of the rewards placed in the boxes. A normally open push-bottom microswitch was wired into the circuit of the motor so that the motor could be started or stopped by pressing or releasing the switch. A section of rubber garden hose was mounted on the outer rim of the disc in order to protect *S* from the rotating disc and to provide *E* with a smooth area to grasp in stopping the disc. The entire apparatus was covered with a heavy coat of flat black paint.

There were two stimuli, each consisting of a set of black-lined concentric circles placed on white backgrounds 4 in. square. One of the stimuli (S-7) has 7 concentric circles, the other (S-5) had only 5. The inner circle in each stimulus was 3/4 in. in diameter; the outer circle, 3 in. The remaining circles were spaced equidistant between the outer and inner circles. Thus, the two stimuli differed in the number and density of concentric circles. Two additional pairs of the stimuli, identical to those described above, were used in the pretraining session.

Experimental design: The experiment was conducted in four distinct phases, all given to each *S* on the same day. In the first phase, the pretraining stage, the stimuli were presented two at a time and *S*s in one group (Group N) were required to call S-5 by the name "five" and S-7 by the name "seven". The second group (Group D) was required to discriminate the stimuli by saying "same" when both stimuli were S-5 or S-7, and "different" when one stimulus was S-5 and the other S-7. In the second phase, *E* familiarised *S*s with the delayed reaction experiment by putting an orange stimulus on one box and a blue stimulus on the other, baiting one of the boxes with a toy coin, spinning the disc briefly, and then asking *S* to find the coin. In the third phase, the test problem, the concentric circles were used as stimuli on the boxes, one box was baited each time, the disc was rotated rapidly for 25 secs., and *S* was then asked to find the coin. Finally, in a check phase, concentric circles were removed from the boxes, one of the boxes was baited, the disc was briefly rotated, and *S* was asked to find the coin. This last step was taken in order to control for the sue of extraneous cues by *S*.

Subjects: The *S*s were 54 children from the Iowa Child Walfare Research Station preschool laboratories. They were divided into two age groups; the younger group of 26 *S*s ranging from 3 yr., 9 mo. to 4 yr., 9 mo.; the older group of 28, from 4 yr., 10 mo. to 5 yr., 6 mo. One-half of each age group was randomly assigned to Group N, the other half to Group D. Seven additional *S*s were eliminated from the experiment following failure to learn the pretraining task in the 72 trials allowed. Of these, 4 were in Group N and 3 were in Group D.

Most of the *S*s had previous experience in name-learning experiments and about 12 had previous experience in a delayed reaction experiment. In neither case, however, were the stimuli and the names of the present experiment used.

Procedure: The *S* was brought into the experimental room by a familiar *E*. The *E* layout two pairs of the concentric circle stimuli on a table before *S*. Group N *S*s were told that the name for S-5 was "five" and that the name for S-7 was "seven". The stimuli were then presented two at a time and *S* was informed that he could tell the difference between "seven" and "five" by the number of circles. The *S*s were not urged to count, although a few *S*s in both groups did count. Four different stimulus settings were used : in one, both stimuli were S-5; in a second, both were S-7; in a third, S-5 was on the left, S-7 was on the right; and in the fourth, S-7 was on the left, S-5 on the right. The stimuli were presented in a prearranged order such that in each successive block of four trials, each of the four settings appeared once. A trial was counted correct only if *S* named both stimuli correctly. Group D *S*s were treated like those of Group N except that they were not told the names of the stimuli and their task was structured for them as saying "same" when both stimuli were S-5 or S-7, and "different" when one stimulus was S-5 and the other S-7. The stimuli were presented in the same order for Group D as for Group N. The *S*s in both groups were continued in the first phase until they made correct responses on 12 consecutive trials, or until 72 trials had been given. In the latter case they were eliminated from the experiment.

In the familiarisation phase, *S* was taken to apparatus described above. A 4-in. square piece of orange construction paper was placed on top of one of the two boxes, and a similar piece of blue paper was placed on the other. While *S* watched, *E* dropped a toy coin onto the wad of cotton in the bottom of one of the boxes and closed the lid. The *E* then asked *S* which box contained the coin. If *S* responded correctly, E immediately spun the disc rapidly and stopped it. The time required to spin and stop the disc was ordinarily about 1 sec. When the disc was stopped, *S* was asked to find the coin. This procedure was repeated with the orange and blue stimuli, in an irregular alteration, until *S* had made three consecutive correct responses.

Before beginning the test problem, *S* was told that he would now have an opportunity to win more toy coins, and that when he had won enough he would be able to buy a toy with them. The orange and blue stimuli were replaced with the concentric circles. Six trials were given to each *S* with the coin being placed in one of the two boxes in the order : S-5, S-7, S-7, S-5, S-7, and S-5. The *E* would bait the appropriate box for that trial and would then ask *S* to point to the baited box in order to assure that he had observed the baiting. Group N *S*s were also asked to name the baited box. When *S* had responded correctly, *E* immediately spun the disc and kept in spinning for 25 secs. at a speed that made it impossible for *S* to follow the baited box visually. At the end of the 25-secs. period, *E* immediately stopped the disc and asked *S* to find the coin. The between-trial interval averaged approximately 1 min.

The check problem was given in order to determine whether or not S's delayed reaction was based on extraneous cues. The discriminal stimuli were removed from the boxes and *S* was given 6 trials with a delay of about 1 sec. as in the second phase. The *S*s' choice were recorded on prepared sheets throughout the delayed reaction phases of the experiment. The *S*s' verbalisations regarding the stimuli were recorded throughout the experiment.

Results

retraining : The number of trials to the criterion of 12 consecutive correct responses was determined for each *S*. The means and *SD*s of these are presented in Table 8.7. It is apparent that both the younger and older *S*s of Group D reached the criterion in fewer trials than did those of Group N. Despite sizeable difference in the means, a treatment by levels analysis of variance failed to show significant differences in the main effects for age or pretraining or in their interaction for either the raw data or a square-root transformation of the raw data ($P>.10$). With some caution, it may be assumed that the two pretraining groups had approximately equal experience with the stimuli during the pretraining task. In any event, all *S*s had demonstrated discrimination between the stimuli at the same high response criterion.[3]

Only nine incorrect responses were made during the familiarisation phase, and so *S* made more than two incorrect choices prior to reaching the criterion of three consecutive correct responses.

Table 8.7
Means and *SD*s in the Pretraining, the Test Phase, and the Check for Extraneous Cues

Group	*N*	*Pretraining Phase: Trials to criterion*		*Text phase: Correct Choices*		*Extraneous Cue Check: Correct Choices*	
		Mean	*SD*	*Mean*	*SD*	*Mean*	*SD*
D-Young	13	20.8	21.2	2.92	1.40	2.85	1.28
D-Old	14	14.8	16.7	5.00	0.96	3.36	1.34
N-Young	13	25.7	17.8	4.77	1.01	3.23	1.17
N-Old	14	25.8	20.1	5.14	1.10	2.79	1.26

Test for extraneous cues : The mean number of correct choices in the six-trial check for extraneous cues is presented in Table 8.7 for each group. A mean of 3.0 is expected on the basis of chance alone. It is apparent that none of the four groups differs markedly from the expected mean and this observation is borne out statistically in a treatment-by-levels analysis of variance. None of the main or simple effects is significant at less than the 10 per cent level. Thus, it seems safe to assume that *S*s were unable to respond correctly, even with short delay, without the use of the discriminal cues on which they had received pretraining.

Test phase : Table 8.7 gives the means and *SD*s of the number of correct responses for the four groups during the critical test phase of the experiment. From this table, it is apparent that Group N, on the average, performs better than Group D; that the older *S*s perform better than the younger *S*s; and that the younger *S*s in Group D perform considerably worse than *S*s in any other subgroup. A treatment-by-levels analysis of these data is summarised in Table 8.8. The significant interaction of age and pretraining suggests the need for an examination of the simple effects. The difference between means for Group N and D was evaluated by a *t* test separately for the older and younger groups. For the older *S*s, $t = .20$ and P> .20. For the younger *S*s, *t* was 3.96, P<. 001. Thus, it appears that the effectiveness of the name-learning was restricted primarily to the younger *S*s.

Table 8.8
Analysis of Variance of the Number of Correct Choices in Six-Trial Test Session

Source	*df*	*MS*	*F*	*P*
Pretraining (P)	1	12.52	8.35	<.01
Age (A)	1	20.24	13.49	<.001
P×A	1	9.78	6.52	<.025
Within cells	50	1.50		
Total	53			

Additional evidence for the relevance of names to the performance in the delayed reaction situation is provided by an examination of the records of *S*s in Group D. The *E* recorded verbalisations of 8 *S*s in this group who used discriminal names to refer to the concentric circles (*e.g.*, "bigger one," "shiny one," "darker one," "wider one," etc.) The mean number of correct responses on the test for these *S*s was 5.38 and the mean for the remaining 19 was 3.42. The value of *t* obtained was 3.15 with P< .005.

Discussion

The results indicate clearly that the pretraining requiring *S*s to learn names for the discriminal stimuli resulted in a performance in the delayed reaction test that was superior to the performance of *Ss* who had pretraining that involved only discrimination of the stimuli. The superiority of Group N appears due primarily to the younger *Ss*, since the older *Ss* in the two pretraining groups did not differ markedly. This interaction of the pretraining with age levels may be attributed to the fact that older *Ss* of Group D were more inclined to invent names for the stimuli than were the younger *Ss*. Six of the 8 *Ss* in Group D who spontaneously verbalised names for the stimuli were in the older age level. On the other hand, the experimentally introduced names provided the younger *Ss* of Group N with symbolic responses to the stimuli that they might not otherwise have attained.

There are two alternative, although not necessarily incompatible, explanations for these results. The first makes use of the hypothesis of acquired distinctiveness of cues (3, 8, 9, 13) which assumes that the learning of distinctive (verbal) responses to similar stimuli decreases the interstimulus generalisation in subsequent learning of other discriminal responses. In the present experiment, the concentric circles were made functionally more dissimilar for Group N by virtue of the distinctive names that had been learned for them. According to this explanation, Skalet's (14) animal forms may have been more distinctive than the geometric figures because the children had names available.

Another explanation of the findings is offered by Skalet's suggestion that the symbolic responses of articulate organisms serve as substitutes for the absent crucial stimuli (*e.g.*, "box 'seven' is baited"). During the delay period, *S* reproduces the name for the baited stimulus, and following the delay, the name serves to direct his choice. This hypothesis is rather well supported by the verbalisations of *Ss* in Group N during the text phase. Nine of the 27 *Ss* spontaneously verbalised the name of the baited box during delay periods, sometimes repeating the name several times during a single delay period. This verbalisation was not observed for *Ss* in Group D. This hypothesis can also be used to account for the results of several experiments (3, 4, 5, 7, 8, 9, 13) in which was found that discrimination learning problems are learned more rapidly by *Ss* who have had verbal pretraining with the relevant stimuli. In this case, the delay period that is presumed to be bridged by means of the names is the intertrial interval; that is to say, the names facilitate *S*'s recall of correct and incorrect stimulus-response sequences on previous trials.

Summary

Fifty-four preschool *S*s were divided into two groups. One group was given training on a pair of stimuli that involved learning distinctive names for the stimuli. The other group was given discrimination training with the stimuli without being required to learn their names. Subsequently, *S*s were given a delayed reaction test involving the pretraining stimuli. The *S*s who had learned names made more correct choices of the baited stimuli following delay than did *S*s who had not learned names, although this difference was due primarily to the younger *S*s. The results were interpreted in terms of a hypothesis that the possession of verbal names for the stimuli permits *S* to produce a representation of the absent stimuli during the delay period.

Notes

1. "Delayed Reaction", pp. 62-79 and Hunter, W.S., "A Reply to Some Criticisms of the Delayed Reaction," *J. of Phil. Psychol., & c.*, 1915, 12, 38-41. See also Watson, J.B.,-Behaviour," 1914, pp. 224-227; and Ch. X.
2. If there is a present determining external stimulus, the reaction is not delayed. A. C. Walton, "The Influence of Diverting Stimuli during Delayed Reaction in Dogs," *J. Animal Behav.*, 1915, 5, 259-291, has shown that dogs can react successfully to three boxes after delays of 30 secs. when they have been distracted during the intervals. This is better than I had been able to show. Before deciding that the dog belongs in a class with the raccoons—as perhaps he does—it will be necessary to have data on the animals' orientations at the moment of response. This Walton unfortunately does not give. The only facts that we have are that the animals did not maintain their orientations during the delays. If it should appear that the animal is able to recover the proper orientation in a large number of instances after a through distraction and can then react correctly, this fact will itself be of great significance and will require careful analysis.
3. Correlations obtained between the number of pretraining trials to criterion and the number of correct responses on the test suggest that even if the difference were significant, it could be safely disregarded for present purposes. The Pearson correlation coefficients for the various groups were: D—O, — .05; N—O, — .05; D—Y, — .27; and N—Y, .03. The correlation for all Ss combined was — .17.

References

1. Allen, C. N., "Individual Differences in Delayed Reaction of Infants", *Arch, Psychol.*, N. Y., 1931, 19, No. 127.
2. Buhler, C., *The First Year of Life*, New York, Day, 1930.
3. Cantor, G. N., "The Effects of Three Types of Pretraining on Discrimination Learning in Preschool Children", *J. exp. Psychol.*, 1955, 49, 339-42.
4. Cantor, J. H., "Amount of Pretraining as a Factor in Stimulus Predifferentiation and Performance Set", *J. exp. Psychol.*, 1955, 50, 180-84.
5. Dysinger, D. W., "An Investigation of Stimulus Pre-differentiation in a Choice Discrimination Problem", Unpublished Doctor's Dissertation, State Univer. of Iowa, 1951.
6. Emerson, L. L., "The Effect of Bodily Orientation Upon the Young Child's Memory for Position of Objects", *Child Develpm.*, 1931, 2, 125-42.
7. Gagné, R. M., & Baker, K. E., "Stimulus Pre-differentiation as a Factor in the Transfer of Training", *J. exp. Psychol.*, 1950, 40, 430-51.
8. Gerjuoy, I.R., "Discrimination Learning as a Function of the Similarity of the Stimulus Names", Unpublished Doctor's Dissertation, State Univer. of Iowa, 1953.
9. Goss, A.E., "Transfer as a Function of the Type and Amount of Preliminary Experience with Task Stimuli", *J. exp. Psychol.*, 1953, 46, 419-28.
10. Hunter, W. S., "Delayed Reaction in Animals and Children", *Behav. Monogr.*, 1931, 2, No. 6, p. 86.
11. Hunter, W. S., "Delayed Reaction in a Child", *Psychol. Rev.*, 1917, 24, 74-87.
12. Miller, N. E., "The Perception of Children: A Genetic Study Employing the Critical Choice Delayed Reaction", *J. genet. Psychol.*, 1934, 44, 321-39.
13. Rossman, I. L., & Goss, A.E., "The Acquired Distinctiveness of Cues: The Role of Discriminative Verbal Responses in Facilitating the Acquisition of Discriminative Motor Responses", *J. exp. Psychol.*, 1951, 42, 173-82.
14. Skalet, M., "The Significance of Delayed Reactions in Young Children", *Comp. psychol. Monogr.*, 1931, 7, p. 82.

CHAPTER 9

Major Factors in Learning and Learning Disorder

Introduction

Watching a normal young infant exploring his environment it is easy to see that his primitive learning consists of a blending of activities. He learns *to* and he learns *that*. He learns *to* co-ordinate his muscular function. He learns *that* sounds occur, *that* light strikes his eyes, *that* things taste sweet or sour, *that* temperatures or pressures can cause a variety of stages of comfort and discomfort. If the infant is seriously ill or grossly immature the extent and quality of learning is severely modified. That simplest description of such a situation which we hear is that the infant 'hasn't the energy to learn', or, 'is too busy surviving'. Though superficially simple, these two descriptions hold considerable significance. We all recognise that producing change demands creation and release of energy. We all recognise that the release of energy must be directed towards the particular change which is required. The simple laws of mechanics remind us of such phenomena as inertia, friction and the conservation of energy, all of which relate to the problems of movement or change. All learning involves a change of state. The first steps demand the initiation of coding processes. In order to teach—or to create situations in which learning can occur—we are bound by the criteria underlying change of any kind. In other words, before beginning to consider the avenues through which learning can occur we need to think of those elements which relate most cogently to change.

Learning at the rate which occurs in the first two years of life requires large quantities of energy, a focusing of attention, normal sensory inputs, an adequate amount of intelligence and, particularly, an environment which is conducive to their most effective deployment. We can, therefore, say that the infant learns *from*, *to* and *that*! One tends to think of early learning as a complicated storage function, which in fact it is. But learning is also an expenditure of energy, a developing perceptual and attentive skill and either depends on, stems from or leads towards a rapid sequence of emotional learning, maturation and gratification. Gratification may arise from what is learned, for instance, that this is the source of food or of comfort, or of security and love. Achievement of learning, for example, the recognition that a problem has been solved or that curiosity is satisfied may be a source of gratification. But such gratifications play only a minor part; a major source of gratification and maturation is the child's own recognition of the *fact of* learning, not so much *what* he has learned but *that* he has learned. One of the most important aspects of knowledge is the awareness that we know. The use of knowledge is facilitated by awareness of its extent and depth but, more important, it is facilitated by recognition that a problem exists, that the problem can possibly be solved, and by some assurance that we hold the solution to it. Such an attitude is not simply a facet of recall because the observer must focus his perceptual skills on the stimulus object or situation before recall can occur. Focusing demands attention; it is based on a prior state of self-regard in which the observer is aware of his skills and his knowledge and has the confidence which is one aspect of the positive reinforcement produced by success. Successful learning is merely one link in the chain. Positive reinforcement is commonly recognised as a result of successful learning; it is less commonly recognised as a reinforcement of the total learning process. Throughout this chapter the ideas outlined above are extended to the consideration of the psychological development of the child in so far as it leads to or is affected by problems of learning.

Information Systems

Although learning is based on the senses and their proper co-ordination there is a danger of over-emphasising the importance of this fact. The processes by which the brain co-ordinates sensory information are at least as vulnerable to stress and disorder as are the sense themselves. It is thus necessary to consider the following processes when thinking of potential learning problems.

1. Perceptual discrimination
2. Conceptual thinking
3. Remembering
4. Reasoning
5. Imagining

These classes are part of the process by which we use the senses to obtain information, to store and organise it, to develop it as the basis for ideas or concepts. The same processes facilitate the testing and ratification of concepts or hypotheses and eventually lead to the formulation of continuous thought processes. The expression of these normally leads to their confirmation, modification or correction and hence it is important to remember that the reasoning processes require expressive as well as receptive functions. Assessment of sensory acuity has now developed into a considerable science but all who work in such fields recognise that acuity is only one aspect of the total sensory process. To illustrate this we need only consider the difference between hearing and listening. Hearing is commonly defined as 'detection of sound by the ear and its transmission to the primary auditory area of the cortex.' One definition of listening is 'the ability to attend to heard sound with the object of interpreting its significance.' Consideration of the latter definition will remind us that the classroom situation is rarely, if ever, concerned with hearing in its strict sense. We are concerned with listening and hence with auditory attention. As soon as we begin to consider those factors which modify auditory attention we are led back to those aspects of discrimination which, even at the auditory level, require remembering, some reasoning, and hence a considerable degree of conceptualisation. The clinician recognises that a mild degree of auditory impairment is commonly associated with a major degree of auditory inattention and that failures of discrimination which lead to error not only undermine confidence but also inhibit and modify recall. Such modification will inevitably introduce delay and impair the whole process of remembering. To distil the whole massive literature on *remembering* into a few sentences is obviously impossible but we can perhaps consider certain of the memory processes in so far as they relate to the problems of learning disorder. At a very simple level we may say that remembering demands a stimulus object or situation which, when perceived by the observer, is related to prior experience and from this relationship some aspect of recall occurs. In thinking of this we can see that the organisation of attention demands a skill in two different directions simultaneously. One feature of attention is focused on the stimulus, the other on the stored codes of previous experience. Following the establishment of some quality of relationship between these events, recall normally occurs. The important point here is that recall demands the ability to maintain this kind of split-level attention, hence in those cases where duration of attention is limited we may expect problems of recall. Recall delays will lead to loss of confidence, leading to loss of attention and so the vicious circle commences. It is important, therefore, to remember that even relatively brief periods of loss of acuity lead to loss of auditory attention and that this commonly persists for a considerable period after hearing has returned to normal. Since it is quite common for certain mild hearing losses to fluctuate for prolonged periods the effect on attention, and therefore, discrimination, should be kept in mind. The child with an almost minimal hearing loss (undetectable without specialised facilities) when seated at the back of the class, loses attention and discrimination which can have the same effect as a much more severe loss. In fact, research in the Royal Berkshire Hospital Audiology Unit has shown that if the child with a 20 db loss is given a speech test while seated at the back of the class, he tends to score as though he has a 60 db loss (for which a hearing aid is normally supplied). This cannot simply be attributed to attenuation of sound-pressure level due to distance but rather to the effects of attention loss and the intrusion of classroom noise between speaker and listener. Mild degree of visual impairment may be expected to produce similar consequences. The spectacle-wearer, deprived of spectacles, sometimes requires a prolonged period of attention-focus before he can begin to use his impaired vision to its best effect. The consequences of undetected visual impairment which used to merit special mention in Teacher Training Colleges between the wars are still as severe, though happily their occurrence is now considerably less common. However, the results of improved testing facilities may have led us to a state of misplaced euphoria due to the emphasis placed on acuity rather than perception or discrimination.

Reasoning was the fourth process mentioned which involves the senses and the brain. This may be described as the application of the cognitive processes to past experience in order to deal with present problems or to plan for the future. It is compounded *inter alia* from the following :

(a) Intelligence
(b) Personality
(c) Physical health (which includes normality of sensory and neurological functions)

(a) Intelligence

Although psychologists recognise that the prognostic value of intelligence testing is considerably less reliable than used to be thought, there is still quite a demand throughout society for such scores. The faulty notion of their accuracy and reliability leads to their continued usage even amongst informed people (*cf.* Mensa, the organisation for that proportion of the population who score highly on test).

Many selection procedures used by banks, the Armed Forces and many educational systems are based on the old idea that in one brief period the applicant can produce a pattern of success which is a consistent and reliable index of future performance. When it is remembered that many intelligence tests demand visual and auditory perception or perhaps reading skill, it is obvious that, particularly in group situations, a candidate may well fail an intelligence test which never gets past the perceptual level. The same comment is, of course, true in the classroom. How many children who make poor reading progress are ever given tests of visual or auditory perception, discrimination, or short-term memory ?

Educationists agree that it is not possible to define intelligence but there the agreement ends. Hence, the following description of intelligence represents no more than a personal preference from those available. Intelligence is sometimes described as a name given to the overall efficiency and level of complexity of an individual's cognitive processes. Whether one agree with Hebb's Theory of Intelligence or not, his description of its availability to test merits attention. He postulates three levels of intelligence. The first, or genetic potential level, he grades A and says that it is non-observable and non-measurable. The observed product in the individual's behaviour between the environment and the genetic potential he describes as Intelligence B. His final distinction is between observed and measured intelligence. This is simply a sample of B scored in intelligence quotients or other units. Since this sampling involves myriads of features ranging from genetic to environmental features on the one hand or from linguistic to perceptual features on the other it is clear that consistency and reliability are, to say the least, vulnerable. Now that children are no longer to be excluded from education on the basis of such sampling (or placed in an environment which would effectively prevent the child from ever disproving the original label) we may feel that reliance on intelligence test scores is no longer a serious matter. However, the challenge to education posed by children with learning disorders poses severe problems of assessment which have not yet been met satisfactorily. Fortunately, we are now sufficiently aware of the importance of interaction between the individual and the environment of encourage educational research into optimal environments and perhaps into levels of specific learning disorder which have not yet progressed much further than the psychological laboratories.

(b) Personality

When we turn to personality features the situation can become unbearably complex. Fortunately, most teachers spend a large part of their professional life either consciously or unconsciously observing and adapting to the personalities of children and so it is feasible to select and specify certain particular elements. We accept that the total social environment has a predictable function. (Bernstein has related this to the level of linguistic development.) We also accept that the social environment of the home has considerable significance. Many claim that the school itself provides another social environment and there is general agreement that at least two, and often three of these, can permanently affect the full maturation of personality. Although concerned more with academic progress than personality, the work of researchers underlines the relevance of a stimulating environment to learning. (The recent award of a RIBA medal to a deaf architect for his design of a school for deaf children which emphasised environmental stimulations is an interesting example of the acceptance of such ideas.) One suspects that any teachers might harbour the wry suspicion that environments may, from time to time, be too stimulating! There is no doubt of the truth of this judgement in the case of children with impaired ability to attend or who are hyperdistractable. Some classrooms which are designed for a child without problems are intolerably distracting for a significant proportion of our children. Since hyperdistractability is not merely a function of low level of intelligence we could well ask ourselves whether the carefully controlled visual conditions of a language laboratory could not be extended to other educational activities. The same comments apply with equal force to auditory distractions. One does not need to live near to London's Heathrow Airport to be aware of the intrusive effect of noise, but there is still room for more specific research into controlled auditory environment for education, particularly when learning disorders pose additional problems.

Physical Health

The above comments lead us to consider the third element of reasoning outlined above. When one talks of the health or functional normality of the child such factors as nutrition and illness are of course, relevant, particularly when they lead to any danger of under-functioning or of time lost in school. Other factors at least equally important deserve special emphasis in this book. These relate to the general, physical, psychological and emotional well-being of the child. Most teachers have had experience of the child who suddenly flags, is given to mysterious loss of energy or who needs periods of rest, particularly in the primary school. Are we always right to blame this on too much television or too little sleep? What of the 'clumsy' child who cannot kick a ball, does not learn to write to our satisfaction as quickly as the rest of the class, is constantly bumping into things in class or requiring first aid in the playground? How many of our class children are severely enuretic? How many children appear to be able to maintain auditory attention but find visual attention unbearable? How many more are 'as good as gold with a book in their hands' but disturb the rest of the class when auditory attention is required? Our present levels of provision are quite inadequate for such children. The School Health Service has concentrated for many years on ensuring that all children undergo a regular, though necessarily rather superficial, investigation. Many authorities are now paying increasing attention to 'problem children' but it will be many years before medical research will really be able to come to grips with these specialised problems of educational paediatrics.

Teachers' Role

The inclusion in this literature of a discussion on Pastoral Care is evidence of the awareness of the need to establish and maintain good working relationships between home and school. The teacher of the child with learning problems need to know the parents, to be able to offer some means of developing the kind of close relationship in which mutual respect and confidence can grow. Domestic problems are one of the major sources of stress on the children in our care and the bewildered, frustrated, aggressive or apathetic states we see (to name but a few) often stem from family relationships which are not conducive to the emotional well-being of the child. We will not really come to grips with these in the busy heartiness of a parent-teacher meeting, yet the arrangement of special interview facilities at school is often difficult or artificial. There is much to be said for home visits which, in the case of deaf children, are recognised as part of the professional function of teachers and are accepted by parents and teachers alike. There is a lot to be said for meeting parents on their home ground. This is not simply because insights are to be gained from seeing the domestic conditions in which the pupil lives but also because the teacher who visits the home has exchanged roles with the parent and so there is a healthier interchange than if the teacher insists on maintaining a role which emphasises dominance and tends to obscure the fundamental role of the parent, without which all our classroom activities will be rendered almost totally ineffective. Usually, however, teachers themselves have not the time to focus attention on the child who may not be reaching potential. Indeed, unless an otherwise bright child shows inexplicable specific learning delays he is rarely a cause for concern in our present crowded classrooms. For instance, in the writer's own clinical experience it is rare to see a child referred because of problems of comprehension without the explicit or implicit assumption that he or she has a low level of intelligence. Yet teachers will commonly describe children who learn well from reading as 'slow readers' because they can not read aloud and are slow to learn auditorily. At one time many such children, referred for hearing test, would have been discharged from the clinic as having normal hearing, although *no* test of auditory comprehension had been used. At one time the orthoptic department in our own hospital saw a number of patients with reading problems though, of course, most of these children had no defect of visual acuity. We all forget from time to time that most learning in the classroom demands an integration of sensory functions. Even though the acuity of the sense may be normal, integrative skills may be impaired. Integration depends not only on maturation and learning but also on the state of the physical integrative systems of the brain.

Reading

To illustrate this point, let us consider the problem of reading. The teaching of reading usually begins with the child looking at a group of visual symbols while listening to a teacher. Quite soon after this he is expected to look to symbols, listen to his teacher and immediately repeat what he has hard in order to develop the association skills. The child with problems of auditory memory or discrimination has already begun to fail. The child with problems of visual attention may continue to succeed in this limited sphere if he has good auditory memory. (To a considerable extent, 'look and say' reading place the onus on auditory memory in the early stages.) The extension of the child's developing skill to new and unfamiliar organisations of the same basic symbolic material tends to prove increasingly difficult in the two instances described above and so we are already faced with two possible sources of error which will cause loss of confidence and therefore failure. Once we recognise that learning to read involves an audio-visuo-vocal function it becomes evident that children can have excellent audio-vocal and audio-visual function, perhaps in certain cases even excellent visuo-vocal function and yet find audio-visuo-vocal function an intolerable problem. Sometime such failures stem from difficulties of attention (see below) and can possibly be helped by special tutoring. It is important to remember that the audio-and visuo-discriminatory processes have different time bases. With a permanent visual stimulus the eye can take time to focus, to extract figure from ground and to have as it were, a number of shots at external and internal scan. The auditory discrimination is essentially fleeting and hence two time-based regulatory systems need a specific skill in co-ordination which will not preclude utterance. Yet how often have we seen even the best reader stammer or stumble against a background of auditory distraction? What then of the child who, throughout his developing years, has perhaps not even advanced to a level of audio-visual parity in terms of attention or inter-sensory function? Other children have fundamental associative disorders or short-term memory problems which, while permitting silent reading, preclude reading aloud. During a period of responsibility for teacher training it was not uncommon for the writer to hear surprise expressed if a child performed better at reading comprehension than at reading aloud. Even now the term 'a beautiful reader' is only applied to the ability to read aloud, yet this is a skill which a minority of adults use. Have we, perhaps, got our emphasis wrong? Even if we have not, can we control the distractions which inhibit the development of those integrative skills demanded by reading? Even in silent reading we are sometimes faced with children who suffer from unusual problems of eye-control and hence of visual track. Some children can track down but not across the page. Some can read from right to left but not from left to right. (The writer once had a patient who could not read from left to right without immediately retracking the same line from right to left. Before this was detected the child was unsuccessfully attempting to match his auditory patterns to a confused agglomeration of visual symbols. Specialised therapy in which the visual stimuli disappeared as soon as the eye had tracked across them from left to right led to considerable improvement.)

Mathematics

From Piagetian studies we are aware of the stages of conceptual maturation and there is increased emphasis on learning concepts. This may pose problems for children who are expected to arrive at mathematical concepts from a study of actual objects or processes. For certain parents (and hence for their children) the notion of mathematical skill still hinges on enumeration or perhaps a parrot knowledge of number bonds. This, of course, ignores the whole basis of the creation of mathematical concepts by experience. Sometimes, indeed, such parents will regard these methods of education as 'just playing about with sand, water and scales'. There are some intelligent children who lack the kind of visual memory that such activities demand and hence are impaired in the development of the relevant mathematical concepts. Yet, at a linguistic (*i.e.* auditory) level, they have no problems of mathematical conceptualisation. Such children will obviously need more time to develop the visual concepts, though the experienced teacher may well decide that if the child can manage problem-solving at an auditory level or even if (as many do) at a symbolic (*i.e.* numeral) level this skill should be encouraged to develop first before returning, should this prove necessary, to practical experience as a foundation for the visual conceptualisation.

Language and Learning

If we consider the significance of language in learning we may draw the threads of research into a clearer pattern. Kirk and Lyle, examining different populations at different times both showed that the subnormal child from the poor or culturally deprived home tends to gain more from additional educational facilities than does the child from a home which offers a stimulating environment. We come close to the key to early learning if we look once more at Hebb's Theory of Intelligence and remember his emphasis on the interaction of 'Intelligence A' and environment. This key lies in the development of language skills. Language, spoken or written, is the meeting ground of minds, the basis for interchange of experience, information and emotion. A most interesting comment on the value and function of language is the emphasis made by Bernstein on its vulnerability and its modification by social factors. Language is a form of nourishment, lack of it will produce effects similar to any other form of under-nourishment, including impaired ability to absorb nourishment. Factors detrimental to language development, even if only temporary, initiate a cycle of inability to absorb. This results in reduced intellectual development which in turn prevents the continued development of skills already present, effect social skill and so holds up social experience and acquisition of information.

While considering development and learning we must remember that the emotional aspects of life are also to a considerable extent a function of learning and maturation. M.M. Lewis, discussing orectic development, described it as 'the progressive organisation of emotions, the emergence of personality, the growth of social life, the differentiation of aesthetic criteria and standards, and the establishment of ethical judgement and conduct.' Russian research has indicated that the development of language may have a regulatory effect on a child's emotional life. As the emotions are given names, the child comes to discriminate them more clearly, to be aware of relationships amongst them, to organise them into relatively stable attitudes or patterns and so in some measure to direct and control them. Above all, language development may well play an important part in stimulating and maintaining the motivation to undertake and persist in particular patterns of behaviour. In thinking of these aspects we remember that communication systems (and in particular spoken language) are inextricably involved in the growth of self-awareness. The child's acts and the expression of his emotions evoke verbal approval or disapproval from others. As a result he becomes more clearly aware of his behaviour and attitudes as set beside those of other people. He realises that he can obtain co-operation and approval or provoke resistance and begins to appreciate that he is as much the object of the behaviour of others as they are of his'.

We recognise that the child prevented from telling us *that* he knows is seriously effected. The child who cannot tell us *what* he knows is even more seriously effected. If he cannot tell us he cannot check his own accuracy. He cannot correct misconceptions, he cannot experiment with hypotheses on a fantasy level. Language is a means of legitimate self-display, it is a form of intellectual preening. Just as preening has a vital function in birds, so intellectual preening is vital to the development of information store, information validation, information extrapolation, vital to cognitive function, and vital to learning.

Learning is a skill—in saying this we are stressing that classroom learning is an acquired function. We learn to learn.

Without communication the growth of learning is stunted. Without language the application of learning is impeded, without spoken language the communication of the fact and content of learning, though not impossible, is incredibly difficult. Our main problem is to differentiate between cognitive and verbal skills. Modification of either will of course lead to greater or less modification of both; we must be scrupulously careful to avoid the conclusion that impaired communication skill invariably springs from, or is an infallible sign of lack of intelligence. The problem is exacerbated by the fact that the majority of intelligence test equate the two, and that as the tests are designed and presented linguistically, language failure is too easily mis-diagnosed. The child with any language modification is in serious difficulties on that basis alone. To compound this by adding an erroneous classification of intellectual impairment is an undeniable tragedy. Not only does it cut the child off from the specialised therapy which he needs so badly but it may well even cut him off from the education or general experience upon which his therapy and his developing language skills must necessarily build.

Conclusions

We have described reasoning as the application of the cognitive processes to past experience in order to make judgements about present or future problems; since it is obvious that language plays a very considerable part in reasoning, our role as diagnosticians, therapists and teachers is surely to ensure that the cognitive processes are given full reign so that past experience will, in fact, be applicable to future living. In other words, unless we have good knowledge of the type and extent of past experience we are in danger of attempting to build on extremely dubious foundations. How does the child develop his experience store? What is the basis of perceptual function, how does this lead to cognitive processes and how are we to encourage the display which has already been mentioned as vital to learning?

As teachers we recognise that we must optimise the child's own prejudgement of success by striving to increase confidence. We set out to convince the child *that* he knows, *that* he can succeed, so that he will put his knowledge to use. Because he knows, he is in a position of potential. Because we know he knows, he is in a position of reinforced potential. If he knows that we know he knows, he is in a position of strength. From this position he can move to a position of confirmation which further reinforces his self-regard, his confidence, his trust in us as supportive agents and his readiness to try again.

Owing to pressures on our psychological services neither the psychologists nor the teachers have been able to give complete and satisfactory service to children with learning problems. In fact, it is true to say that in a very large percentage of cases the needs of both children and teachers have not really been met. We need a clearer picture of the avenues of learning, of basic perceptual skills and in particular of specific assets and deficits. Non of these, of course, will be given to us as a result of repeated requests for, or dependence on, Intelligence Quotients. The same situation will be equally true if we simply expect *scores* on the new Learning Aptitude scales. It simply is not good enough to show that a child scores. We need to know by what process he has scored and how such processes can be put to work in the classroom. In attempting to assess perceptual or cognitive potential we need to keep in mind the following facts about children with problems of learning. First of all each child is an individual with individual assets and deficits. These deficits are the result of an interaction of conditions and events and hence one would make a firm plea that we stop talking about '*the* backward', '*the* retarded' or '*the* slow learner'. The terms imply a homogeneity which does not exist. If it did the title of this contribution would be a different one and much of what has been written would be unnecessary. Children with learning problems may face some or all of the following conditions to a greater or lesser extent. These they master with variable success and so pose problems for the teacher which demand observational and descriptive skills of a high order if the optimum co-operation between teacher and psychologist is to develop.

A child may suffer from damaged sensory activity or inter-sensory organisation, giving rise to impaired perceptual processes. This reduces experience and precludes or diminishes potential memory store. Reduced memory store results in low capacity to recall or encode and hence in reduced coding skills, which in turn leads to underdevelopment and hence to lack of further growth. In addition the child may have difficulties in discrimination and consequent problems of comparison between new stimuli and developed codes, where such exist. Diminished power of attention will lead to reduced expressive goals which will prevent full development expressive skills. This is accompanied by modified attention at inter-sensory and sensory-motor level and results in reduced self-appraisal and the continuous self-awareness so necessary for further development.

All the factors described above may stem from psycho-physical or possibly neuro-motor conditions. Readers could, no doubt, produce a similar set of problems in motivational, social-emotional, intellectual or personality fields. All of these are intrinsic to learning and may well lead to learning delay or disorder. It is now more than twenty years since Magdalen Vernon stated that, 'We need tests of analytical skills by means of which we can identify strengths or weaknesses in the abilities to analyse constituent units or to organise them into the correct sequence or configuration. From this we could look for weaknesses or skills in generalising rules of combination and hence to re-synthesise or re-figure the constituent units in accordance with these generalised rules.' These comments, taken from her earlier book on *Reading Backwardness*, still apply equally well to all aspects of learning disorder.

From their own experience teachers will recall the child who for no apparent reason has given up and 'settled for failure', the class buffoon, so beautifully described by Morris; the child who decides that any answer is a sign of willingness and that willingness is a pathetic substitute for knowledge; the child who craves attention and has not the skills to earn it legitimately. He will also recognise the child who must be first, who cannot wait for a context to reveal itself but leaps in to identify on the basis of the first familiar cue. Does the teacher recognise equally readily the child who finds visual stimuli an intolerable distraction, auditory stimuli a barrier to continuous thought, concentration on neuro-motor functions a bar to integration of other sensory inputs (most typically present in the child with minimal cerebral palsy or other neurological damage) or the one who needs prolongation or repetition of familiar situations or materials as a basis for security? Do we really know enough about the children in our care? How reliable is this knowledge? How is it obtained? What means of assessment are available to us? How objective are they? How are they recorded? Can we use these measures as a reliable and consistent means of objective measurement of progress? What size are our classes? How many classroom assistants are available? How many are needed? Would it be helpful if we did have someone to take over while we do concentrated individual work with children who require it? How are we to achieve the rigorous consistency and repetition some children need? Are the various mechanical or electronic audio-visual aids at present available to us a satisfactory substitute for the solid hard grind which is at present demanded of the teacher? How are we to achieve the minute specific gradations of progress which certain children seem to need? Would it be feasible to develop learning programmes which, while meeting individual needs, would prove sufficiently flexible to apply to other children without proving prohibitively expensive? Can we bridge the gap between laboratory research and classroom practice to the benefit of the children rather than the laboratory? How are we to persuade our educational administrators that without research no progress will be made while solving the practical and ethical problems that such research engenders?

Finally, in meeting the challenge posed by the child with problems of learning, can we make a clear assessment of the reality of our ambitions for the children in our care? What are we really aiming for? Are we intent on joining the struggle because we enjoy a struggle? Do we see sufficiently clearly what we ourselves have to offer? What in fact, is the balance sheet of our individual assets—and liabilities? What in the end are we aiming for—the well-being of the child or our own gratification? One hopes that the answer is 'both' but that the latter will be based on a realistic appraisal of the former.

References

B. Bernstein, *A Socio-linguistic Approach to Socialism* from *Directions of Socio-linguistics*, Eds. J. Gumperz and D. Hymes, Holt, Rheinhart and Winston.

D. O. Hebb, *The Organisation of Behaviour: A Neuropsychological Theory*, Wiley.

S. A. Kirk, *The Early Education of the Mentally Retarded: An Experimental Study*, Urbana, University of Illinois Press.

M. M. Lewis, *Language and Personality in Deaf Children*, N.F.E.R.

J. G. Lyle, "The Effect of an Institution Environment upon the Verbal Development of Institutionalised Children", (II) Speech and Language (III) The Brooklands Residential Family Unit, *J, Ment. Def. Res.*, 4, 1-13, 14-23.

R. Morris, *The Quality of Learning*, Methuen.

J. Tizard and S. C. Grad, *The Mentally Handicapped and their Families: A Social Survey*, Oxford University Press.

M. D. Vernon, *Backwardness in Reading: A Study of its Nature and Origin*, Cambridge University Press.

P. E. Vernon, *Intelligence and Cultural Environment*, Methuen.

S. Wiseman, *Education and Environment*, Manchester University Press.

CHAPTER 10

Educational Approaches and New Technologies

What is known about practical procedures for teaching is not a recent discovery. The expository methods of the Sophists might perhaps be contrasted with the Socratic method, in which the student to some extent directs his own learning by seeking answers to significant questions. The approaches of the Sophists and of those who pursued the Socratic method represent differences in procedure related to the achievement of different goals. Thus, even from the earliest days, various technologies were produced for achieving different goals. The earliest aspects of technology developed were those that would be described in modern times as teaching methods. Later developments involved the invention of procedures for the duplication of materials for the student and teacher. The early forms of printing involved the cutting of print in the surface of blocks of wood, together with some ornamentation, and these blocks could then be used for making many copies of the documents engraved on them. Manuscript copying was, of course, a common occupation of those who spent their lives in monasteries, but it hardly provided a means for the widespread dissemination of educational materials.

Gutenberg did not invent the printing press, as many commonly say he did. What he can be given some credit for inventing is type that could be set up for printing and then be disassembled and reused. Dutch printers had almost certainly already used movable type on a small scale, but Gutenberg was able to incorporate the idea into the consummation of an ambitious project—the printing of the Bible. Like all contributions to technology, Gutenberg's represented one step forward in a long sequence of steps that included the development of small type castings, the means for producing paper, and the production of inks. Gutenberg received support for his enterprise because it was coupled with the great educational enterprise of disseminating the Bible. The success of the printing press, in this respect, established it as the prime development of all time of educational technology.

Experimentation with the format in which subject matter was presented was common in the Middle Ages. The best known example of such experimentation was the catechism, a step-by-step systematic development of the ideas to be mastered. The catechisms of monastic education resemble the step-by-step presentations of modern programmed materials. The idea that subject matter needs to be analysed by the teacher and then organised in an optimum sequence is a very old idea that has been many times rediscovered by those concerned with education. The concept of sequencing of subject matter played an important part in the thinking of the philosopher Johann Frederick Herbart, who had a profound influence on the development of educational ideas. Maria Montessori also viewed the problem of sequencing as a matter of crucial importance in pre-school and elementary-school instructions. Many of the Montessori materials represent attempts to provide carefully sequenced materials. Thus children learn to classify materials before they engage in ordering materials into scales. The present emphasis on the sequencing of subject matter is just continuation of a long tradition.

The technology of behaviour related to teaching placed emphasis, in the early stages of its development, on developing procedures for the teacher to follow and materials for the student to study. Only within the last century has there come to be some recognition that a technology of education has to take into account still other factors. Perhaps the most significant of these is the behaviour of the pupil. Not much more than a century ago did some educators come to recognise that pupils were not like empty vessels to be slowly filled with the elixir to knowledge, but that pupils had purposes of their own of which account had to be taken if learning was to proceed with efficiency. Slowly there evolved a conception of the learner as a person who had to play an active and central role in the direction of his own learning. The old technologies of education had little to say about how to arrange effective learning for a person who was to choose his own goals and largely direct his own activities.

The view commonly held until as late as the present century was that the child had the responsibility to learn whatever the adult proposed and that failure to learn could only happen if the child did not try hard enough. According to this conception of the nature of the child, academic failure was moral failure. The treatment for failure was punishment, which was supposed to result in the child becoming sufficiently motivated to accomplish the goals set for him. Teachers who held this theory were not discouraged from applying it when the failing child, punished for failing, continued to fail. The theory and its related practices were abandoned, not so much because of obvious ineffectiveness, but because research slowly produced a changing conception of man. Teachers and other concerned with education came to recognise that individuals of school age differ in their capacity to learn and that such differences are important.

Much of the technology of present-day education, that is its practices and procedures, evolved before research related to human behaviour had even begun. Even some of the more modern aspects of educational technology have been developed without any impact from the behavioural sciences.

Perhaps the most important single technological development related to education in recent years has been the development of motion pictures and film strips. Most of this has occurred because manufacturing firms have seen the schools as a new market, but it has had only the most limited support from scientific research. Surprisingly little is known about how children respond to motion pictures, what attracts their attention in them and what they ignore, and what they ultimately retain. There has been some agreement that the passive role of the pupil observer is not a desirable one, and various attempts have been made to convert this role into a more dynamic one, but these have not been very successful. One technique has been that of stopping the film in various places and then presenting the pupil with a problem to solve related to what he has seen and heard. Projection devices have also been simplified so that the children themselves can operate the equipment. The advantage is that with such equipment all children do not have to view the material simultaneously, but each child can show it to himself when he is ready. Parallel developments in the area of speech and sound have also had impact, the most sophisticated devices being the language laboratories, which were highly fashionable in the 1960s, but many of which have fallen into disuse in recent times.

An overall evaluation of such mechanical and electronic devices cannot be given. As a minimum contribution, one can say that they have provided some variety in classroom procedure, and this is excellent. They have probably made the classroom a more interesting place. How effective they are as teaching devices is controversial, for often they are used as substitutes for effective teaching. The teacher may spend the afternoon running films through the projectors because that is they easy thing to do.

Educational technology is not, in itself, good or evil. The author would reject strongly the position taken by Skinner (1971) that the evils of an industrial and manufacturing technology can be counteracted by the development of a behavioural technology that is somehow expected to provide a balance. A technology of behaviour has already shown itself to be capable of propagating extraordinary evils. Anyone who doubts this statement should read the article on the subject by Wolf and Jorgensen (1970), which documents some of the nefarious purpose for which a technology of behaviour has already been used. They cite, for example, the project undertaken in Southeast Asia on the control of the behaviour of native populations The recommendation of the project was that the behaviour of natives could best be controlled through the control of food, but that food control could not be used effectively until all crops and other sources of food had first been destroyed. The behavioural sciences have great capacity for establishing new milestones along the path of human disgrace. The impact of behavioural technology is not necessarily going to be good.

Technology of education, as it has emerged in recent years, has been developed along two distinct lines. The predominant source has been operant psychology and must be traced to Skinner's interest in the development of improved ways of controlling learning in the classroom. Skinner's (1954) original conception of how this should be done involved the idea that the kind of equipment used to control learning in the laboratory should provide an excellent means of controlling classroom learning. The adaptation of this equipment led to the development of what have been called *teaching machines*, though these machines were eventually to involve much more than simple adaptations from the laboratory. The idea of using mechanical devices for the control of pupil learning was not new, having been advanced much earlier in the century by Pressey (1932). However, Pressey drew his analogy for the new technology of education from industry, whereas Skinner thought in terms of adapting laboratory procedures to educational use. Both Pressey and Skinner assumed that a technology of education should be based on scientific knowledge and seemed to imply that a technology could not be developed without such knowledge. This assumption is obviously nonsense in view of the fact that most educational technology, like that of other fields, was developed long before scientific knowledge had been developed. Whether at this stage of educational development, scientific knowledge is crucial to educational technology remains controversial. Ultimately, such knowledge must surely become important, but there is probably still much scope for educational invention that is only remotely related to basic science.

Operant psychology makes assumptions about the nature of man that are not acceptable to many persons of scientific competence. Hence there are alternative viewpoints that can supply the basis of a technology. Psychologists engaged in research on perceptual problems and on problems related to man's ability to receive, organise, and retain information offer one alternative. Those concerned with such problems have viewed the pupils in the classroom as a creature who seeks out information, actively organising the information discovered. Such models of pupil behaviour have generally been described in the literature of pedagogy as *discovery models of learning*. Around such models of pupil behaviour a limited but new technology has also begun to emerge.

Technology and New Learning Models

The operant approach to the development of an educational technology has been intimately related to attempts to build machines to handle aspects of instruction. Sidney Pressey began during World War I to develop mechanical devices that would test and instruct at the same time. Pressey did not envisage that machines would take the place of many traditional instructional procedures but believed that they would supplement the more typical procedures. His position is to be contrasted with that of some of the recent enthusiasts for teaching by machine who have taken the position that the teacher is obsolete and will soon be replaced by a mechanical device. Nearly forty years after Pressey's early experimentation with his classroom devices, Skinner (1954) quite independently came to the conclusion that what was needed to improve education was proper instrumentation related to teaching. Skinner was unaware of the fact that his proposals were not new. Later, as he became cognisant of the work that had preceded his, he began to ponder the question of why the early devices had not produced the revolution in schools about which Pressey had written. He came to the conclusion that the reason was that the Pressey machines had come before a science of learning could have provided the knowledge necessary for designing them correctly. Skinner believed that by mid-century a body of knowledge had been built and that his devices would succeed where others had failed.

Skinner built teaching machines on the basis of principles of learning derived from a study of lower organisms, particularly pigeons and rats. The two main principles incorporated into their design were that the learner should always have to perform the response himself, in contrast with just choosing a response, and that feedback or reinforcement should be immediate. Skinner was probably much too quick in generalising these principles to all of human learning behaviour, for the fact is that they have not proven themselves to be particularly valid. Human beings do learn by merely watching other human beings, and without making the responses to be learned, and reinforcement is often more effective when it is delayed. Skinner's machines were ingenious but not designed on the basis of any well-established scientific principles of human cognitive learning. Indeed, it is doubtful whether they would have been any less effective if designed on the basis of common-sense. Whereas the Pressey machines had merely asked the pupil to make a choice between answers presented and then told him whether his choice was correct, the Skinner devices required the pupil to construct an answer and then the machine showed the pupil the answer he should have given. Skinner, like other operant psychologists who followed him, believed the difference to be important, but in practice it has not been shown to be so. Skinner was also quite concerned with designing machines that would not permit the learner to cheat, but this also has turned out to be a matter of no great consequence.

Certain newer concepts related to the design of teaching machines can be viewed as of much greater consequence. One important concept is that of the adaptivity of machines. A review of the development of this concept is provided by Stolurow (1961). Teaching machines are more or less adaptive to the needs of the learner; no machine, and perhaps no teacher, is completely adaptive to the learner's needs. For example, if a pupil said to me "I want to know more about the civilisation of the *Upanishads*!" I can probably do nothing to help him. I do not know who the *Upanishads* are. I do not know whether they are living today or died out long ago. Generally, I am able to adapt by suggesting places where he can locate information and sometimes by giving him information. If he does not understand the material to which he is referred, then he can come back to me and I will send him to more easily understood sources. Any effective teacher has to be at least partially adaptive in this respect, and the designers of teaching machines have attempted to make their devices adaptive to the learning needs of the pupil.

In a sense, teaching machines are inevitably minimally adaptive, in that they provide teaching related to fixed objectives. Unlike the human teacher, they are not adaptive to the objectives of the pupil but only adaptive in how the objectives are achieved. A pupil who tells the teaching machine that he doesn't want to learn the addition of fractions, or any other aspect of mathematics, cannot expect any positive help from the machine. The teacher, who is somewhat more adaptive in this respect, may be able to offer constructive suggestions, perhaps giving him some problems to work on that interest him and will eventually require some mathematics for their solution.

Adaptivity in teaching machines is generally limited to keepin track of how the pupil is doing on a series of problems and changing the instructional programme to help the pupil overcome difficulties he encounters. The type of device that provides the greatest flexibility in doing this is the computer that has been arranged to function as a teaching device. The computer can feed information to the learner, present him with problems, check his answers, and decide whether he has or has not demonstrated skill in solving the problems. If he has not demonstrated adequate skill, then he can be given additional information or he can be helped to correct his errors. If he has solved the problems successfully, then he can be introduced to new information and a new set of problems. The machine can even offer the pupil a range of topics to study.

The statement is commonly made that teaching machines, unlike live teachers, make no assumptions about learners, but this is a specious claim. Although machines make no assumptions, the designers of machines do, and the machines reflect the assumptions built into them. Such machines are generally built on the basis of the assumption that correct education is that which takes the pupil through a prescribed intellectual routine, diagnoses the difficulties he has along the way, and, by various means, ensures that certain specific goals are achieved. The assumption is implicit that the pupil makes few, if any, significant choices. At the best, he can choose among the limited array of repertoires provided by the machine. Because machines are built after the designer has made very important assumptions about the nature of the learner, they operate within a very limited and prescribed area of education, but perhaps an area within which they have legitimate functions.

Technology and New Curricula Design

The idea that the elements in a curriculum should be arranged in the best order, if teaching is to be easily accomplished, is an idea that has long intrigued teachers and educational planners. The catechisms of the Middle Ages were attempts to order subject matter in ways believed to be effective for teaching. In the last few decades, there has been an interest revived in this problem, largely because those interested in machine teaching are preoccupied with questions of efficiency, and the ordering of subject matter is believed to have potential for contributing to effective education. In addition, the approach of operant-conditioning psychologists to the learning of skills involves the analysis of the skills into components that should be learned in a definite order. The operant psychologists have typically attempted to apply to the classroom the techniques they have used in the laboratory. In addition, other psychologists, notably Gangé (1970), have taken the position that learning involves the acquisition of a hierarchy of skills and that the only path of effective learning is to start instruction with the skills at the bottom of the hierarchy and slowly move to the top. Thus, in the acquisition of reading, the pupil has to be able to discriminate common simple shapes, such as squares and circles, before he can begin to discriminate the complex forms involved in the recognition of letters and words. Later, he will learn to recognise words by using information derived from the context and perhaps using no more of a cue than the first letter of the word that is being recognised.

The typical example given of how subject matter, if properly organised for teaching, falls into a hierarchy is in mathematics. One can easily understand that addition has to be learned before multiplication, that number series have to be learned before addition, and that the concept of number has to be acquired before any of these. All this makes sense and has provided the basis for many studies showing that mathematical concepts are better acquired in some orders than in others. Curriculum developers have tended to assume, on the basis of studies of mathematics and mathematics teaching, that all subject matter can be arranged into the best order for teaching purposes. Now there can be no doubt that subject matter can be arranged in orders that seem reasonable to both learners and teachers, but whether there is one optimum order is an open question in most subject matter fields. The order that can best be justified may depend on many factors, including the age of the learner.

Because instruction by means of a teaching machine requires that the subject matter be divided into units to be presented and that the units be presented in a particular order, some means has to be found for doing this. The usual basis for ordering subject matter for this purpose is intuition. The subject-matter expert looks over the material to be formulated into a programme to be run through a machine and arrives at an order he believes is a useful one for instructional purpose. The process is basically intuitive in that the structure of most subject matter is not particularly evident and certainly very complex.

In a programme to be presented by machine, information is presented in units called *frames.* The size of a frame has long been controversial. Skinner and many of his followers have taken the position that a frame should include only a small amount of information. Others have suggested that this is an ineffective way to teach, suggesting instead that each frame include a substantial amount of information, perhaps as much as that provided by several hundred words. The argument is that the large unit of information gives the learner an overall concept of what he is attempting to learn and a broad group of what it is all about. The small unit of information may be dull and uninteresting, and its significance may escape the learner. The notion that the unit should be small comes from animal training, which generally involves taking the animal through small steps of the skill to be learned. However, human beings have the capability of grasping complex situations and do not necessarily have to have them broken down into small components.

In programmed learning, each presentation of information is followed by an exercise in which the learner has an opportunity to use the information he has been given. This, of course, is a revival of the old idea that activity related to whatever is to be learned is important. In programmed learning, the activity is an attempt to perform either a component of the skill to be acquired or the complete skill. Then, after the performance has been completed, the learner is given an evaluation of his performance. This is referred to as *reinforcement* by operant psychologists, who have also held the questionable belief that reinforcement should occur without delay. When computer-based teaching machines are used, the device may keep track of a pupil's progress. If it does this, then it may provide additional study for those who have less than a certain percentage of correct answers.

The programming of materials for presentation through teaching machines led to asking whether the machine is really necessary at all. Those who doubted the necessity of the machine proposed that the material be presented in book form. Various devices were proposed in connection with the book form of programmed learning that would prevent the pupil from seeing the answer until he had completed the problem. The simplest of these devices involved no more than a piece of paper, slowly moved down the page of the text as the pupil worked, which presented him from uncovering the answer to each problem until he had entered it on the sheet.

In the early 1960s, there was a proliferation of textbooks published in programmed form. Materials thus presented tended to be extremely bulky and, for this reason, quite costly. A pupil taking a first course in a foreign language might have to purchase as many as three volumes of such materials, a factor that limited greatly the use to which such materials could be put. Just because of the cost, enthusiasm, for programmed textbook materials was quite brief and their use is declining. There is also perhaps a second reason to account for their limited use—the absence of any literary skill in their production. They tend to be humourless, dull and lacking in any of the real skills of the writer.

All kinds of variations have been introduced into teaching machines. Some machines have the capacity of showing motion pictures as a part of the instruction provided. Some can show slides. Some may show pictures and have a recorded voice narrative. The learner may solve problems by pointing to the correct picture, because many devices have been developed that permit the machine to record which is pointed at. Thus the subject matter may be presented in a variety of forms, and these devices do provide great flexibility in this respect. The subject matter does not have to be presented in the verbal form that constitutes the main material used in textbooks.

Nevertheless, the point must be made that programmed materials designed for teaching machines, like all materials produced by the new technology, are always removed one step from the real world. There is a fundamental difference between seeing an experiment undertaken in a film presentation and seeing the same experiment undertaken before one's own eyes. In the real situation, the student can examine the materials involved, do the experiment again with certain variations, check on whether the results just represent some artifact, and obtain a great diversity of information that he could not obtain from a film. Even the most realistic materials presented in films and other devices are one step removed from the real world, but education would bring the pupil into close contact with the real world. It should not provide only substitutes.

Computer Assisted Teaching

The concept of teaching by machine has resulted in a proliferation of invention, but most of this invention is of experimental interest only. Many devices permit experiments on teaching to be undertaken with a high degree of experimental control, and, although they may not be ready for use in the classroom on a regular basis, they should not be written off as useless. There is also the possibility that experimental devices may ultimately become of value for day-to-day use in the classroom. However, teachers have difficulty in finding out just what is the status of these experimental devices, because they are promoted by Madison Avenue techniques. For example, company interested in promoting its computer system for use in instruction in schools used prime advertising time on a television network to tell the audience that its system taught more efficiently than any other method. The president of the same company is quoted as using similar promotional lines at the ceremony opening the facility that was going to handle the teaching system. All this is unfortunate and may serve to prevent such devices from serving whatever useful purposes they may be found to have.

In computer-assisted instruction, the pupil sits at a terminal. The information he receives from the computer may be typed out on a teletype, or it may appear printed on a screen much like a television screen. The pupil types his responses on a standard typewriter keyboard. The pupil can work best if he has some familiarity with the typewriter keyboard, but in giving the answers to mathematics problems, for which such terminals have been mainly used, the pupil probably only has to type out a number to give his answer. If the answers are to be given in works, then they involve very few words. At present, it is not feasible to present problems that require long answers, for computers have difficulty in handling and analysing sentences of any length, except for those that form part of a standardised repertoire of sentences with which the responses can be matched. Single-word responses are those that the computer can best analyse, next to numbers. In contrast, the verbal outputs of computers can be extensive, for the devices are capable of printing out hundreds of lines a minute. Perhaps, in this respect, computers are much like human beings—good at producing verbiage but quite poor at receiving verbal information and analysing it. Human beings may well have a tendency to design machines that include inherent human weaknesses.

One of the most ambitious and best-documented programmes of computer-assisted instruction is described in a volume by Suppes *et al.* (1968). The programme took place mainly in schools near Stanford University in California, and the experiments were confined to the elementary grades. The content taught was mathematics and spelling. The programme was an adjunct to more typical instruction and consisted of lessons lasting four to six minutes. Pupils were assigned to the teletype booth, one at a time, to take their lesson on the teletype. A very careful initial orientation was necessary in order to overcome anxieties related to the new method of instruction. Pupils had to learn that information would come to them through the teletype and that they would type out their answers on the machine. They learned to type out their names when they first entered the telephone booth and then to type out numbers indicating their answers to problems. The materials used in the instructional programme are described as "drills" and were, presumably, supplemented by regular classroom instruction.

Just what to make of this particular experiment and the findings is difficult to say. The responses of pupils to working on the teletype tended to be favourable, though some pupils were highly negative and the report calls attention to instances of "crying," which are described as "normal" school behaviour. How normal this is beyond the first grade is questionable. One would generally expect children to respond favourably to a new gadget in a gadget-oriented society. In a way, the experiment plays with loaded dice in that exposure to the teletype was brief, and most children will respond positively to any variation in the usual classroom routine. Classrooms typically lack sufficient variation in activities, but whether computer-assisted instruction is the best way to introduce variation is a matter for study. Another serious question that may be raised is whether the complicated and expensive equipment used in the experiment does anything much more than present rather typical workbook materials through a mechanical channel. It is very hard to see from the account of the study how the teletype terminal and computer equipment provided any real advantage over the old-fashioned workbook. Indeed, many might say that the old-fashioned workbook, together with a device permitting the pupil to check his answers, might have advantages of simplicity and ease of use. The idea that machine teaching prevents the pupil from looking up the answer before he has solved the problem is a point of doubtful strength in its favour. Some of the promoters of machine teaching have emphasised this point, but there is little evidence that pupils using work-books cheat themselves out of education by looking up answers rather than solving problems. Common observation in the classroom suggests that they do not.

A point to be noted in the present connection is that work-books can be arranged so that pupils who fail to achieve mastery of particular units of work can be given additional help. The type of programmed text known as a Crowder text is of this character. A pupil using such a text reads a page or more for information, attempts to solve a problem, and then checks his answer. Beside his shown answer is a number indicating the page to which he is to turn. If he has not solved the problem correctly, then he is given some pointers about where he went wrong and is referred back to the problem. When he solves the problem correctly, he is allowed to proceed with the next unit of work. Books and work-books do not have to manifest the inflexibility they have in the past but can be designed to undertake all kinds of teaching procedures.

Perhaps a more serious objection raised about the entire procedure in the Stanford project is that the work-book has long been regarded as one of the inferior procedures used in teaching. The teacher's reliance on the workbook often results in a degeneration of classroom procedures. The pupils work the problems, and the teacher sits and watches. Often everybody likes the procedure. The pupils are happy because the teacher is "off their backs," and the teacher is happy because the pupils are busy and do not cause too much trouble. The teacher also does not have to think up answers to difficult questions the pupils may ask. The procedures have the virtue of eliminating tensions but have little else to recommend them. Pupils engaged in workbook assignments do not ask interesting questions and rarely have the opportunity to explore issues except those raised by the workbook. The Stanford project mechanises this kind of procedure.

A final question that has to be raised in the evaluation of computer-assisted instruction is cost. At the time of writing, the cost is far above that of conventional teaching. The enthusiastic supporters of the enterprise take the position that cost will decline as computers become more widely used, but this prediction is of doubtful validity. Experience up to this point indicates that as computers become more complicated and can come nearer to undertaking highly useful teaching functions, they also will become more expensive. For example, in order to develop computer-assisted instruction further, it is necessary to have a machine that will permit the pupil to communicate freely with the machine in ordinary language. Such a device can be built, but the expense involved is likely to be enormous. There is no basis to the argument that computers can correct the work of pupils quite cheaply, for the use of paraproffesionals in the classrooms has already provided a cheap means of undertaking such chores. An even cheaper method is to let the pupil score his own tests, an activity that he will engage in competently so long as he is not under pressure to compete with other children.

There are other questions that need to be raised in relation to computer-assisted instruction. Although the human being is likely to be fascinated by a mechanical gadget for a short time, one wonder how long pupils would remain intrigued with learning in isolation. Man is a primate and, like most primates, does not typically enjoy activities undertaken in isolation. He likes group work and group participation. The isolation booth of the computer terminal is not well designed in terms of man's nature. Perhaps the booth permitting two pupils to work together might be better designed in terms of human qualities. Although much thought has been given to problems of attaining academic goals, little concern has been shown for the matter of how to achieve them in ways compatible with man's essential nature. The isolation booth of the computer terminal seems to be particularly poorly designed in this respect.

Programmed Instruction: A Review

Programmed instruction and the design of teaching machines developed in a flurry of enthusiasm. Leaders in the movement proclaimed that the new development would increase the rate of learning by many times, some even predicting that through use of such devices doctoral degrees would commonly be acquired by the age of twelve. Kindness leads us to avoid documenting the latter statements in detail and telling who said what and on what occasion. Enthusiasm for a new development is good provided it does not interfere with sober evaluations of what is actually being accomplished. Studies soon began to accumulate comparing the outcomes of programmed instruction and the outcomes of machine instruction with those of instruction along more traditional lines. Hundreds of studies, mainly doctoral dissertation, were done in the 1950s and early 1960s, and although no single one of these studies is of any great significance, the studies taken altogether provide a consistent picture.

Hartley (1968) reviewed studies of programmed instruction undertaken up until up mid-1960s. Of the 162 studies located, 37 per cent favoured the use of programmed materials, 49 per cent showed no significant difference between programmed methods and traditional methods, and 14 per cent favoured the traditional procedures. Zoll (1969) reviewed studies in mathematics that made similar comparisons. Of these thirteen studies, three showed a significant difference favouring the programmed procedures, three showed a significant difference favouring the traditional procedures, and seven showed no significant difference. The trend of the studies is typical of studies conducted in education. Whatever is considered the new method has a slight edge over what is considered the more obsolete method. This trend reflects a novelty effect more than anything else. Both learners and teachers respond with enthusiasm to new methods of instruction and, for a short time, pursue them with renewed energy. Unfortunately, the initial enthusiasm wears off and so too does the apparent efficiency of the new invention. Students learn through the use of programmed materials and through machine teaching, of that there can be no doubt, but these new devices cannot be credited with any startling efficiency in comparisons with the older methods. This should not lead the reader to say that the new methods should necessarily be discarded, for they can provide a variation in activity in the classroom, and variation generally promotes learning. Any device that shakes the routine of the classroom out of a rut is likely to be advantageous and help to keep both pupils and teachers alive. Classrooms filled with virtually dead pupils and dead teachers lack, more than anything else, variation in the procedures and tasks undertaken.

The discussion up to this point should not be interpreted as implying that the evidence is now in and it can be stated conclusively that programmed instruction or teaching machine instruction is no better or no worse than traditional instruction. There are difficulties associated with making such comparisons that are not evident on the surface and that were not evident to most of those who have undertaken the research in the area. The difficulties have become apparent as the research has proceeded. Let us consider briefly what some of these difficulties are.

One difficulty has already been noted, namely, that a new instructional method tends to evoke positive responses from learners so long as the method is new. The novelty effect is a plague for the educational researcher, though a boon to the teacher, who can arouse new interest in pupils by varying procedures. Another difficulty involves the way in which materials are developed for the experimental comparison. Suppose that an experimenter is going to compare the effectiveness of teaching a unit on the addition of fractions by two methods, one involving a programmed text and the other involving a presentation by the teacher followed by the pupils' attempts to solve some problems of adding fractions. The lessons are prepared in the two forms, but let us suppose that the person who does this is not very good at writing programmed materials. This immediately produces a bias in favour of the traditional method of teaching. The writer of the materials might also have been very good at writing programmed materials, in which case the bias would have been in the opposite direction. There is inevitably bias of this sort. Also, however good one set of materials may be, there is still the possibility that a better set of materials might be written for the other method. Experiments of the kind considered are primarily comparisons of the cleverness of the writers of material rather than comparisons of methods. What this means is that studies comparing two methods do not give very clear answers concerning their relative virtues. The best one can conclude from the studies of programmed learning is that the new method does not seem to provide any very striking improvements over the older methods. The differences are certainly not the striking ones predicted by the early enthusiasts.

Other difficulties are shared by all studies that compare two methods of teaching. One of the most important of these is that teachers have prejudices and are likely to favour one method over another. In some studies, teachers may be assigned to the method they prefer, but who can genuinely say he prefers a new method he has never tried? Also, most studies compare the effectiveness of teachers who are using an old method with which they are thoroughly familiar with the effectiveness of teachers using a new method with which they have had little experience. A teacher needs time with a new method to gain the experience required to use it to full advantage.

Another difficulty faced by such studies is that there may not be simple answers to the question "Which method is best?" Many research workers have long suspected that some methods are more effective with certain groups of students than with others. For example, very slow learners require an enormous amount of repetition in teaching. They have difficulty in transferring information of permanent memory, and repetition helps them in this connection. There is, perhaps, the possibility that pupils highly rigid in their thinking may respond more positively to very structured teaching than do more imaginative pupils, who may require more opportunities to think freely. Bracht (1970) has summarised some of the studies indicating that the effectiveness of a teaching method is influenced by the characteristics of pupils. Some positive evidence suggests that the phenomenon is a real one. For example, Bracht touches on the very substantial evidence that, in the case of attitude change, high IQ students change more if some effort is made to present both sides of an argument, with refutation of the "wrong" side. The low IQ students seem to become confused when both sides are presented.

Context of Educational Technology

The immense enthusiasm that has been shown toward the development of an educational technology is strange in view of the fact that it is taking place at a time when there is considerable disillusionment concerning the value of technology as a whole. At the present time, there is much more concern with matters related to the control of the ill effects of modern technology than there is any rejoicing with the bounties that it may have brought us. Many seek to escape from the impact of technology, some by returning to simpler ways of life involving the growing of their own foods, some by purchasing only products that will not harm the environment, and some by seeking political action that will reverse the trend toward destruction of the planet. The search of escape from the evils that technology has brought represents one of the vigorous movements of they day. There is a paradox in the fact that educational technology is being promoted with enthusiasm in an age characterised by disillusionment with the world that technology has produced.

Technology, in itself, is neither good nor bad. It can serve many ends, and the ends may sometimes be worthwhile. However, one cannot pass over lightly the point made by Mumford (1970) that most of the great advances and developments in the humanness of man have come from sources other than technology. Great ideas, such as the idea that man should be free or that all men should receive an education, did not emerge as a result of any technological development but were the result of the development of a conception of what is worthwhile in life. Athens' contribution to posterity was not a contribution to the building trades but a contribution to how man viewed himself and the universe. The worthwhile contribution of technology has been in matters related to the provision of food, shelter, clothing, and health rather than a direct contribution to the mind of man or to the development of the political institutions that make civilised life possible.

Let us consider some of the more obvious potential sources of negative effects of the new educational technology. One of the obvious ones is that it is likely to be designed to eliminate any kind of pupil initiative. The kind of programme designed by Suppes *et al.* (1968) in the field of computer-assisted instruction illustrates this. The behaviour of the pupils in the booth equipped with the computer terminal is completely dominated by the programme on which the computer is run. When events in a classroom are completely dominated by the teacher, one is likely to comment that such a classroom is very old-fashioned and out-of-date. The use of a computer to perform the same class of actions does not make the classroom any more up-to-date. Presumably, those who design such classrooms consider them *avant garde* rather than obsolete—a very curious viewpoint. The unfortunate feature of this situation is that the pupil is submitting himself to a situation in which he virtually renounces all control of what happens except for quite trivial aspects of his actions.

From this author's viewpoint, the situation has features that have little please in a well-designed educational programme. Education, from the author's point of view, should concentrate on giving the pupil opportunity to make decisions for himself and for him to be very independent of machines and other people in the decisions he makes. Education should provide opportunities for pupils to make significant decisions related to what they are going to accomplish and what they are going to learn. An educational programme in which all significant decisions are made by adults is hardly education but would be more appropriately described as indoctrination or training. Educators have long held out the hope that schools would become places where pupils and teachers work together. The kind of technology that is given the greatest support at this time is one in which teachers are the planners and pupils are those whose behaviour is controlled by the planners. What a caricature of education!

Andrews and Karlins (1971) have pointed out that education based on behaviour-control principles is designed to produce adults who will fit docilely into an industrial system and who will have little concern for making decisions for themselves. In such an "advanced" world, the people of Russia, China, and the United States will all be cogs in their great industrial machines. The peoples of the different countries will probably differ only in some of the things they say but not in what they do and not in what controls their behaviour. Peoples will not be slaves to a class, or slaves to a state, but slaves to the technology that has acquired control over every phases of their lives.

Related to this overwhelmingly serious criticism of modern educational technology is the fact that educational technology has been, to a marked degree, tied to the goal of the efficient achievement of traditional objectives. The objectives may have little significance for the new generation. The high-school diploma is, for many, a means of becoming eligible to belong to a union, but what is learned in high school may have nothing to do with what it takes to be an efficient union worker. Furthermore, the high-school curriculum may have little to help workers enrich their lives outside of work. The usual attempts to introduce English literature have little long-term value for students who turn to television for recreation and who are unlikely to read books for pleasure. The learning of mathematics is probably "irrelevant" to most students, who will not even have to work out the amount of change coming to them in the supermarket, for the cash register does this automatically. Most mathematics taught to the masses is taught so that the few will have the background needed in some college science courses. For the others, it has little functional value in their lives. Machine methods of handling numbers have taken over for man most of his mathematical tasks of only a generation ago. The pupils can see that education in the modern world is not there to enrich their lives, but that it is only a prolonged ritual that will enable them to obtain a union card. The present emphasis of educational technologists on finding efficient ways of teaching mathematics is hardly a channel of innovation likely to endear education to the modern generation. Most of the more significant problems of education are not those of how to make education more efficient but how to change its goals and purposes so that it will enable a person not only to enjoy education as one of life's great experiences but to see education as a source of enrichment for his entire life.

This leads to the question of why educational technology has fallen into the same rut as other technologies and with at least as devastating potential side effects. Why has not educational technology sought to enhance man's freedom through education? Why has not educational technology sought to convert education into a wonderful, inspiring, and freedom-giving experience?

The answer to this question is not simple, but one of the major factors in the unfortunate trend of much innovation in education is that it is to a great extent politically sponsored. The largest single set of enterprises directed toward educational innovation is the chain of regional laboratories funded by the Federal government. These enterprises, as Chase (1970) points out, are largely engaged in the development of educational materials and these materials are designed almost exclusively for the purpose of achieving traditionally endorsed objectives with greater efficiency. These organisations, as Chase also points out, exist to serve a public purpose, and, although they have their own boards controlling them as corporations, they are subject to review and evaluation by the United States Office of Education. The result is that their programmes must conform to government policies. New government policies are only rarely concerned with social change but are generally directed toward making the system, as it is, run more smoothly by eradicating the problems produced by elements that do not function well within the system. Educational technology has become the tool that government can use to help eradicate behaviour that prevents the system from running smoothly.

For this reason, the major direction of effort of the government-sponsored educational technology has been to develop educational tools that can be used to produce conformity in the main nonconforming sections of our society. The poor, the underprivileged, the black, the Latin Americans, the Eskimos, and the Puerto Ricans belong to this category. These are the groups that the government sees as misfits, and it views the problem as one of educating them in such a way that they will conform to the rest of society. The problem is viewed as though it were one of modifying some of the human components in the great industrial machine so that these components will fit better. Education, through the new technology, is viewed as the means whereby some degree of uniformity in the human component can be achieved.

There is, of course, nothing new in a government developing a technology for particular political purposes. Indeed, much of technology has developed so, typically to the detriment of man. The Romans developed the metal industries as a means of arming the legions and extending imperial power. The nobility of the medieval period developed the use of the horse for military purposes, inventing both the stirrup and the horse-shoe. In contrast, the so-called barbarians were the main developers and exploiters of first the water wheel and later the harnessed horse and iron plow—devices from which the great bulk of humanity benefited. History gives us little hope that a government-developed technology will be of any great value to the people, for such technologies have generally served only the most immediate ends of a relative few. Whether a federally sponsored technology in education can do anything more than achieve some goal of producing uniform educational products remains to be seen. That such a technology can be developed there seems to be little doubt, but there are real doubts whether such a technology can genuinely contribute to the overall quality of life. Indeed, it might be expected to produce a deterioration.

Scope for New Trends

The developments in education that have been considered in this chapter have been criticised because of their tie to very short-term political goals, and the reader has a right to ask what the alternatives are. In considering these, the point must first be made that the author is not against all technology in a educational field. In education, as elsewhere, technology may serve worthwhile goals of the mass of humanity, or it may serve the purposes of the few and be damaging to the many. Technology may also serve the immediate goals of the many but have damaging side effects that are not identified until much harm has been done. The author believes that an educational technology is needed that serves the mass of humanity on a long-term basis, and that it should be an instrument whereby man builds up his individuality. In the development of this technology, the greatest sensitivity should be shown to possible harmful side effects, and no project should evolve without some attempt being made to assess potential damage as well as potential worth.

The technology of education needs to be more closely associated with the independent type of invention occurring outside of the federally sponsored machinery for educational progress. There is a need, for example, to develop a technology related to the open classroom. In particular, there is a need to develop rich sources of materials that children can explore. There may well be a greater need for this than there is for the rather dull packaged material that constitutes the main product of the so-called educational industry. A few manufacturers are producing interesting classroom exhibits and related materials that children can explore and that they can be given the choice of exploring or not exploring in a free environment. The design of a classroom in which there are real opportunities for exploration, rich sources of information that the pupil can consult, and opportunities for making significant decisions offers a real challenge to the educational technologists who have not become preoccupied with turning out pupils to meet very precise specifications.

One of the chief deterrents to such a programme is cost, and this is a serious deterrent at a time when there is so much preoccupation with the matter of producing more education for the same or less money. The affluent American society has not learned that good education is expensive and is far different from the cheap mass-production model. A rich educational environment means not only the ready availability of extensive sources of information but also very large quantities of natural objects for the children to study and work with. These facilities, in turn, mean that there has to be a far better pupil-teacher ratio than there has been in the past and also better-qualified teachers.

Closely related to this kind of development is the development of situations in which pupils can make real and significant choices. Almost nothing is known about what children learn when they are given amounts of time during which they have to choose among learning activities. Such periods should be times to make explorations that the pupil has wanted to make, but the environment must provide real alternatives for exploration. The alternatives also must not be blind alleys. A pupil who chooses to study the balance of life in a tank must be helped to continue this exploration and to pursue at subsequent times the problems he has encountered. Too often, such free exploration periods are terminated with some statement by the teacher that enough time has now been wasted and it is time to get back to real work. There are problems of space and money related to equipping a school that will provide the kind of educational environment envisaged, but a beginning needs to be made in working out the details.

An educational environment that teaches the child to be free and independent must also make him recognise that some aspects of community life require conformity to regulations and self-discipline. He must come to recognise this limitation on his freedom as a necessary evil, but one to be kept to a minimum. Just as teachers and pupils have to arrive on time in order to have an organised school, so too do workers in factories and other places have to submit to similar controls. However, the pupils must learn, through the example provided by the school, that one submits to such controls only temporarily and for the purpose of enjoying opportunities for freedom. The school should be the place where the alienation from society produced by such controls exercised on a massive scale comes to be resolved. This must be accomplished through the pupil becoming not the willing recipient of such controls, as he is at present, but one who accepts them on occasion, with reluctance, as a means of achieving more worthwhile goals.

How far children can learn to avoid becoming subservient to a controlling technology of the world of work and the world of governmental control remains to be seen. No serious and extensive effort has, as yet, been made in this direction, and most of the recent effort in educational reform has involved a trend in the completely opposite direction, which, over the years, can be expected to increase alienation of youth. The political pressures are all in the direction of producing an education that will bring man more and more under the control of the great machine, or monster, he has created. Perhaps education must seek to free itself from such control as a first step.

One step that schools can begin to take as a part of their own liberation process is to end meaningless educational requirements. For example, many unions require their members to have high-school diplomas, even though the education provided by high schools has no relevance to performance on the job. The purpose of the requirement has been to exclude members of minority groups from the union. The result, of course, is not only social injustice but a degradation of education. Under such circumstances, students can hardly be expected to seen a high-school education as anything more than a political gimmick of questionable morality. If students are to view education as a life-relevant activity, then education must cease to be a mere political tool of power groups but must become a means of personal self-development in a society where man truly values freedom from unnecessary control.

Related to this matter is a matter long ago discussed by John Dewey, namely, the extent to which the school can become a model for society by providing opportunities for learning the democratic process. Unfortunately, the school has become much more a model of a factory than a model of a free and democratic state. This is an area in which sociologists and social psychologists need to devote efforts to the development of social organisations within the school that will provide useful experiences. Certainly, the traditional systems of student government appear to be as obsolete as much of the rest of the curriculum.

Such problems are not going to be solved overnight. Large sums of money need to be made available to particular schools, over long periods of time, to work out experimental procedures. Perhaps twenty years is not too long a period for the evolution of a highly different form of school system and a technology of education entirely different from the present one, with its preoccupation with developing a packaged curriculum to be used for producing a uniform pupil product.

CHAPTER 11

Child Development Perspectives and Mass Media

Much has been written on the concerns of society for the growing child in the modern electronic and television age. The dichotomies are obvious; on the one hand, there is violence and sex on TV and their ill-effects on impressionable minds, while on the other, children cruise freely on the cyberways.

A major feature of the studies of the influence of mass media is that they are focused on the here and now. That is, the attempt is to determine what happens to audience in a more or less immediate time frame. Moreover, only the direct influences of the mass media are the subjects of investigation.

But it can be easily suggested that the significance of mass media in the society lies not only in the direct and short-time influences but perhaps mass media leave long lasting impressions on the minds of the people. The results of these impressions are manifest not in the immediate future but indirectly they contribute to the process of personality formation of the individuals and hence mass media can be suspected to have an indirect and lasting effects on the society.

There seems to be three reasons why the impact studies of mass media remained tied to direct and short-term effects only. Firstly, the theoretical basis for the studies mostly comes from psychology which concentrates on the uncovering of the immediate influence of independent variables on dependent factors at a specific point of time. It is postulated that the congnition, sub-cultural and social characteristics of individuals shape the selective patterns of attention, perception, recall and overt actions of the individuals response to mass communication

Secondly, the methodology used to conduct the impact studies of mass media also led to the determination of the immediate effects only. The experiment method of psychology and sample survey interviewing in sociology could not throw any light on such effects of the mass media that are likely to influence the structural and functional aspects of the human organisation and behaviour.

Study Findings

Another reason for the failure of the social scientific for ignoring the long-term effects was also the commercial use of the findings of the media studies. Exposure patterns of the audiences lead to change in the advertising media-mix strategies and rating structures. Bits of information on the change of human consumer behaviour led to change in the marketing strategies and more important in the replication of same kinds of messages. Results of the media research are required in a hurry and so there is neither time nor the intention of looking beyond present or perhaps immediate tomorrow.

Study of the process of socialisation is one area where the significance of the long-lasting role of the mass media has been recognised. Socialisation is process that brings members of the society into sufficient conformity so that the social order, predictability of the behaviour and continuity of culture can be maintained. Socialisation is essential for perpetuation of the society. Through death society loses its members and by birth it enrols new members. But unlike other animal forms the new entrants need to learn the ways and means of living in the society. This is neither genetically inherited nor is it intuitional. This learning is accomplished by transmission of the foundation of social organisation and general culture to successive generations via the socialising process. From individual point of view it is by the process of socialisation that one learns about various norms and role-sets. In a way individual gets prepared for any future performances. Parents, family, kin, peers, schools, teachers, folk tales and epics work on the individuals to inculcate the society-culture. But the process in most societies is non-institutional and is different from formal learning situations.

In traditional societies the life cycle of an individual is clearly marked. With each stage of the life-cycle there are associated roles and status that are almost fixed for each individual. Even the process of teaching the young ones the role expectations and choice of behaviour, possible punitive actions for non-compliance are all woven in the normal social life. The socialising agents are identified and their roles well defined.

But as the process of de-tribalisation begins the norms of social behaviour are no more so rigid. Yet there is a need to learn to identify with the social groups and adopt the group-norms. The learning process is no more precise and well-defined.

In the contemporary societies the process of socialisation is by no means clear. "Competing and often contradictory sources of information ranging from peers to corporations vie for the attention of the individual to provide definitions and directions as to what behaviour to imitate, what rules of actions are important and what meanings to attribute to events. Conspicuous among these competing sources of information are the mass media".

Integrated or Integral?

The examination of the role of the mass media in socialisation of the individuals thus becomes an important aspect of the study of long-term influence of the mass media. Mass Media provides multi-point references to the members of the society with which to learn and regulate the social life. But mass media themselves are not external agents in the society. They in fact constitute a sub-system of the social system. So it will not be wrong to say that the society by communicating through mass media facilitates the perpetuation of the accepted values, attitudes, norms as also tends to socialise the members continuously and through all age groups.

So, theoretically speaking mass media seem to have made their place along with the parents, peers, teachers as the primary agents of socialisation. This has been largely possible by the advent of Television in the home situations. Newspapers have a limited role, perhaps in the perception of the political events, Radio listening, though an intimate experience, does not have much potential of mass influence. Films and television with moving images become very important for those who have access to them. Studies have shown that in societies where television programming is quite advanced, children spend more time watching television that they spend in school or in outdoor activities. With the advent of computer and mind absorbing computer games the children are reported to be spending most of their leisure time glued to the gadgets. Greater the exposure more are the chances of long-lasting impressions on the minds.

Traditionally, in Indian families the process of socialisation goes differently for male and female children. Male child is the favoured one. This is not only the consequence of the way the elders or the parents have been socialised but it also acts as a model for the new learners. Males learn to expect dominating roles for themselves, whereas females accept to perform subordinate and secondary roles.

Does the advent of mass media supposedly 'modernising agents' act as equalising factors or do they just reinforce the conflicts between the traditional socialising factors like parents and teachers, on one hand, and mass media, on the other?

A systematic way of answering these questions is attempted by examining the issue under following heads:

1. Process of ownership of the media.
2. Freedom of operate radio and television sets.
3. Personal ownership.
4. Choice of Programmes.

First the ownership of the media. A very small fraction of the Indian households subscribe to newspapers or magazines regularly. Even in subscribe households it is mainly a male decision whether to subscribe and what to subscribe to. Event the educated urban housewives role in this process is not very dominant or active.

Radio ownership presents an interesting socialphenomenon. A transistor set has become an essential item of the dowry. One can see beautifully covered transistor sets being exhibited along with other items of dowry like cot, steel-box, cycle etc. In more affluent families it is the television set black and white, or colour with or without VCR/VCP. Perhaps next in the list to be included in the dowry is the home computer.

Therefore, in many families radio or television ownership is through a gift where bride is the main actor. But she has no say in the selection process. She acts just as a carrier. Case histories of some dowry deaths reveal that the first item of demand was a television set, black and white or colour depending upon the economic condition of the husband's family (not or bride's parents).

Once the instrument is in the family all members of the family do not have free and equal access to it. In rural situations the radio and TV are normally placed in a room which is the domain of the males only. The females are deprived of the access to the instrument.

Rural Change

A new phenomenon is emerging in some parts of the country. It is mainly because of the erratic or uncertain power supply to the tubewells. So the farmers start developing mini household around the tubewells, and gradually the younger farmers shift to the houses in the fields away from the actual village along with the wife and children. The overall social climate in these dwellings is of freedom and females have more constructive role. They have also more access to radio and television.

Under normal situations the freedom to switch-on or switch-off the radio or television does normally lie with the senior male members of the family. Senior female members of the household are generally unaware of the basic operations and even if they want to listen or watch some programmes they have to depend on others to operate the instruments. In urban middle-class families the housewife has an equal access to operate the instrument. But both in rural and urban situations female child has limited access to radio and television.

There are indications that in affluent urban families personal ownership of TV and VCR/VCP in becoming prevalent. Similarly in some rich rural families young males are going more and more for personal radio sets. But among the rural young females this is hardly observed.

There is not much family radio listening, in rural or urban areas, normally either listening is personal or in groups of peers of males only. Group listening by female is a rare phenomenon.

On the other hand, television watching in majority of the rural and urban households is a group activity, mostly confined to family or family plus neighbours. But here also the choice is male dominated and females have little say.

What programmes children should see and what they should avoid watching is decided by the parents or the elders. Here also the female child is prone to more controls and guidance than the male child. Direct telecasting or special broadcast of tennis, cricket or football matches are all male targetted programmes. Hardly you see special programme where primary targets are females.

These are some of the ways media interfaces with the other socialising factors in a family situation. It is evidently clear that though the mass media are both the agents of socialisation and also of social change, their advent in the family situations reinforces the anti-female child practices rather than the break them. The sub-ordinate position of the females gets validated.

However, more important than how radio or television sets are handled in the family are the images that these mass media dissemination in the society. What is the long-term impact of these images on the female child ? Answer to this question will further elaborate the role of mass media but it is beyond the scope of this book.

Concerns for Girl Child

The following lines are about the plight of the girl child in our countries. The song is in fact saying many of the same things which research findings have been saying. Research findings need to be communicated more widely and in different ways. Scholarly papers, articles, speeches are important but they have their limitations. The medium of songs is what we have been using to convey the findings of research to challenge existing stereotypes, to create new role models, songs, theatre etc. appeal not only to our minds—also to our emotions and feelings. They touch people's hearts and minds both and therefore have a stronger impact.

When, in a country daughters are disrespected and demeaned tell me truly, can that country be called free ?

At the birth of a son there is joy and celebration but shunned are the mothers who by mistake give birth to a daughter.

Her own mother gives the girl less of everything. She craves for justice even in her own home.

A girl is the young plant that gets neither light nor water. She is the flower that would have blossomed but could not.
Half fed and half heartedly educated she gets only half a wage for her labour. The country got its freedom but she continues to be bonded.

Media and Their Role

Media are all the methods and means used to communicate, to spread messages, information, values.

Face to face communication in small and big gatherings of people are one kind of media the oldest media for transmitting messages and information. Religious congregation, songs, scriptures, customs, traditions, are all media. Very strong, very deep-rooted and omnipresent. Religion as a medium has a tremendous presence and outreach. Sayings, proverbs, social customs, folk songs, folk stories are other form of media, transmitting messages all the time. Then of course there is what we call mass media which includes print media (newspapers, magazines, books, children's literature, etc. Radio, TV, cinema.)

In the context of media one significant fact to remember is that almost all media have been created by men. Religious texts, mythologies, have been written by men and they are also interpreted by men. For the last 2000 years or so creation of knowledge has been largely in the hands of men. So, it is men who have defined everything for us—religion, science, development, psychology—all. Men have defined what is good what bad, what is superior, what is inferior, what is moral, what immoral, what is male, what is female. It is men who have told us who a good women is, what her duties are. It is men who have defined our psychology and our sexuality. We, women, have been only the recipients, and often the victims of this male knowledge and male dominated media.

It is only during the last century that women have slowly started sneaking into the male domain of creating knowledge. Women have now started questioning male knowledge and challenging accepted facts. Women have started looking at religion and psychology and science and development from a women's point of view. This is one of the most revolutionary things. I believe, which is happening all over the world. Women's studies, feminist research is looking at things from a fresh angle and often putting things upside down.

Media-based Ideology

The main function of media is to create ideology. It makes up people's minds. It interprets events and reality for people. It is a very powerful instrument and that is why those who have political and economic power always control media. Most media—religious media, mass media—is controlled by the upper classes and upper castes. Radio and TV are controlled by the state because of the power media has.

In the context of the girl child what role does media play?

Let us look at the world into which a daughter is born. Girls are born carrying the burden of patriarchy; carrying the burden of a history of subordination. They are born in a world which does not treat them as equal, which considers them less valuable and less able than men. Some unfortunate ones may feel the hostility while they are still in the womb.

Most families in our countries hope and wait for a son. In many areas of Northern India women fast and pray for sons. The traditional blessing for a pregnant woman is "*Dodho Nahao-Pooto phalo*" or may you have prosperity and sons. In many rituals connected with pregnancy a son is desired. Most pregnant women dream of having male children. The most popular and fond image of a child is that of "*krishna*"—the male child. Most songs and lullabies talk of "*beta*" "*Chaand*", "*Aankhon ka tara*" *Raja*"—all male images. In such a socio-cultural atmosphere a girl can hardly feel welcome.

And once the suspense is over, the secret is out, she can hear sighs, moans, harsh words, or deathly silence. "Its only a girl," "I knew this woman is capable of nothing better." "Better luck next time," "start preparing for a dowry" etc.

Some communities refuse to accept these unwelcome "surprises". They kill the unwelcome daughter using the most effective, locally available and locally acceptable method—stifling with a heavy blanket, feeding them some poisonous herbs, drowning them. The more modern ones kill them before they are born using advanced science and technology. It is not easy to say which method is more brutal, more primitive, which killers are more humane.

A village in Rajasthan is proud of the fact that no *baraat* (Bridegroom's party) has entered their village for several decades. By killing all the girls born in their village the proud Rajputs have escaped the insulting situation of being somebody's *Saala* (wife's brother). For them being a *Saala* is more insulting and a bigger crime than being a killer.

Such is the atmosphere into which we girls are born. The question is why this hostility against girls, why this insult? The contractors of religions have declared women to be unclean, vile, vicious, breeders of sin. Religious men are often advised to shun women. There are sects around where the *Maharajajis* (the saints) are not to look at women. Women have to clear out when the "*Maharajajis*" arrive.

Strong and knowledgeable women are perceived by religious men as threatening. Hence they prescribe subordination as the utmost virtue for women. *Pati Vrata, Sati Savitri*, cow-like, docile, homely are all virtues for women. Those who dare not to follow the norms, those who dare to be strong-willed, knowledgeable are given names like "*Kulacchini*" (ill-mannered). "*Kalyugi*" (modern). The still stronger ones are declared to be "*chudails*" or witches and burnt alive. In Europe thousands of women were burnt alive by "religious" men and their equally "religious" and moral congregations. In our villages "*chudails*" are still stoned or burnt to death.

Our daughters breathe such cultural air. They are fed with such stories at bed time in the name of cultural education or entertainment. They dream of superior men and inferior women. Their self-image is determined by such patriarchal values, traditions and religions.

Girls born in modern, educated, secular homes may escape pure religious preaching but they cannot escape media—the modern perpetuator of patriarchy. Whatever our girls may pickup—children rhymes, *amar chitra kathas*, story books, text books, folk tales the message is the same—man is superior, women inferior, man is the master, women the subordinate. There is no escape from such messages.

One would have expected that mass media controlled by the so-called "educated", "forward looking", "scientific minded" classes would have challenged old stereotypes and would have taken the girls and women towards equality. But unfortunately the reality is the opposite.

Studies done on women and media in India, Pakistan, Nepal, Sri Lanka show that the state controlled media, the commercial media are all one in portraying women negatively. They are promoting the same old characteristics for women—the housewife, the mother—with no other role, no other aspirations. They are preaching the same old characterisations for women—self-sacrificing, self-effacing, submissive, shy, dependent. These are never prescribed for men. They are promoting the notion that the most important thing about a woman is her body.

A woman is being reduced to a commodity, a thing on sale. There was an advertisement of a 14" TV on the front page of an Indian daily. A girl of 14-15 years was shown wearing very revealing clothes and the copy said, *"A beauty of 14. Keep her in your living room. Take her to your bed room or take her to the office."* This was in the *Indian Express,* the champion of human rights and justice.

In our media there is an increasing amount of violence against women in the form of rape, sexual harassment. All this influences reality. All such portrayals influence people and their behaviour. Such media affects women's self image. Violence which we see on the screen spills out to the roads, to our homes. Once woman is equated to a body a commodity, it becomes easy to tease her, beat her, rape her, burn her to death or perpetually harass her. If she is considered male property then the owner can treat her as he likes. Media, by and large, is reinforcing such attitudes.

With this kind of media all around our daughters, you can imagine what happens to their self-image, their psyche, their aspirations and dreams. Patriarchy, or the rule by men, is deeply embedded in our culture, in our religion, in the social norms. It has the sanction of education, laws and the state.

By and large media ignores facts that girls and women, in all working class homes are economically productive, that they produce 50 per cent food of the world, that they collect all the fodder and fuel and water, that they run the homes of the country, that they are farmers and labourers. While media bemoans the fact that rural girls do not go to school, their literacy levels are low, they get married at an early age, it keeps totally silent on her contribution to the family, to society and to the nation. The girl child in a working class home has no childhood. She works, behaves and contributes to the household and other work like any adult. Her contribution to the national GNP is never calculated and never highlighted.

Reality is distorted and misrepresented. Such misrepresentation leads to distorted thinking and planning. There are indeed some good articles written and TV programmes produced but unfortunately they are outnumbered and overshadowed by the overall negative image of women.

Text books and other children's literature unfortunately does exactly the same—it shows only in stereotypical roles. Text books promote the same patriarchal values, instead of challenging them. Even when the girl child goes to school she receives these limited messages. Her esteem does not necessarily increase, her dreams don't expand. I analysed some literacy primers for adolescent girls and women. They all promoted stereotypes. None of them showed women as workers, as farmers.

The girl child has really no hope from media because she sees that whether it is religion, or cinema, or her text book the message is the same—you are inferior, your dreams should be limited, you are subordinate, you have limited opportunities, in any case you will go to another family, it is only the son who will look after us in our old age, etc. Messages from all around force the girls (from middle and upper classes) to spend much more time and attention on their looks. While boys play outside, develop their physique and motor functions, little girls dress up in clothes which stifle them physically; they spend hours putting nail-polish or henna or doing their hair. Little girls are much more dress conscious. There is much less pressure on them to excel in studies, to prepare for a career, to be independent and fearless. All this affects their development, their dreams and aspirations. Media reinforces these ideas. The million dollar cosmetic industry, clothes industry are all interested in perpetuating these notions.

Coping with Change

This present state of affairs does need to be challenged. Fortunately many women and many organisations are already taking steps to change the situation. Some of the things which many more people need to do are:

* To learn to look critically at all media, including religious media. Our children need to be taught this too so that they learn to deal with the media onslaught. They should know that what media tell them is not necessarily the truth, it is the interpretation of reality by those who control media. This is true as much of news as of advertisements.
* We should increase our protest against media which perpetuates stereotypes about women and men, which degrades and insults women, which is offensive. Only a strong public opinion can lead to a change in media negative portrayal of women.
* We should put pressure on the Governments to weed out anti-women and sexist contents from all those media controlled by the Government, *i.e.* radio, television, text books etc. The government should be constantly made aware that sexist portrayal is against their own constitutions which preach equality between sexes and non-discrimination on the basis of sex.
* A number of studies are being done on media, girl child, women's issues etc. The outcome of these studies should be disseminated more widely in different ways. Let us tell everyone, for example, how much work women do, how much they contribute to the GNP. Let us tell everyone that women also are and can be farmers, labourers, craftsmen, sportsmen, chairmen. Let us look at our languages also which are very sexist and biased.
* Religious texts and mythologies, religious and cultural customs which preach and justify male superiority need to be challenged. This is indeed an area which we should tread cautiously but tread it we must. It is an area which will not change overnight but if we keep silent about it, it will never change. Let us start saying that all religions and customs are man-made, that all scriptures are written by upper caste, upper-class men, at a particular time in history. These can and should be changed, rewritten, reinterpreted by us in keeping with

the present reality. Religions which justify caste, class, gender, hierarchies cannot be accepted uncritically in the present day and time.

* We should create new texts from the point of view of women. What about writing a *Sitayan* from the perspective of all the women in *Ramayan*? We should modify old festivals like *Karva Chauth, Raksha Bandhan,* which perpetuate the notion of women's dependence on men. We should start celebrating the birth of a girl child in the same way as we celebrate the birth of a male child.
* We should continue to demand equal inheritance rights and property rights for girls as well as prepare girls for economic independence.
* An area where we need to do a lot of work is children's literature. We need to write non-sexist rhymes and stories for children. We need to give to our girls positive role models. I have written two books of children's rhymes and the response to them has been very positive.

We need to organise more workshops, conferences, camps, women's *Melas* (fairs) to talk about all these issues. What is encouraging is that such alternative media is being produced. There are women's magazines, films by women, street plays, songs, posters, exhibitions. These need to be disseminated widely. We cannot really keep silent any more because:

If we were just one or two we might have been silenced. But if this country is half full of men the women are one whole half too.

CHAPTER 12

Understanding the Value of Children

Findings are reported from a comparative study of the value of children that was carried out in six counties—Japan, the Republic of Korea, the Republic of China (Taiwan), the Philippines, Thailand, and the United States (Hawaii). For each country, results are presented for three contrasting socio-economic groups: urban middle class, urban lower class, and rural. These result are based upon interviews with young husbands and wives with at least one child; about 360 respondents were interviewed in each of the Asian countries, 557 in Hawaii to permit comparison of Caucasian, Japanese, and Filipino ethnic groups.

The value of children is defined as having two basic dimensions: positive value or satisfactions, and negative values or costs. In this study, the economic, social, and psychological components of the satisfactions and costs of children are analysed. Cultural and socio-economic differences in the value of children are described and the implications of these findings for population policies are discussed.

Introduction

The value of children is at once simple and complex; obvious and surprising; changing and timeless. Some of the ways in which children are valued by parents are universal, while other ways are specific to cultures, social groups, or individuals. For many parents, children serve to preserve and perpetuate tradition; for other parents, children are the agents of change, pointing the way toward different life styles and a new social order. Children may be valued for themselves, as intrinsically precious beings, or they may be valued as a means to an end, as an instrument of economic gain or as a vehicle to carry on the parent's name or identity. Some children are wanted, others are not; some are loved and protected and even spoiled, while others are exploited and even abused.

How can the value of children be assessed? It cannot be measured only in dollars or pesos or yen, although the financial costs and benefits of children are an important part of their value. The exchange of affection between parent and child is also important, as are the emotional stresses of childrearing, but these are difficult to assess. And what of such subtle matters as confirmation of one's sex role through having children? It might be argued that, rather than dealing with these psychological components, the best way to measure the value of children would be to count the number of them that a parent has or wants. That can hardly be a valid procedure, however, if contraception is imperfect or if value can be expressed through quality rather than quantity.

Despite these complexities and difficulties, research on the value of children is needed to understand better the determinants of human fertility and to suggest guidelines for policies through which societies may bring about regulation of fertility. This assertion is elaborated upon below, after which the concept of "the value of children" is defined, some findings from a cross-cultural study of the value of children are presented, and the policy implications of these findings are discussed.

Population Issues and the Value of Children

In a finite world population growth must eventually case. The only legitimate questions are how and when population stabilisation will occur. The question of "how" has three components: births, deaths, and migration. For a particular locality, the growth rate can be reduced through fewer births, more deaths, or movements of people to other localities. The last alternative, migration, has no effect on growth from a global perspective and only slight effects for most nations because of legal restrictions on international migration.[1] An increase in deaths to reduce population growth is an alternative that few people would favour. It is a reduction in births, then, that must be the aim; this is the "how" of population stabilisation.

The question of "when" population should stabilise is much more complex and allows no definitive answers. There is no consensus on an "optimal" population level, although most experts would agree that optimal levels will be exceeded in many countries by the end of this century it current growth rates continue. If that position is adopted as a standard, then the "when" of population stabilisation is "soon," in historical perspective; moreover, a reduction in births is needed now, because even when birth rates are reduced to replacement levels the size of a population continues to grow for some time. For example, Frejka (1968) has shown that the population of the United States would increase by 37 per cent over the next 70 years even if replacement-level births (2.1 per woman) were achieved immediately and continued indefinitely.

It is perhaps obvious in this context why it seems important to study the value of children. Knowledge of this topic will help us to understand why people want children, and why they choose to have children over available alternatives. Research on the value of children can provide information about the factors influencing the decisions of couples to have a certain number of children, decisions which, in the aggregate, add up to a "population problem".

Demographers and economists have for some time been interested in the effects of the value of children on fertility, but their interest has been expressed more in theory than in empirical research. Before presenting a psychological approach and related research findings, we will briefly describe demographic and economic perspectives on the value of children.

The demographic transition describes an important change over time in a society, from high mortality and high fertility to low mortality and low fertility. Most demographic explanations of this transition concentrate on societal-level variable, such as urbanisation or, more generally, socio-economic modernisation. These explanations are supported by correlational data.

When demographers attempt a micro-level explanation of the transition, the changing value of children often cited as a basic causal element. Specifically it is noted that in a more modern society children cost more economically, because of such factors as higher educational requirements, and they provide fewer economic benefits, because of such factors as child labour laws and the reduced availability of productive roles in family farms or businesses. It is also postulated that more educated, modern parents are increasingly aware of attractive alternatives, such as leisure activities or consumer goods; in addition, the care of children is viewed as more of a burden for nuclear families in urban settings than for extended families in rural settings. It is thought also that the relative isolation of nuclear families may reduce pro-natalist pressures from the older generation. Through a variety of mechanisms, then, it appears that social change should bring about changes in the way children are valued by parents, resulting in actions taken by parents to restrict family size.

Economists have approached this topic in a more systematic way, initially by regarding child-bearing as similar to the purchase of goods and applying the framework of household consumer choices. In this approach, decisions about having children are made on the basis of anticipated costs weighed against resources, within the context of preferences applied to children and to alternatives. In bare outline, the economic theory seems too simple and mechanistic to be applied to the complexities of sexual behaviour, contraception, and children as living, growing, interacting beings. In fact, however, elaboration of the theory in recent years have expanded the basic economic dimensions and moved toward a broad, behaviourally-oriented theory of human fertility decisions. For present purposes, it is sufficient to note that the core of the theory is, indeed, the value of children, as perceived by parents. The basic postulate of the theory is that parents will make decisions about whether to have children based on their expectations about the utility to be derived from children, in relation to perceived alternatives.

The demographic and economic approaches have in common that they treat the value of children as a basic causal element in the determination of societal fertility. This common focus is hardly surprising, since children are after all the tangible outcome for parents of the births that are counted by demographers. What is surprising, though, is that this consensus on the importance of the value of children has led to so little research. We have no systematic knowledge about the value of children to parents, or at least have not had such knowledge until recently. (For current reviews of work in this area, see Fawcett, ed., 1972; Schultz, ed., 1973.) In the sections that follow, a social-psychological approach that encompasses demographic and economic perspectives is presented, and illustrative research findings are discussed.

A Social-Psychological View

The value of children may be viewed functionally, from the perspective of parents, and the functions served can operate at different levels of conceptualisation. In the framework of the psychology of individuals, the functional approach would be reflected in the question : What are the needs of individual parents that are fulfilled by having children? Or, if childbearing is viewed as a social phenomenon, the question may be cast in social-psychological terms: From the perspective of parents, what are the functions—social, economic, and psychological—that are served by having children?

The phrase "the value of children" appears to emphasise the positive functions, or the satisfaction, of having children. It must be recognised, however, that dysfunctions or costs are also involved. The reality of childbearing is that one cannot have the satisfactions without also incurring some costs. Thus, two basic dimensions are involved: positive values or satisfactions, and negative values or costs. Conceptually, the value of children refers to the net balance between these opposing forces. For research and policy purposes, however, it is desirable to examine the diverse components of satisfactions and costs, rather than to seek a single index of the value of children.

A useful set of categories has been provided by Hoffman and Hoffman (1973). Their essay analyses and systematically describes the positive functions served by children, within a psychological framework. (See also Berelson, n.d.). The Hoffmans developed nine types of values that are intended to cover comprehensively the social and psychological needs met by having children:

1. Adult status and social identity (women's major role).
2. Expansion of the self, tie to a larger entity, "immortality".
3. Morality: religions; altruism, good of the group; norms regarding sexuality, impulsivity, virtue.

4. Primary group ties, affection.
5. Stimulation, novelty, fun.
6. Achievement, competence, creativity.
7. Power, influence, effectance.
8. Social comparison, competition.
9. Economic utility.

In the total scheme developed by the Hoffmans, the nine values are part of a larger framework that takes into account the costs of children, alternatives to children for fulfilling these values, and societal barriers and facilitators affecting realisation of the values. The Hoffmans' work was very influential in the development of the cross-cultural research described below; as a result of that research, however, a different set of positive and negative values that fits rather closely with the empirical findings has been developed:

Positive Values

1. *Emotional benefits*: Happiness, love, companionship and fun; also viewed in reverse as relief from strain, avoidance of boredom or loneliness.

2. *Economic benefits and security*: Benefits are derived from children's help in the house, business, or farm, from care of siblings, and from sharing of income; old-age security for the parents, including psychological security, is often a distinctive aspect of this value.

3. *Self-enrichment and development*: Learning from the experience of childbearing; becoming more responsible and mature; incentive and goals in life; being viewed as an adult, a grown woman or man; self-fulfillment; feeling of competence as a parent.

4. *Identification with children*: Pleasure from watching growth and development of children; pride in children's accomplishments; reflection of self in children.

5. *Family cohesiveness and continuity*: Children as a bond between husband and wife; fulfillment of marriage; completeness of family life; continuity of family name and traditions; to produce heirs; to have future grandchildren.

Negative Values

1. *Emotional costs*: General emotional strain; concern about discipline and moral behaviour of children; worry over health; noise and disorder in household; children as nuisance.

2. *Economic costs*: Expenses of childbearing; educational costs.

3. *Restrictions or opportunity costs*: Lack of flexibility and freedom; restrictions on social life, recreation, travel; lack of privacy; restrictions on career or occupational mobility; on time for personal needs and desires.

4. *Physical demands*: Extra housework; caring for children; loss of sleep; general weariness.

5. *Family costs*: Less time with spouse; disagreements over rearing of children; loss of spouse's affection.

These ten broad categories seem to represent fairly well the way people in a variety of cultural setting think about the satisfactions and costs of children. They do not of course represent the total sphere of motivations for and against childbearing. Biological drives or maternal needs are not represented, for instance, and these empirically-derived categories encompass mainly conscious. admissible reasons for wanting and not wanting children. The deeper, less verbalizable motivations stressed by psychoanalysts do not appear here, nor do some of the socially less desirable motivations, such as proof of sexual potency or the need to dominate others. Moreover, these categories pertain especially to reasons for wanting children, in the context of children versus no children. When values related to family size or reasons for wanting another child are considered, at least the following categories should be added :

Large-Family Values

1. *Sibling relationship*: Desire for another child to provide companionship for existing children; to enrich the lives of children; to avoid an only child.

2. *Sex preferences*: Specific desire for a son or daughter; desire for a certain combination of sexes among children.

3. *Child survival*: Concern that existing children may die; need for more children to have enough survive to adulthood.

Small-Family Values

1. *Material health*: Concern that too many pregnancies, or pregnancy beyond a certain age, is bad for the mother's health.

2. *Societal costs*: Concern about overpopulation, that another child would be a burden to society.

The 15 categories described above encompass most of the descriptive findings from a recent comparative study carried out in Asia and the United States. The research was not designed to test a formal model, but to provide basic knowledge about how people in different cultures perceive the satisfaction and costs of children. Implicit in the research, however, is a conceptual scheme in which the value-of-children dimensions are seen as a set of variables that intervene between background factors, situation variables, and general psychological orientations on the one hand, and fertility attitudes and behaviour, on the other. This conceptual scheme is tested through multivariate analyses in the project report (Arnold *et al.*, 1974) but will not be discussed in detail here. It should be noted, however, that multivariate analysis do reveal the value-of-children dimensions have a substantial predictive effect, independent of background and situational factors, on such fertility variables as desired and ideal family size.

The Value of Children Project

The research that provided a basis for deriving the 15 categories given above was a cross-national exploratory study, carried out over the past two years by co-operating social scientists in six countries—Japan, the Republic of Korea, the Philippines, the Republic of China (Taiwan), Thailand, and the United States (Hawaii). The research was a collaborative effort from the outset, with all co-investigators participating in the design of the study and the construction and pre-testing of the questionnaire, as well as in data collection and analysis.

In each country, comparable data were collected from young couples having at least one child. Husband and wife were interviewed separately. Country samples consisting of three contrasting groups were studied: urban middle class, urban lower class, and rural. About 60 couples were interviewed in each group, giving a sample of about 360 respondents in each country. In Hawaii a somewhat larger sample was chosen to facilitate ethnic comparisons among Caucasian, Japanese, and Filipino parents. Table 12.1 summarises the basic characteristics of the samples in the six countries. Altogether, more than, 2,500 respondents were interviewed in this exploratory study. The interview itself was intensive and multifaceted; it took about one and a half hours to complete, on the average, and about half of that time was devoted to various measures of the value of children.

Because the samples are not strictly representative of the national populations from which they are drawn and because the three equal size subsamples do not reflect the proportions of those groups represented in the populations of the various countries, the results for sub-groups cannot be combined to give results for any country as a whole. Rather, the analytic approach used here is to compare similar socio-economic groups across countries, then to look at the patterns that emerge for each of the three groups. Since the socio-economic groups were sampled by similar criteria in each country, and because the study is regarded as exploratory, this seems to be a reasonable approach. Primary attention is given in this paper to describing and interpreting the value-of-children dimensions, since that is the main focus of the exploratory study.

Open-ended questions were relied upon heavily in the study to elicit the dimensions of the value of children that were salient to respondents in the six countries. Structured questions developed on the basis or pre-test experience were also used, so that results from different types of questions could be compared. It should be noted, however, that to avoid excessive redundancy in the interview, the questionnaire was designed so that the context as well as the format varies for different questions. For example, an open-ended question asks about advantages and disadvantages of having children, compared with not having children; a structured set of items asks about reasons for wanting another child; a set of attitude items asks about the degree of importance of various values associated with children. Each of these questions gives a slightly different perspective on the value of children. Moreover, similarities in the pattern of response to different questions enhance confidence in the validity of the

Table 12.1

Characteristics of Samples: Number in Sample, Education, Age, Years of Marriage, and Number of Living Children, by Country and Socio-economic Group

Country and Characteristics	*Urban middle*		*Urban low*		*Rural*		*All groups*	
	Mean	*Standard Deviation*	*Mean*	*Standard Deviation*	*Mean*	*Standard Deviation*	*Mean*	*Standard Deviation*
Korea								
(Number in sample)	(120)		(132)		(126)		(378)	
Education[a]	15.4	1.4	8.1	3.4	6.3	3.4	9.8	4.9
Age	33.3	3.8	31.8	4.6	31.9	4.6	32.3	4.4
Years of marriage	6.6	2.5	7.3	3.9	9.2	4.2	7.7	3.8
Living children	2.5	0.8	2.7	1.1	3.4	1.4	2.8	1.2
Taiwan								
(Number in sample)	(144)		(144)		(144)		(432)	
Education[a]	12.2	3.4	6.0	2.0	4.7	3.1	7.6	4.4
Age	30.2	5.5	30.3	5.0	28.8	4.2	29.8	4.9
Years of marriage	5.3	3.0	6.9	3.7	7.8	4.5	6.7	3.9
Living children	2.2	1.1	2.9	1.1	2.8	1.2	2.6	1.2
Japan								
(Number in sample)	(136)		(134)		(142)		(412)	
Education[a]	12.3	2.4	11.5	2.3	10.6	1.6	11.4	2.2
Age	32.6	4.5	30.4	4.4	31.8	3.4	31.6	4.2
Years of marriage	7.2	3.1	5.7	3.7	8.2	3.8	7.1	3.7
Living children	2.0	0.7	1.6	0.7	2.0	0.6	1.9	0.7
US (Hawaii)								
Japanese								
(Number in sample)	(98)		(76)		(0)		(b)	
Education[a]	13.6	1.8	12.3	1.3	na	na	b	b
Age	30.8	4.5	29.3	4.9	na	na	b	b
Years of marriage	6.6	3.6	7.4	4.2	na	na	b	b
Living children	2.0	1.4	2.0	1.0	na	na	b	b

Caucasian								
(Number in Sample)	(95)		(87)		(0)		(557[b])	
Education[a]	13.4	1.8	11.7	1.5	na	na	11.7[b]	3.1[b]
Age	29.4	3.6	28.8	4.7	na	na	30.1[b]	4.9[b]
Years of marriage	7.6	2.9	7.1	4.5	na	na	7.5[b]	4.4[b]
Living children	2.0	1.0	2.5	1.7	na	na	2.3[b]	1.5[b]
Filipino								
(Number in Sample)	(0)		(126)		(84)		(b)	
Education[a]	na	na	10.7	3.1	7.0	2.8	b	b
Age	na	na	30.6	4.6	33.6	5.7	b	b
Years of marriage	na	na	6.9	4.8	11.1	5.2	b	b
Living children	na	na	2.4	1.5	3.2	2.0	b	b
Philippines								
(Number in sample)	(136)		(126)		(127)		(389)	
Education[a]	12.6	3.5	9.9	3.6	7.0	3.6	9.9	4.2
Age	30.2	5.1	30.5	5.5	31.4	5.7	30.7	5.5
Years of marriage	6.6	4.8	7.9	4.3	8.3	4.9	7.6	4.7
Living children	3.0	1.9	3.4	1.9	3.3	1.9	3.2	1.9
Thailand								
(Number in sample)	(120)		(120)		(120)		(360)	
Education[a]	13.8	3.2	5.6	3.6	4.2	2.0	7.9	5.2
Age	34.0	4.7	28.6	5.2	31.8	6.1	31.6	5.8
Years of marriage	6.8	3.8	7.6	4.2	9.4	4.8	7.8	4.4
Living children	2.2	1.2	2.8	1.6	3.3	1.5	2.8	1.5

na—not applicable because subsample did not include persons in this socio-economic group.
a—Years of formal education.
b—Figure for Caucasian includes Filipino and Japanese.

results especially when similarities are shown also in comparisons across countries. The data presented here are organised to facilitate such comparisons.

Each of the tables presenting the descriptive result from the study has three components: the pertinent dimensions of the value of children; the three subgroups that were sampled in each country (urban middle class, urban lower class, and rural); and within subgroups, the six countries. In the case of Hawaii, separate results are shown for Caucasian, Japanese, and Filipino respondents.

General Observations

The diversity of both satisfactions and costs is striking. The cross-national data confirm the commonsense notion that children, who are complex, growing, interacting beings, fulfil many needs of parents but also create many difficulties in parents' lives. It is important to note that most parents in all six countries are quite aware of these conflicting aspects of having children and are able to articulate them, at least to some extent.

With respect to the three broad categories of satisfactions and costs—psychological, economic, and social—the data show that each emerges as important in its own right.

1. Psychological or *emotional benefits*, such as happiness and companionship, have very high salience generally and are particularly strong for certain economic and cultural groups; *emotional costs* are also salient but they show less differentiation across groups.
2. Perception of *economic benefits* from children are shown to be clearly related to the socio-economic setting of the family, with strong urban-rural contrasts, while *economic costs* of children are shown to be a potent influence overall but not related so strongly or so simply to the setting.
3. *Social benefits* pertain mainly to the welfare and integration of the family unit, rather than to larger social aggregates, and vary by both culture and socio-economic group; *social costs* pertain especially to restrictions on interactions with persons other than children, including both the spouse and others outside the family, and are most salient for urban respondents.

Different sets of values emerge in the context of different types of questions. When asked about the advantages and disadvantages of having children, parents tend to cite personal satisfactions and costs—that is, they describe the ways in which children either fulfil or interfere with the needs of the parents themselves. When respondents are asked about advantages and disadvantages in relation to number of children, the concern shifts to the children or to the family unit—*i.e.*, responses pertain to sibling relationships, rearing of children, and providing for children. In questions about the advantages and disadvantages of sons and daughters, both personal and familial motivations emerge and strong differences are shown reasons for wanting sons and daughters. These sets of values each shows some relationship to family size and they are of course related to each other.

While the results from different countries are far from identical, some striking cross-cultural similarities are shown in the data. These similarities seem especially impressive in the responses to open-ended questions, where instrument or measurement influences are minimised. Similarities are naturally to be expected in studying aspects of human behaviour that have intrinsic uniformities, as is true for childbearing and childrearing. Nonetheless, the limited appearance of culturally distinct values in our data is surprising.

On the other hand, the relationships among value-of-children variables and other variables do vary considerably across countries, in nature and in degree. Perhaps it is in these patterns that cultural influences assert themselves. Such patterns are shown most clearly in correlational analyses that are contained in the project report but not included in this paper.

The analyses show that husbands and wives share a broadly similar orientation toward children. For that reason we have adopted for this report the simplification of presenting results only by socio-economic group and not by sex of respondent. Some specific sex differences are noted below however.

In the paragraphs that follow, a composite profile of the three socio-economic groups is drawn, based on all of the available data. The profile reveals the main findings of the study but necessarily obscures some important differences among groups. Following the generalisations significant exceptions are pointed out, but the appendix tables themselves should be consulted for a more complete picture.

Satisfactions

In the *urban middle-class group,* psychological or emotional advantages of having children are emphasised. These include happiness for the individual parent or the family, feeling of personal growth and development of the parent that is associated with childrearing, and pleasure in the companionship and fun provided by children. Values related to specific aspects of family life, such as continuity of the family name and a strengthening of the bond between husband and wife, are shown to be important for the middle class in some countries but not in others. Economic benefits of children are not generally salient for middle-class respondents.

When middle-class respondents describe reasons why other people want children, rather than their own reasons, two interesting differences occur: continuity of family name emerges as the most important reason in Korea and Taiwan, and in four countries respondents frequently mention that it is "instinctive" or "natural" to have children.

Daughters are wanted mainly for psychological reasons, especially as companions for the mother and because of their positive personality or behavioural qualities. Sons are wanted mainly for continuity of family name everywhere but in Japan, middle-class respondents also see psychological advantages of having sons similar to those of having daughters, but when sons are discussed there is an increase in responses pertaining to economic or practical benefits.

With respect to reasons given as important for wanting another child, the pattern of strong emotional-psychological values and weak economic motivations among the middle class is generally maintained, and continuity of family name and sex preference are also shown as important. Values related to the respondent's desired family size include providing companionship for other children or avoiding an only child, as well as sex preference or a desire for balance between sexes. A common response for the middle class in four countries is "can afford that number or am able to raise that number," which may suggest that overt, rational planning of family size in relation to family resources is more common for this group.

Urban lower-class respondents, like those of the middle class, stress psychological or emotional benefits provided by children, but there is an increase of economic motivations for this group and some evidence of a stronger orientation toward continuity of family name. The differences in economic dimensions and family continuity show up more clearly in the reasons for wanting sons and daughters than in the general advantages. Similar to the middle class, the lower-class respondents attribute strongly to others the motivation of continuity of family name and also that it is "instinctive" or "natural" to have children.

In reasons for wanting another child, the similarity between urban middle-class and urban lower-class respondents is again shown on many dimensions, but with the same increased emphasis in the lower class on economic benefits and family continuity. Concerning motivations related to family size, the lower class is distinguished from the middle class mainly by an increase in the specific desire for more boys.

For the *rural group*, the economic utility of children comes to the fore, with respect to both current economic contributions and security in the parents' old age. This emphasis shows up in a variety of items: the general advantages of having children, the reasons for wanting both sons and daughters, the perceived motivations of others for having children, the reasons for wanting another child, and in responses to specific questions on old-age support. Economic motivations are thus most salient for the rural group, somewhat less so for the urban lower class, and least salient for the middle class. The "traditional" value of family continuity shows this same trend, again reflected in responses to several types of questions, including the attitude scale labelled "continuity, tradition, security."

Emotional benefits remain salient to rural respondents in all countries, but their significant diminishes both in relation to other benefits and by absolute frequency of mention. This does not mean, of course, that rural parents do not enjoy their children; it does seem to suggest that, given their socio-economic setting, the emotional benefits of children are much less important than the economic benefits. It is of interest that a particular type of psychological benefit emerges as important for rural respondents in three East Asian countries: "pride in children's accomplishments" and "children to carry out the parents' hopes and aspirations." Perhaps these rural parents are especially frustrated by their own life circumstances and hope for better for their children.

Costs

Financial costs are very salient even to the more affluent *middle class*. This finding presumably reflects their desire for children of high "quality" at a greater cost per child, as well as the generally higher costs of raising children in an urban setting. While the level of concern about financial costs tends to be somewhat lower for the middle class than for other socio-economic groups, the importance of financial considerations in relation to other costs is shown clearly in middle-class responses to questions on the general disadvantages of having children, reasons for not wanting another child, reasons for limiting the family to the desired size, and the perceived financial burden of having three children.

Restrictions of various kinds, or opportunity costs, are important to middle-class respondents in all countries. In tabulations of spontaneous responses by major coding categories, restrictions show up as more salient than financial costs for middle-class respondents in all countries except the Philippines and Thailand. The relative importance of restrictions diminishes, however, in a structured item on reasons for not wanting another child, possibly because opportunity costs are significant in the decision to have children or not have children, but less so in decisions for more children after the first child has been born.

Emotional strain from rearing children and such associated factors as noise and disorder in the household show up as salient to middle-class respondents in all countries. Health problems of children and general rearing problems are also salient in most countries. In the decision to have another child, parents are also concerned about not being able to give enough care and attention to existing children. Problems of pregnancy and maternal health are cited with modest frequency by middle-class respondents as reasons for restricting family size. In Japan, housing problems are the second-most important reason for limiting the number of children, for all urban respondents.

Lower-class respondents in general show greater concern than the middle class about financial costs of raising children. In fact, in some countries the data suggest a trend toward curvilinearity, with the urban lower class more concerned about costs than either the middle class or the rural group. This is not surprising, since the urban lower-class respondents tend to have more children and lower income than the middle class while being exposed to the same high urban cost factors, and to have higher costs and fewer benefits than the rural group.

Restrictions on alternative activities are also important to the lower class, although generally less important than for the middle class. Rearing and health problems are fairly similar across the middle and lower class, and likewise there is little difference with respect to emotional costs.

Rural respondents in all countries show a strong awareness of the financial burden of children. Although the costs of raising children should be lower in rural areas, rural respondents tend to have many children to raise on relatively low incomes. Restrictions on alternative activities of the parents are less salient in rural areas, but restrictions on work do rank as somewhat important among rural respondents in Taiwan and Thailand, and other types of restrictions are cited in Japan and by Filipinos in Hawaii.

Rural respondents in several countries mention physical work, tiredness, and emotional strain caused by children, both as a general disadvantage and as a reason for restricting family size. This pattern of responses is probably related to the greater amount of physical labour required of both husbands and wives in rural areas.

Discussion

Most striking in the profiles described above is the contrast between psychological benefits of children emphasised by the middle class and economic benefits emphasised by the rural respondents, with the urban lower class falling between. This finding may be in part a function of different styles of response related to the education of respondents, but the pervasiveness of the trend in different types of questions suggests that the three groups have genuinely different orientations toward the value of children. The difference in expected economic benefits is, of course, quite consistent with explanations of the demographic transition that have been advanced.

Results pertaining to economic costs are more complex, and this study probably has not dealt adequately with that aspect of the value of.children. Among other things, better indicators of parents' aspirations for quality of children are needed to understand the effects of costs.

Opportunity costs, it appears, may not play a very significant role in determining family size, once the decision has been made to have children. This finding seems reasonable, since the major restrictions and change in life style occur with the birth of the first child and additional children have relatively slight impact.

While a general similarity between husbands and wives in their orientations toward children was noted, some significant differences emerged. Wives, especially in urban locations, tend to emphasise more the affectional relationship with children and the companionship they provide. Expectations for economic help from children are consistently higher among wives, compared with husbands, perhaps reflecting the generally greater degree of economic dependence of women and their longer life expectancy.

Husbands are more likely than wives to stress the benefits of continuity of family name, pride in children's accomplishments, and family happiness. In general, husbands are more concerned about financial costs than are wives.

Preference for sex of children, or the desire for a balance of sexes, is a pervasive influence on family-size decisions. The desire for sons appears strongest in Taiwan and Korea.

Reasons for wanting daughters and reasons for wanting sons show strong similarities across countries, presumably reflecting certain universal in sex-role prescriptions. It appears that daughters are wanted for qualities that apply mainly when they are still children and still living with the parents, whereas sons are wanted for reasons that apply more when they have become adults—for example, continuity for family name and economic security for the parents.

The pattern of results for the Philippines differs substantially from that of the other countries. The perceived economic benefits from children are higher and are spread more evenly across socio-economic groups in the Philippines; large numbers of children are seen as less of an economic burden; there is more emphasis on emotional gratification from children; restriction on parents are less important. This pattern is quite consistent with the higher fertility evident in the Philippines.

In most countries major differences appear between all urban respondents (middle and lower socio-economic groups combined) and rural respondents. In Thailand, a greater contrast is found between middle-class respondents and the other two groups (urban lower and rural).

ANNEXURE

EXHIBIT A

Major Code Categories and Specific Code Categories used in the Content Analysis of Responses: Advantages and Disadvantages of Having Children

Advantages

Happiness, love, companionship
Companionship, avoidance of loneliness
Love, affection
Play, fun with children; avoidance of boredom
Relief from strain, distraction from problems
Happiness for individual Parent (general)
Happiness for family
Uniqueness, specialness in parent-child relationship

Personal development of parent
Character development, responsibility, maturity, morality
Incentives to succeed, striving to provide for children
Fulfilment of self, completeness as person
Extension of self
Learning from experience of childrearing motherhood, fatherhood; adulthood
Proof of fertility, masculinity, femininity

Childrearing satisfactions
Pride in children's accomplishment
Pleasure from growth, development of children
Children to carry out parent's hopes, aspirations
Opportunity to teach, guide, instill values

Satisfaction in one's childrearing ability, accomplishment
Satisfaction in providing for children

Economic benefits, security
Economic help in old age
Companionship, comfort, care in old age
Unspecified help in old age
Economic help (old age not mentioned)
Comfort, care (old age not mentioned)
Help in housework, family chores; practical help
Sharing financial responsibility; insurance, security
Help in family business, farm
Help in taking care of other children
Unspecified help (old age not mentioned)

Benefits to family unit
Children as bond between spouses
Children as reason for, fulfilment of marriage
Children as family life, complete or close-knit family

Kin group benefits
Continuity of family name
Continuity of family traditions
Enhancement of reputation of family
Having future grandchildren
Children as heirs, someone to inherit family wealth
Religious rituals, ancestor worship
To increase strength, power of kin group
To satisfy desires of spouse
To satisfy desires of other kin

Social, religious influences
Conformity to social norms
Conformity to religious norms
Children as benefits to society

General, intrinsic value of children
Children as treasure, wealth, assets
Instinctive, natural to have children
General wanting, linking children

Other advantages

Disadvantages

Financial costs
Educational costs
General, other costs

Emotional costs
Responsibility of parenthood
Discipline, moral behaviour
Health problems of children
Concern over children's future success, happiness
Concern about satisfying children's present wants
Noise, disorder, nuisance
General rearing problems
General emotional strain

Physical demands on parents
Health hazard of pregnancy; maternal health
Physical work, tiredness caused by children

Restrictions on alternative activities
Restrictions on time
Restrictions on travel
Restrictions on social life, recreation
Restrictions on job, career
Restrictions on personal wants
Restrictions on privacy
General lack of flexibility, freedom

Marital problems
Less time, interaction between spouses
Disagreements over children
General marital problems

Kin group costs, problems of inheritance
Disadvantages relating to, affecting kin group

Societal costs, overpopulation
Disadvantages relating to, affecting society; concern about overpopulation

Other disadvantages

TABLE

Advantages of Having Children : Percentage of Under Each of Specified Major Code Categories,

SES group and country	Major Code Category·			
	Happiness, love, companionship	*Personal development of parent*	*Childrearing satisfactions*	*Economic benefits, security*
Urban Middle				
Korea	69	39	54	12
Taiwan	88	10	9	6
Japan	61	29	37	7
U. S. (Hawaii)				
Japanese	74	48	47	15
Caucasian	73	66	61	14
Philippines	79	34	17	80
Thailand	67	35	8	20
Urban Low				
Korea	72	39	42	25
Taiwan	89	3	8	29
Japan	69	21	36	9
US (Hawaii)				
Japanese	84	55	43	22
Caucasian	66	54	55	13
Filipino	86	22	13	76
Philippines	83	29	21	84
Thailand	35	6	3	80
Rural				
Korea	56	22	42	45
Taiwan	51	3	19	53
Japan	63	17	46	19
U.S. (Hawaii)				
Filipino	90	19	5	96
Philippines	68	17	20	91
Thailand	25	3	3	76

* Less than 1 per cent

A1

Respondents who Mentioned at least One Advantage by Socio-economic (SES) Group and Country

Benefits to family unit	*Kin group benefits*	*Social, religious influences*	*General intrinsic value of children*	*Other advantages*
25	15	5	5	1
14	20	4	6	*
28	3	4	1	*
51	21	4	17	7
40	23	8	15	5
26	8	5	6	*
42	23	5	1	7
30	23	2	1	1
3	46	4	7	2
35	4	1	2	*
33	18	1	17	1
34	17	1	18	5
20	21	*	3	2
17	16	8	6	*
6	18	4	1	4
4	32	11	6	2
5	35	5	4	1
14	11	1	3	*
6	12	*	4	*
13	6	4	6	*
4	37	13	1	0

TABLE

Disadvantages of Having Children : Percentage of Under Each of Specified Major Code Categories,

SES group and country	*Major Code Category*		
	Financial costs	*Emotional costs*	*Physical demands on parents*
Urban Middle			
Korea	41	56	15
Taiwan	33	59	11
Japan	42	38	6
U. S. (Hawaii)			
Japanese	31	50	12
Caucasian	49	66	12
Philippines	60	82	15
Thailand	44	56	15
Urban Low			
Korea	69	60	8
Taiwan	48	71	11
Japan	40	49	9
U.S. (Hawaii)			
Japanese	42	45	16
Caucasian	43	51	3
Filipino	68	74	23
Philippines	56	75	12
Thailand	61	38	9
Rural			
Korea	46	63	7
Taiwan	67	57	18
Japan	43	45	5
U.S. (Hawaii)			
Filipino	90	82	30
Philippines	57	74	12
Thailand	54	36	31

* Less than 1 per cent

A2
Respondents who Mentioned at least One Disadvantage by Socio-economic Group and Country

Restrictions on alternative	*Marital problems*	*Kin Group costs, problems of inheritence*	*Societal costs, over population*	*Other Disadvantages*
51	24	*	*	3
40	4	*	*	*
57	12	*	*	*
70	7	1	*	5
79	15	*	1	5
37	2	*	*	1
19	*	1	*	2
25	6	*	1	2
32	2	*	*	*
54	2	*	*	*
82	9	3	4	3
63	8	*	2	6
50	1	*	*	3
33	3	*	1	1
18	*	*	*	8
21	4	*	*	2
22	*	*	*	*
33	3	1	1	2
57	*	*	2	1
23	*	*	*	*
21	1	1	*	2

Table A3

Advantage of Having Children: Five Most Frequently Mentioned Advantages Ranked According to Percentage of Respondents Mentioning them, by Socio-economic Group and Country

SES group and country	1 Advantage	%	2 Advantage	%	3 Advantage	%	4 Advantage	%	5 Advantage	%
Urban Middle Korea	Happiness for family	42	Incentives to succeed	25	Satisfaction in one's childrearing abilities	25	Pleasure from growth, development of children	23	Play, fun with children; avoidance of boredom	20
Taiwan	Play, fun with children; avoidance of boredom	44	Companionship, avoidance of loneliness	22	Continuity of family name	19	Happiness for individual parent	13	Happiness for family	13
Japan	Happiness for family	41	Prime value of life[a]	35	Pleasure from growth, development of children	24	Children as bond between spouses	22	Children to carry out parent's hopes, aspirations	14
U.S. (Hawaii) Japanese	Companionship, avoidance of loneliness	37	Play, fun with children, avoidance of boredom	32	Children as family life, complete or close-knit family	30	Pleasure from growth, development of children	28	Learning from experience of childrearing	25
Caucasian	Pleasure from growth, development of children	39	Love, affection	31	Learning from experience of childrearing	29	Children as family life, complete or close-knit family	25	Character development, responsibility, maturity, morality	25
Philippines	Happiness for individual parent	38	Help in housework, family chores; practical help	36	Unspecified help in old age	33	Happiness for family	33	Incentives to succeed	24
Thailand	Companionship, avoidance of loneliness	38	Children as bond between spouses	28	Character development, responsibility, maturity, morality	23	Incentives to succeed	20	Continuity of family name	20

Urban Low										
Korea	Play, fun with children; avoidance of boredom	37	Happiness for family	33	Incentives to succeed	27	Children as bond between spouses	26	Pleasure from growth, development of children	19
Taiwan	Play, fun with children; avoidance of boredom	52	Countinuity of family name	44	Companionship, avoidance of loneliness	38	Unspecified help in old age	24	Love, affection	14
Japan	Happiness for family	49	Prime value of life[a]	41	Children as bond between spouses	27	Pleasure from growth, development of children	19	Children as family life, complete or close-knit family	16
U.S. (Hawaii) Japanese	Companion-, ship, avoidance of loneliness	45	Play, fun with children; avoidance of boredom	43	Pleasure from growth, development of children	28	Children as family life, complete or close-knit family	25	Character development, responsibility maturity, morality	24
Caucasian	Pleasure from growth, development of children	40	Companionship, avoidance of loneliness	28	Play, fun with children; avoidance of boredom	28	Learning from experience of childrearing	22	Children as family life, complete or close-knit family children as bond between spouses	21 21
Filipino	Happiness for individual parent	45	Help in housework, family chores; practical help	38	Companionship, avoidance of loneliness	28	Companionship, comfort, care in old age	27	Play, fun with children; avoidance of boredom Unspecified help in old age	16 16
Philippines	Help in housework, family chores; practical help	39	Happiness for individual parent	37	Unspecified help in old age	34	Play, fun with children, avoidance of boredom	25	Economic help (old age not mentioned)	22
Thailand	Unspecified help in old age	49	Companionship, avoidance of loneliness	23	Unspecified help (old age not mentioned)	22	Help in housework, family chores; practical help	17	Continuity of family name	14

(Contd.)

Table A3 *(continued)*

SES group and country	1		2		3		4		5	
	Advantage	*%*	*Advantage*	*%*	*Advantage*	*%*	*Advantage*	*%*	*Advantage*	*%*
Rural Korea	Play, fun with children; avoidance of boredom	30	Continuity of family name	25	Happiness for family	18	Pleasure from growth, development of children	18	Pride in children's accomplishment	16
Taiwan	Unspecified help in old age	39	Continuity of family name	33	Play, fun with children; avoidance of boredom	32	Pride in children's accomplishment	16	Companionship, avoidance of loneliness	15
Japan	Happiness for family	46	Prime value of life[a]	42	Children to carry out parents' hopes, aspirations	23	Pleasure from growth, development of children	18	Companionship, avoidance of loneliness	12
U.S. (Hawaii) Filipino	Help in housework, family chores; practical help	66	Companionship, avoidance of loneliness	64	Happiness for individual parent	63	Unspecified help in old age	42	Companionship, comfort, care in old age	13
Philippines	Help in housework, family chores; practical help	48	Unspecified help in old age	35	Happiness for individual parent	32	Economic help (old age not mentioned)	27	Companionship, comfort, care in old age	23
Thailand	Companionship, comfort, care in old age	43	Continuity of family name	28	Unspecified help in old age (old age not mentioned)	18	Companionship, avoidance of loneliness	13	Comfort, care (old age not mentioned)	13

Note: Responses have been coded by category (see Exhibit A). In cases where two or more advantages were mentioned by the same percentage of respondents, indentical ranking is indicated by the omission of vertical rules.

a Translated from the Japanese expression *iki-gai*—literally, "one's life worthwhile." The response is similar to the English expression "goals and incentives from children," but because it implies an emphasis on present satisfactions for raising children it has been coded as a country-specific response category.

Source: Derived from a content analysis of responses to question 4 of the VOC questionnaire.

Table A4

Disadvantage of Having Children: Five Most Frequently Mentioned Disadvantages Ranked According to Percentage of Respondents Mentioning Them, by Socio-economic Group and Country

SES group and country	1		2		3		4		5	
	Disadvantage	*%*	*Disadvantage*	*%*	*Disadvantage*	*%*	*Disadvantage*	*%*	*Disadvantage*	*%*
Urban Middle										
Korea	Financial costs (general, other)	39	Noise, disorder, nuisance	22	Health problems of children	22	Restrictions on time	22	Restrictions on travel	19
Taiwan	Financial costs (general, other)	31	Noise, disorder, nuisance	27	Restrictions on time	20	General lack of flexibility, freedom	17	Health problems of children	16
Japan	Restrictions on time	24	Financial costs (general, other)	20	Health problems of children	15	General emotional strain	15	General lack of flexibility, freedom Restrictions on social life, recreation	12 12
U.S. (Hawaii) Japanese	General lack of flexibility, freedom	46	Financial costs (general, other)	31	General emotional strain	21	Restrictions on social life, recreation	18	General rearing problems	14
Caucasian	General lack of flexibility, freedom	64	Financial costs (general, other)	49	General emotional strain	24	General rearing problems	22	Restrictions on job, career	14
Philippines	Financial costs (general, other)	50	Discipline, moral behaviour	42	Health problems of children	31	Financial costs (education)	24	Noise, disorder, nuisance General rearing problems	18 18
Thailand	Financial costs (general, other)	39	General rearing problems	28	General emotional strain	18	Physical work, tirendness caused	13	Responsibility of parenthood	9

(Contd.)

Table A4 *(continued)*

SES group and country	1 *Disadvantage*	*%*	2 *Disadvantage*	*%*	3 *Disadvantage*	*%*	4 *Disadvantage*	*%*	5 *Disadvantage*	*%*
Urban Low Korea	Financial costs (general, other)	58	Noise, disorder, nuisance	35	Financial costs (education)	25	Health problems of children	20	General emotional strain	19
Taiwan	Financial costs (general, other)	42	Noise, disorder, nuisance	38	General lack of flexibility, freedom	17	Health problems of children	15	General rearing problems	11
Japan	Restrictions on time	29	Financial costs (general, other)	21	Health problems of children	19	General emotional strain Restrictions on job, career	13 13	Noise, disorder, nuisance General lack of flixibility, freedom Restrictions on social life, recreation	13 13 13
U.S. (Hawaii) Japanese	General lack of flexibility, freedom	61	Financial costs (general, other)	36	Restrictions on job, career	21	Discipline, moral behaviour	16	Restrictions on social life, recreation	16
Caucasian	General lack of flexibility, freedom	49	Financial costs (general, other)	37	Discipline, moral behaviour	17	Health problems of children	15	General rearing problems	14
Filipino	Financial costs (general, other)	65	General lack of flexibility, freedom	40	General rearing problems	33	Discipline, moral behaviour	30	Noise, disorder, nuisance	23
Philippines	Financial costs (general, other)	46	Discipline, moral behaviour	46	Health problems of children	25	Financial costs (education)	25	Noise, disorder, nuisance	21
Thailand	Financial costs (general, other)	61	General rearing problems	20	General emotional strain	14	Physical work, tiredness caused by children	9	Financial costs (education)	8

					Discipline, moral behaviour 8 Restrictions on job, career 8 General lack of flexibility, freedom 8
Rural Korea	Financial costs (general, others) 44	Financial costs (education) 38	Noise, disorder nuisance 32	Health problems of children 29	Discipline, moral behaviour 18
Taiwan	Financial costs (general, others) 64	Health problems of children 24	Noise, disorder nuisance 22	Physical work, tiredness caused by children 17	Restrictions on job, career 14
Japan	Health prob-lems of children 22	Financial costs (general, others) 21	Restrictions on time 15	General emotional strain 12	Noise, disorder nuisance 12
U.S. (Hawaii) Filipino	Financial costs (general, others) 90	Health problems of children 57	General lack of flexibility, freedom 33	Discipline, moral behaviour 31	Physical work, tiredness caused by children 30
Philippines	Financial costs (general, others) 44	Discipline, moral behaviour 36	Health problems of children 26	General rearing problems 22	Noise, disorder nuisance 20
Thailand	Financial costs (general, others) 42	Physical work, tiredness caused by children 31	Financial costs (education) 18	Discipline, moral behaviour 17	Restrictions on job, career 11

Note: Responses have been coded by category (see Exhibit A). In cases where two or more reasons were mentioned by the same percentage of respondents, identical ranking is indicated by the omission of vertical rules.
Source: Derived from a content analysis of responses to question 6 of the VOC questionnaire.

Index